BONFIRES
ON THE
HILLSIDE

An Eyewitness Account of
Political Upheaval in Northern Ireland

BONFIRES
ON THE
HILLSIDE

An Eyewitness Account of
Political Upheaval in Northern Ireland

JAMES KELLY

FOUNTAIN PUBLISHING

BELFAST

To my wife Eileen and daughters Patricia,
Grainne and Eileen, without whose encouragement
this book would never have been written.

Published 1995
by Fountain Publishing

© 1995 Fountain Publishing
ISBN 0-952556-502
ISBN 0-952556-553

Printed by ColourBooks Ltd, Dublin
Cover and Design by Dunbar Design

CONTENTS

PREFACE

IN NEW YORK EVEN the Jewish yellow-cab driver *en route* from Wall Street to the Lexington Hotel was able to discuss intelligently the sad state of affairs in Belfast. It did not take him long to find out where I had come from and offer his own solution to the madness he had read about in the papers.

Earlier when my wife and I visited our daughter in Halifax, Nova Scotia, two local radio stations and a television station tracked me down to tell my story of the violence – twenty bombs in and around my office with 'two minutes to get out'. Our diffidence about mentioning that we hailed from one of the earth's most notorious townships was soon dispelled by the evident sympathy of our transatlantic friends. At a reception a university lecturer, inevitably to write a thesis on James Joyce on a visit to Ireland, asked us in all seriousness 'How are things in God's own country?' Poor sad old Belfast, torn apart by conflict and terror.

It was almost comforting after flying across the Atlantic to hear strangers thousands of miles away identify with the Falls Road, the Shankill, Ardoyne and all the traditional green and orange battle-grounds, victims of misfortune, the mistakes of history, the mythology of bloody old flags.

It has often been said that the definitive book on Belfast has yet to be written. It may take many books to tell that mangled story.

This is just one man's story, written after much heart searching and not a little prodding from friends and colleagues. Inevitably, a newspaperman of long experience picks up many a story or anecdote behind the scenes, some bizarre, some hilarious. A growing number of my friends over the years have been saying 'Why don't you write these experiences down?' Others, adopting a more truculent attitude, have been heard to remark after some reminiscent exercise over a drink on times past, 'If he doesn't write them we bloody well will!'

THE LAST LOVELY SUMMER

HOW TO SORT OUT one's confused love-hate relationship with the place that gave one birth? That's the problem. There's that fat old dame, Queen Victoria, glowering from under hooded eye-lids, the big squat statue outside the Belfast City Hall, the unamused monarch who, the story goes, gave more money to the Battersea Cat and Dogs' Home than to the starving Irish victims of the Famine.

Down at the bottom of High Street is the Memorial to her beloved Albert, the Town Clock, now leaning over slightly as the waters of the culverted River Farset, degraded to a sewer, suck the salt-marsh from the foundations, another relic of grim Victoriana handed on by bewhiskered City Fathers who, in their search for brass in the form of rates, built up and shut out the beauty of the surrounding hills and the green shores of an entrancing Belfast Lough.

In the days when spirits were cheap New Year revellers crashed their whiskey bottles against the clock-tower as twelve midnight tolled out over the city. They did not share the respect of the city burghers who left behind a rash of streets and squares named after the old Queen and her German consort. Further down the social scale, outside the Academical Institution, once the home of liberal thought, stands another sentinel in stone, the 'Black Man', now going green with age, Dr. Henry Cooke, D.D., the Presbyterian Divine and progenitor of all the bigots, the man who incited the mobs to attack Dan O'Connell on his visit to the city as the Catholic Liberator. Cooke sowed the seeds of the religious hate which grew like a foul weed to plague subsequent generations.

As boys wandering Belfast's streets we wondered about the Sunday sermons on 'The Whore of Babylon' and 'The Scarlet Jezebel of Rome' emblazoned on the bill boards outside the churches and little mission halls throughout the city. Who were they and why did we not hear about them from our pulpits?

One's memories of those days of innocence are jumbled. The band playing among the trees in the lovely old Falls Park while young men in straw boilers and blazers flirted with youngdamsels in long flowing white frocks. The smell of the new-mown hay in the upper slopes of the park with its sweeping vista of the Divis mountain providing a mysterious back drop to be explored some day in summer. In winter bare-footed boys, some with legs as red as Highland red-shanks, splashed through the puddles in the street after the rain in contrast to their better-off friends in knickerbockers, long black stockings and laced boots. Others cut a dash on Sundays in sailor suits or Eton jackets and celluloid collars, sometimes to the derision of the corner boys.

A farthing would still buy sugar-candy from the sweet bottles on display in the local corner shop. Soon it was to disappear along with the sovereign and half-sovereign and the sweets began to go too, for there was a War on which was to change everything.

The picture of the so-called 'Great War' of 1914-18 in Belfast to me was one of black-painted street lamps, for fear of Zeppelin raids, a terrifying prospect against which the darkened gas-lamps seemed a pathetic protection. The warm golden glow which the friendly lamp-lighter with his wooden pole provided each evening was replaced by sinister dark shadows and rising fears of dreaded Prussians with spiked helmets who, it was whispered, impaled unfortunate little Belgian babies on their bayonets.

There was talk among the grown-ups of 'the trenches' and colourful posters, on the hoardings of William Allen, showed rubicund soldiers cheerfully sipping their steaming Bovril in comfortable sand-bagged dug-outs on the 'Western Front'.

From Bundoran, County Donegal, one August I still have the memory of my younger brother trotting alongside a detachment of khaki-clad soldiers singing 'Tipperary' as they clumped along the dusty road past Harte's long whitewashed cottage – where we boarded – *en route* to 'the Front' from the nearby Finner Camp. The sweet odour of the milking cows in the byre beside the iron pump where we washed in cold water and the sunlit days on the beach with its sudden swirling tide and the red sails of the ketches dancing on the sun-dappled horizon remain abiding memories of those days when so many young warriors marched away from Ireland never to return.

Back home in Belfast in darker days as the military bands and the singing stopped I heard talk about the headlines in the newspapers day after day – 'The carnage at Verdun', about 'Little Willie', the German Crown Prince, and 'Disaster on the Somme'. Young as we were the tragic waste of war cast its dark shadows on our minds for each day we could see the survivors from the Front back home to the Belfast War Hospital at the corner of the Grosvenor Road, struggling along on crutches in 'hospital blue' uniforms, pale, emaciated, some shell-shocked, some minus limbs, no longer smiling, the wreckage of war.

Years later a senior newspaper colleague, Albert Withers of the *Irish Times* Belfast office in Donegall Street, told me about the fateful day of July 1, 1916, when 6,000 local men fell at the Battle of the Somme. He said that everywhere throughout the city that day there was the sound of weeping as the dreaded telegrams, 'Killed In Action' flooded into the little houses. Carson's Volunteers who joined up for a different war, for 'God and Ulster', went over the top to their deaths alongside the Catholics of John Redmond's 'Volunteers',

3

the forgotten grey ghosts lured into the war to fight for a small nation like Ireland, 'gallant little Belgium'.

For a few hundred yards of territory, those men were sent to their deaths in an inferno of shell-fire over an impassable terrain of barbed wire and mud. A German general commented that they were 'lions led by donkeys'. That same year I have a vivid recollection of my first sight of an aeroplane circling over West Belfast dropping recruiting leaflets. The wine-press of Armageddon was running dry. More flesh and blood was needed for the 'War to end War'.

Earlier that year at Easter time I heard people talking about the 'Rebellion' in Dublin and how the trains had stopped but I cannot say it made much of an impact in Belfast although there was the spectacle, dimly remembered from a few years before, of green-uniformed Irish National Volunteers parading up the Falls Road past Beechmount, complete with a cycling corps. Were they Redmond's Volunteers mobilised to defend Home Rule?

At my maternal grandmother's home at 1 Almeda Terrace on the Falls Road, opposite Beechmount Avenue, there was news of three of my uncles who, like many others of their generation, rallied to Redmond's call to Irishmen to go out to fight for 'Catholic Belgium' and the defence of humanity. My uncle Justin had joined the Irish Guards and was wounded in the Retreat from Mons. Despite his wound he walked with stiff shoulders and back as straight as a ramrod all his life, as if still on the parade ground. His younger brother, Tom, a gangling six-footer, received a serious chest wound at Gallipoli with the Dublin Regiment and was invalided back to a hospital in Edinburgh. Then there was the eldest of the Magauran family, my long-lost uncle Johnnie who had gone off years before to seek his fortune in Cape Town, South Africa. All trace of him had been lost but the prodigal son turned up unexpectedly one day to join his sisters and brothers announcing that he was 'on leave' from the Front where he had been serving with a South African regiment in the trenches. Came the excitement of Armistice Day, 1918 and this bronzed giant wearing a jaunty cowboy style felt hat with upturned brim was shipped back to South Africa. A letter home saying that he was working in a diamond mine at Johannesburg was the last the family received from him. He was never heard of again.

After the war came the halcyon days of long summers and peace at Clowney Street off Beechmount on the outskirts of the city. It was a long quiet street of 'parlour houses' and tiny gardens of shrubs, daffodils and nasturtiums. It reached up to the sloping fields of long grasses where cows grazed for O'Hare, the milkman, on the Whiterock Road. The fields were not yet despoiled by the giant excavations encroaching steadidly from McGladdery's big brickyard. The tree-lined Riddell's Demesne and its large mansion owned by a city ironmonger flanked the waste ground at the back of the houses. Its well-stocked orchard proved a considerable temptation for the youth of the district. The widow Riddell, an old lady dressed in black, used to issue forth daily in a coach driven by her gate-lodge keeper, Johnston. In her will she was said to have instructed that the place must never be sold to a Catholic.

Alas such is the irony of fate that in later years the estate became a Catholic Hospice run by the Sisters of Mercy. On our bird-nesting expeditions up to the heather-clad hills we stole curious glances at the courting couples lying in the meadow grass wrapped in the voluminous black shawls worn by the mill girls against the cold. Little brooks tumbling down from the hills were crossed by stepping stones on our way to the looming Divis or Black Mountain, on fire at Easter with bonfires of blazing heather. In the little pools we gazed at the tiny fish we called 'spricks' and envied the lads who had brought jars to catch them and bring them home.

At the top of the steep rocky mountain lane from the Whiterock a flood of crystal-clear water poured from a subterranean limestone well. Groups of climbers, hot with exertion, lined up for the ritual slaking of thirst from a white enamel cup thoughtfully provided by a nearby thatched cottage, before ascending by the narrow stony

5

path across the side of the mountain to the Hatchet Field. Here, in an ancient habitation under a clump of trees swaying in the wind, an old gentleman with a long ginger beard kept a few cows grazing in two small triangular fields cut out from the gorse-covered slopes. By evening time he could be seen trudging down the hillside with two milk churns slung over his shoulders. He was a bit of a mystery. Nobody knew who he was or his story. When he died the cottage fell into ruin and the cows were no longer seen on the hillside. An ancient muddy path led past the cottage to what we called 'the Gully' described on local maps as 'Windy Gap'. Here another mountain stream tumbled down to the tree-lined Colin Glen over a waterfall at Toneroy where in the summer heat children from the west of the city dived and swam in a deep icy pool worn into the rocks.

On the other side of the gap in the hills which in winter formed a kind of tunnel for the roaring south-west wind blowing across Ireland from the mouth of the River Shannon, a grassy path, railed off on the right for a city merchant's shooting rights, led downhill to the tiny hamlet of Hannahstown. At school we listened to hair-raising stories about youngsters who jumped the fence into the forbidden boggy fields to emerge flying from an irate game-keeper who did not hesitate to fire salt pellets at their retreating backsides. At Hannahstown, nestling between McQuillan's quarry and the quietest little church in Ireland surrounded by old moss-covered gravestones, Brennan's pub provided liquid refreshment for thirsty adults and lemonade and Abernethy biscuits and cheese for the young ones.

My first school-days were at the parish school of St. Paul's on Cavendish Square adjoining the church where the much-loved Archdeacon, 'Father Pat' Convery, was a real shepherd of his flock, an old-time Father O'Flynn, 'who had a wonderful way with him', regarded by young and old with a mixture of awe and affection. Trailing his old blackthorn stick as he patrolled the district, Father Pat met a boy carrying a jug of whiskey, scolded him and told him to be off to school and taking the jug delivered it to his abashed mother without a word.

At St. Paul's school, a dapper little man with a small waxed moustache, Pete McGivern, the Principal, ruled with a rod of iron as he and his staff laboured over the task of licking an indifferent herd of boisterous boys into shape as educated young Christians. The sing-song voices, learning the arithmetic tables by rote, rose and fell from the classrooms throughout the day. At noon the Penny Catechism confronted First Class, under master Billy Reid, with the question 'Who made the world?' A nervous child from Clowney Street replied 'The brickyard men' and blushed with shame when the class laughed. When Mr. Reid told him that the answer was 'God', a cheeky cub interjected 'Sir, who made God?'

Long thin canes were used to inflict stinging welts across the palms for misdemeanours of any kind. Some masters were less free with the cane than others and we all loved John Derby, an amateur goalkeeper in his younger days, who sportingly threw dusters expecting the offending pupils to hurl them back so that he could illustrate his old goalkeeping skills. On the whole discipline was maintained at a high level by Mr. McGivern. After the lunch hour he lined us up in military formation in Cavendish Square while he rang his large brass hand-bell before marching us back to our long desks.

Every Friday afternoon he visited each class to collect pennies and halfpennies for the African Mission's 'Black Babies' or for the Chinese babies in the 'Far East'. We were full of pity for Chinese baby girls who we were told were unwanted and 'thrown out' by their parents. During the big 'flu epidemic when people were dying like flies and all the Belfast hospitals were crammed with victims, the schools were closed down. When we returned Mr. McGivern would appear in the afternoon with a big spray of disinfectant and spray each class thoroughly to keep the germs at bay.

Over the Easter holidays I was greatly excited when my father, a Kilkenny man, who had come north in his young days, announced that he was taking me for my first trip to the south of Ireland to introduce me to his family in John Street, Kilkenny city. They lived on the main street leading from the railway station to the lovely old Kilkenny Castle on the banks of the River Nore. The castle was the seat of the Earl of Ormond, descendant of the almost legendary Butler family whose history spanned the centuries from the Norman invasion of Ireland down to modern times.

Arriving at the Great Northern Railway terminus at Amiens Street, Dublin, I got my first glimpse of the southern metropolis from the roofless top of an old Dublin tram as it creaked and swayed under railway bridges impelling me to duck suddenly as each loomed in sight. The broad O'Connell Street was still in ruins after the 1916 'Rising'. Where shops and hotels once stood were great mounds of rubble levelled off by the wind and the rain. Up the quays past the metal Ha'penny Bridge over the rather smelly River Liffey we looked down on the colourful Guinness barges loaded with barrels of stout chugging down to the docks. My father remarked something about 'Dear, dirty Dublin' but it looked alright to me.

At Kingsbridge Station, an impressive building at the head of the river, he pointed to the trees at Phoenix Park and promised some day to take me to the zoo there. We had little time to spare and boarded the Great Southern Railway train for Kilkenny. It stopped at Kildare but the 'Refreshment Room' was like old Mother Hubbard's cupboard, no sandwiches, just stout, lemonade and digestive biscuits.

It was dusk when we arrived at last in Kilkenny. When the affectionate greetings were over we sat down to a splendid meal home-baked bread before a blazing sizzling fire of local Kilkenny coal, hotter than any fire I had experienced. Coming from gas-lit Belfast I found the flickering shadowy light from the household oil lamps a strain as I peered at my comics on the big living room table to follow the adventures of 'Weary Willie' and 'Tired Tim'. I was puzzled when one of my aunts introduced me to visitors as the 'little

Orangeman from Belfast' and everyone laughed. She asked me if it was true that the initiation ceremony for an Orangeman consisted of sitting on a red-hot poker or riding on the back of a billy-goat! It sounded daft to me but I resolved to find out some day.

Somehow the spectacle matched the prevailing atmosphere of the ancient city with its old friaries, black abbey, winding streets and historic buildings. The centuries-old St. Canice's Cathedral which I visited many years later was full of Plantagnet knights in stone lying outstretched in full armour on the tombs of the Butlers. These were the Norman-Irish, the settlers London punished for 'going native'. If they became 'more Irish than the Irish themselves' it was different back in Belfast. Visiting Englishmen arriving at the old air terminal in Glengall Street, Belfast, were confronted with the embarrassing bill-board over the Ulster Unionist Party headquarters 'Ulster is British'. When a visitor remarked 'Methinks you protest your loyalty too much' it was decided, wisely, to remove the slogan. In later years it was replaced in amended form 'Keeping Ulster British'.

There was a flutter of excitement for me one evening when the Lord of the castle arrived by train in Kilkenny from London. Peeping through the curtains of the front window we saw his coach drawn by horses clip-clopping along John Street to the ivy-covered castle just beyond the John Street bridge.

Before the 'Troubles' of the early twenties came there were the uneventful times when life seemed to run smoothly. There were the weekly visits to the local cinema, the Clonard Picture House, or even into town to the Royal Avenue Picture House to see another instalment of Pearl White in the 'Perils Of Pauline', with our heroes or heroines being snatched from death from under the wheels of oncoming express trains hurtling towards us, from tight-ropes across two skyscrapers, a mystery for the rest of the week how they would escape once more from a sticky end.

At the Boys' Holy Family Confraternity at Clonard Redemptorist

Monastery we sang in the church with great gusto 'Faith Of Our Fathers ... we will be true to thee till death' after Benediction in the odour of sanctity and incense. Death did not make much impact then in spite of the fact that both the Protestant City Cemetery and the Catholic Milltown Cemetery were situated on opposite sides of the Falls Road and we had the daily spectacle of black funeral hearses, drawn by trotting black Belgian horses frothing at the mouth, passing to and from the last resting places of our fellow citizens that in a divided city they all ended up at the top of the Catholic Falls.

One child, with wonder in his eyes, claimed that at Protestant funerals the minister ended the graveside dismissal service with the words 'Dust to dust, and if the Lord does not take you the divil must.' We nailed this awful lie very quickly by crawling up to a City Cemetery graveside under the legs of the mourners. We listened intently to the clergyman and were afterwards able to denounce the bearers of such lying tales.

Our next-door neighbour was a nattily dressed compositor with long white cuffs, a respectable Protestant. My particular childhood friend was his eldest son, Sam, a cheerful little fellow with fair hair and a winning smile. We played together in the open fields and on summer days lay in makeshift tents of tree branches and leaves, sucking the stems of long grasses and gazing up at the cotton-wool clouds sailing majestically across the blue sky from the western hills. Occasionally the silence was broken by a distant piper practising his art on the slopes of the mountain. The drone of the pipes and the song of the lark overhead lulled our thoughts to a feeling of contentment.

There must have been much unemployment in that part of the city in those days for there seemed to be many able-bodied men wandering about aimlessly, some with children and others with dogs. We wondered about all the jokes we heard of something called the 'Buroo'. One day on an excursion into the hills with cans of rice, fat raisins and milk, we blundered suddenly into a clearing at Glenalina on the left of the Whiterock Road to find scores of scantily dressed men and youths swimming in a muddy lake while others sunned themselves, bare-chested, beside the surrounding hawthorn hedges.

Glenalina, with its rushing hilly streams and pathways, was used during the world war for stabling mules and horses needed for the battle-fields of France and Belgium. We often saw cavalrymen riding up the Falls Road with three riderless mules on either flank. The animals with the letter 'S' branded on their hide looked scared and difficult to handle and some said they had been 'shell-shocked' and sent back from the war for rehabilitation.

DAYS OF FEAR

FOR ME THE 'Troubles' began the morning I awoke to the sound of someone beating a bath-tin in the back yard next door. Above the din I could hear the childish voice of young Sam repeating in a sing-song voice 'No Home Rule for Ireland'. It was the Twelfth of July, 'Orangeman's Day' and above the rattle of the bath-tin across the open fields from the direction of the distant Shankill Road came the dull menacing roll of big Lambeg drums, rising and falling on the breeze.

Later that day I heard adults whisper that Carson, the great Protestant leader, had arrived from London and it was feared that there would be trouble. He was to address a huge Orange demonstration after a triumphal march through the city. I sensed the tension in the air that morning. Everyone seemed convinced that Carson's brand of reckless oratory would blow up into serious disorder. Trouble there was, and plenty, that day and thereafter. The dreaded pogrom had begun in Belfast. It was the end of our happy carefree days. We became aware very quickly of a new fear in our young lives. Violence and terror overshadowed our play that lovely summer.

While on an errand to Fleeton's shop at Springfield Road corner I saw a fleet of cars and taxis conveying workmen with bloodstained bandages around their heads to the nearby Royal Victoria Hospital. These were the Catholic workers, beaten up and 'expelled' from the two great shipyards on the Lagan. A telegram from Sir James Craig MP in London said 'Well done, big and wee yards.' The unfortunate shipyard workers were the victims of the speech-makers like Carson, the reaction of the bigots against the Sinn Fein revolt in the rest of Ireland. Some had even been pelted with iron bolts and thrown into the tide to swim like rats to the safety of the slob-lands. We heard of hardly anything else that summer but IRA ambushes and of the hideous 'reprisals' on innocent civilians by the British Black-and-Tans and Auxiliaries in the south.

Up north we feared the Specials. There were three categories of Special Constabulary – 'A', 'B' and 'C' Specials, masquerading as police but, in actual fact, Unionist party followers, many of them sectarian thugs armed to the teeth in uniform. The signal had come from Winston Churchill in London to arm the Protestant population to 'hold Ulster' and the Unionist party leaders took the cue.

All hell was let loose one night when some lunatic tossed a bomb into a tramcar packed with shipyard men homeward bound for the Shankill. By 7 o'clock the sunlit streets were empty, football games in the fields were abandoned and cricket stumps were pulled up and packed away for another day. At Beechmount a pitched battle raged for hours between tender-loads of 'B' Specials armed with rifles and local IRA snipers firing down from the fields. A British Army Whippet armoured-car intervened at twilight firing a heavy Maxim gun but the sporadic shooting continued all night as we lay for safety beneath the windows, fearful of the crossfire.

Shocked and bewildered by it all we children fell asleep towards midnight, worn out by fear and trembling. We awoke in the early morning light to the desultory crack of revolver fire but it died away by breakfast time. When at last we issued forth expecting to find the streets littered with bullets we found nothing but a few pock-marked walls. Only one person, a male 'staller' had been wounded at the local brickyard. The people we called 'stallers' were the pathetic 'meth' or 'blowhard' drinkers. About a dozen of them, men and women, could be seen each night stumbling along drunkenly to the brickyard where they 'stalled' for the night in the still-warm kilns from which new baked bricks had been cleared. They were homeless and forgotten in their misery. They sang meaningless snatches of songs as they lay, their clothes covered with the red dust of the kilns. This was the only abode these outcasts knew. In the morning before work resumed at the brickyard they would be gone. Occasionally they might leave behind some abject wreck, man or woman, too far gone to move. Mercifully, an ambulance would appear to remove the victim to hospital.

My friendship with young Sam came to a sudden and sad end. One evening the blow fell. Groups of men came knocking on the doors of the small number of Protestants living in the area. They looked grim-faced and determined. They told the Protestant families, all decent folk who lived in peace with their neighbours, that they would have to clear out immediately to make way for dispossessed Catholic families who had been forced by mobs to flee from other parts of north and east Belfast. Some had been 'burned out' and left with only the clothes they wore. Later that night, about 11 o'clock, I saw the white face of poor Sam as he sat looking bewildered on a coal-cart carrying his family's furniture and belongings out of the street. We did not even have time to say 'Goodbye' and I never saw him again. As the horse-drawn cart rumbled off down the street I felt heart-sick. New neighbours appeared next door. They were English Catholics from Lancashire who had been put out of their Belfast home because of their religion. I missed Sam and for a long time resented the new neighbours.

Many years later I was able to look back at the moment in time when the manipulators of the electoral boundaries in Belfast were able to boast that they had 'tidied up' their political maps marked orange and green.

At night we were sometimes awakened by the noise of a raiding party looking for members of the Republican 'Flying Columns' from the south suspected of hiding out in a friendly household. First there was the rumble of a heavy lorry as the vehicle slowed to a halt outside. Its headlights cast shadows on the window blinds as we lay quaking, listening to heavy foot-falls approaching. They stopped at a house a few yards from us on the opposite side. Then came the sound of fists pounding on the door followed by a crash as they burst in. Many footsteps ascended the stairs and we could hear shouts and screams as if a struggle was going on. Then again the noise of feet on the stairs as if one or two men were being manhandled. The door slammed closed and the engine of the lorry started up and soon it was moving out of the street. Who were they? Was it the police or the military? Could it be the Murder Gang of whom we had heard such fearful tales? Would some more victims be found lying out on the wet grass of the Daisy Hill in the morning with bullets through their heads and placards round their necks saying 'Sinn Feiners Beware'?

Going into the city with one's parents to the big stores in Donegall Place, High Street and Royal Avenue was at times an unusually hazardous exercise. The old red and yellow coloured tramcar swayed, whined and groaned over the rails down the Falls Road. There were certain danger points when it passed Cupar Street, Conway Street, Northumberland Street and Dover Street, long streets leading from the Falls to the Shankill. Across these streets, at moments of tension, the report of rifle fire rang out as snipers on both sides opened up. The tram speeded and clanked past these streets as the driver crouched down on the deck behind the controls. The passengers took their cue and huddled down on the floor which the Tramways department thoughtfully provided with a carpet of straw. There were always audible sighs of relief when the neutral Castle Junction hove in sight. Life went on in spite of the perils. We lived dangerously. When the Civil War broke out in the south over the Irish Treaty, most of the leading northern Republicans left to join in the fratricidal strife. The famous Michael Collins, who had become a legend in his own lifetime, was killed in a Cork ambush while Arthur Griffith, President of the 'Provisional Government' in Dublin died suddenly, it was said, of a broken heart. Up north we all sensed the feelings of despair and abandonment which prevailed at the time. A sinister British brasshat, the saturnine Sir Henry Wilson, the jack-booted intriguer of the 1914 war, arrived in Belfast as military adviser to the new northern Unionist administration led by Sir James Craig. He devised the so-called 'Block-house system' of repression under which the Specials entered the Catholic areas to dominate the largely defenceless population and bring them into submission to the new Orange rulers. There was little resistance when these undisciplined forces, armed to the teeth, moved in to seize St Mary's Hall and other strong-points throughout West Belfast. The Falls Baths were occupied and fortified, and near us the big Beehive Bar, owned by the McKeown family, was taken over and turned into a sandbagged fortress.

The open hostility of these swaggering louts was soon manifest as they flaunted their guns threateningly at every opportunity. Innocent people felt intimidated by their murderous reputation. Further up the Falls Road they were thwarted in their plans to take over another spacious pub, O'Neill's Rock Bar. Before they could move in with their paraphernalia of guns and sandbags the place was destroyed by a landmine. This was the only show of resistance. At the Beehive Bar we had the curious spectacle of a Special standing sentry behind the sandbags armed with a clumsy-looking Lewis gun, no less.

Once a month, on paynight, a minor reign of terror descended on the district. The danger signal was the sight of barrels of Guinness stout being rolled across the road from Paddy Hynes's pub and into the Beehive. About 8 pm, after several hours' boozing, the Specials issued forth swinging their rifles, and into their Lancias and caged armoured cars for a night of fun 'shooting up' the area and teaching the Fenians a lesson. Speeding along Beechmount Avenue they fired volley after volley up the long streets where neighbours gossiped and children played. As they fired at random, women and children ran in terror or dropped down out of sight in the little gardens. Door after door slammed shut and in spite of the bright summer evenings nobody risked going out, even though the officlal curfew hour was not due until 10 pm.

About this time British troops, who had maintained a semblance of fair play and decency in the sectarian confrontations, were withdrawn to barracks, a strange decision by some sinister influence at the top. It seemed that the powers-that-be in London were letting the Specials loose to cow the minority population. The disaster of the vicous and stupid civil war in the south had played neatly into their hands.

One of the odd, almost folk, heroes of the time was a dashing young Englishman, a lieutenant of the Norfolk Regiment, a regiment said to have Catholic sympathies. At moments of danger for the civil population he would appear from nowhere with a small squad of soldiers running at the double into the firing line. Many stories were told about his coolness in awkward situations. He sported a small clipped moustache and had a public schools' accent with a dry laugh which earned for him the nickname 'Ha-ha'. Women, terrified by some inexplicable shooting incident, used to cry out with relief 'Oh thank God, here comes Ha-ha'. But now 'Ha ha' and his men were being recalled by their masters in London. Britain was washing its hands of the six Ulster counties, abandoning its responsibility to a bigoted new regime, a one-party state which had chosen the weapons of repression and discrimination to bolster up its seizure of power.

SEND HIM UP THE RIVER

IN THE EARLY twenties an uneasy peace settled over the country as the civil war ended in the south and the northern government, composed of men who had taken up arms against Home Rule, took over control. Those Sinn Feiners who had not been lifted and interned in either Belfast Prison or the old wooden prison ship *Argenta*, first moored off Carrickfergus in Belfast Lough and later towed to Larne Lough, had either fled to Dublin or emigrated to America.

On the other side several known Orange gunmen, who had openly boasted of 'notches' in their guns for the Sinn Feiners they had shot, were quietly provided with cash and one-way tickets to Canada. A few who, it was said, had embarrassed their former leaders by indulging in private bank robberies and hold-ups, were put behind bars under internment orders when they threatened to 'tell all' if charged in open court. Sir Dawson Bates, Minister of Home Affairs, in charge of police and prisons, was plagued for much of his subsequent career in the northern parliament by his old enemy, John W Nixon, MP for Woodvale, and an ex-police inspector who continually reminded him of one such Protestant internee. At odd intervals over the years Nixon used to bellow across the floor when Bates spoke 'What about James Mulgrew?'. Sir Dawson, the keeper of many political secrets, never answered.

In the new desire for public respectability and to keep face at Westminster, the criminal elements among the Loyalists had to be dispensed with, but it was not easy. There were mutinies by some of the worst elements among the Specials when they were told that cash resources from Britain were drying up and that the irregular forces were being reduced by disbandment.

It was about this time that my parents decided to transfer me to St Mary's Christian Brothers' School at Divis Street, a school with a great reputation, the *alma mater* of many leading figures in the north, judges, barristers, journalists, politicians and clergymen. Pictures of a selection of these distinguished old boys adorned the walls in the ground-floor classroom. One of them evoked more interest among us than the others. This was a picture and story of a boy named Corr who had invented a ray in his home at Holywood, County Down, on the shores of Belfast Lough. Corr had focused his ray on the opposite County Antrim shore and succeeded in setting fire to a haystack. We were told that Corr was scooped up by the War Office in London in its quest for a weapon to combat the wartime threat of the German Zeppelins.

At first I was scared of the stories I had heard about St. Mary's and particularly because of dark hints about a mysterious punishment called 'the mossy' said to be meted out by the brothers. These fears proved to be groundless. The Brothers were tough, but so were we, and only 'sissies' complained. My first experience there was under a kindly old Limerick-born Brother known as 'Old Mac', Brother McSweeney, a man of many ingenious ideas on education, not to mention personal fads such as handwriting by the Cremer system which permanently ruined my earlier rounded copy-book style.

For his half-hour religious instruction each morning he used a wooden motto device rather like a mechanical desk calendar. Turn the knob and up would come the subject for a talk such as 'Holy Purity' or 'Death, Judgment, Hell, Heaven'. Then would come a down-to-earth, man-to-man, chat on subjects rarely mentioned previously. But he often digressed to other matters, for example the latest headlines in the morning newspapers about a terrible Welsh mining disaster or the story of a shipwreck or some other calamity. He never mentioned politics but it was an open secret that he was a personal friend and supporter of Joe Devlin, the famous Nationalist MP for West Belfast. A great orator in his day, 'Wee Joe' was the darling of the girls in the West Belfast linen mills. Dubbed at Westminster the 'Vest-pocket Demosthenes' Devlin's election brakes were followed by hundreds of enthusiastic beshawled mill-doffers. They laughed and sang a ribald Belfast ditty 'We'll send him up the river with his ya-ya-ya ...'.

Old Mac was proud of the fact that Devlin was once a pupil at St Mary's, living in a humble home around the corner. He started his career washing bottles in Kelly's Cellars, the city's oldest pub in Bank Street, a narrow lane, close to Castle Junction. His natural gift as a public speaker soon brought him to the fore in Home Rule politics. His impassioned speeches, delivered in the harsh accents of Belfast, swayed gatherings of thousands, and even, by all accounts, electrified the sophisticated members of the British Commons.

Young as we were we imbibed a feeling of pride in the old smoke-blackened school, built from ancient bricks, salvaged we were told, from the old artillery barracks in the adjoining Barrack Street. It was heartening to think that one could emerge through the ruck, as Devlin did, to the very pinnacle of fame in the wider world far from our native city.

My family had moved by this time to the larger rambling Victorian house, No. 1 Almeda Terrace, formerly the home of my Magauran grandparents. There I slept in the 'Returning Room' at the top of three flights of stairs, listening to the gurgling Clowney River flowing at the bottom of the adjoining garden. The rear windows looked on to the fields at Willowbank where we were told the old huts, still remaining, had once been occupied by dragoons during the riots of the last century. Across the broad meadow where cows grazed was Celtic Park, headquarters of Belfast's famous soccer team, Belfast Celtic. It was in Celtic Park that Winston Churchill addressed a monster Home Rule gathering away back in 1912 after Orangemen had seized the municipal Ulster Hall and barred the doors against him. So the venue was changed and Winston, after being mobbed outside the Grand Central hotel by angry Unionists, sped up the Falls Road in a taxi being cheered by women in shawls and pursued by the inevitable barking dog. For years I carried a picture of this scene as Winston's taxi drove past the Clonard Picture House. Churchill was then Home Secretary in the Liberal Government and had threatened to send a battleship to Belfast to deal with Carson's rebellion against the government's Home Rule Bill.

From Almeda Terrace it was a halfpenny tram ride down town to St Mary's in the mornings. The old-fashioned lurching and bucking tram was so packed that one had often to sit in the freezing cold of winter in the exposed front or rear section of the upper deck, guarding one's precious books, secured by a strap, from the pelting rain.

Our education at St. Mary's was interrupted for a few years when we passed over to a preparatory course for secondary or grammar school at St. Patrick's in Donegall Street, a dark and dingy building hemmed in on one side by the grim Gothic St Patrick's Church and a rumbling flour mill on the other side. Here a handsome athletic teacher from the south, later to become a member of the Dublin Dail and father of a Cabinet minister, swore at us in a rich Clare brogue as he raised his eyes to heaven at our efforts to absorb 'Elementa Latina' and 'Amo, Amas, Amat', I love, You love, He loves. Paddy Lenihan's skill at athletics and his salty humour invoked a kind of hero-worship and we were all saddened when he left to take up a post in the Irish civil service.

At St. Patrick's we were introduced to the mysteries of Euclid and the 'pons asinorum', Scott's *Lay of the Last Minstrel*, Physics, the Principle of Archimedes, Algebra and Logs. Our early enthusiasm for the Irish language was dampened by the frustration of the irregular verbs. Master of Arts, Tom Ivory, who took us for History, was a popular teacher and his asides on historical figures opened our eyes.

He described James I, who came down from Scotland to take the English throne, as an 'oul slobber' who dribbled at the mouth so much that courtiers were forced to open up their umbrellas to avoid the flying spits when he addressed them! I remembered this piece of imagery many years later when one of William Whitelaw's civil service advisers at Stormont ruminating over a drink on why 'Ulster' was such a 'pain-in-the-neck' to London blamed it all on James I, the 'wisest fool in Christendom'. Said he: 'In my book King James was a bloody idiot. Wasn't he responsible for the Ulster Plantation, the source of all our troubles in Ireland?'

The senior Christian Brother in charge at St. Mary's was Brother Murray, a good-hearted but tough martinet whose bark was worse than his bite. As a young man he had taught at a Christian Brothers' school in far-off Newfoundland. He was quick on the draw with his thick double-sown black strap and used his gold-rimmed spectacles as a rear-view mirror to detect cheeky youths who made faces behind his back. Lugubrious offenders were familiar with his favourite expression of disgust 'You've a face like Pontius Pilate's horse! Hold out your hand' and then would come down three on either palm.

Our days at St Patrick's were enlivened at lunch-hour some days by expeditions to the docks to inspect the tug-boats at the lower harbour, or past the gangways leading up to the saloons of the big cross-channel passenger steamers for Liverpool, Heysham, Glasgow and Ardrossan. At Great Patrick Street we gazed in the window of a pawn shop at mariners' sextants and brass clocks and compasses for sale. At the deep-sea docks there was the smell of salt-water and the sight of Russian grain ships and once a huge three-masted sailing ship from Finland with its furled sails and miles of cordage to stir our imagination.

Soon all that episode was to end for we were now equipped for the final stage of our school career back to Junior Grade at St. Mary's, upstairs among the big fellas with incipient moustaches and deepening voices. First Smithfield was ransacked for cheap second-hand Latin classics and prescribed Maths. Few could afford the large batch of books required and Harry Hall's or Greer's in Smithfield was the recognised source for Caesar's *Gallic Wars* or Virgil's *Aeneid* and such like.

Our introduction to the Latin classics was an excruciating experience. From Julius Caesar we learned that all Gaul was divided into three parts, that the Roman dictator was bald and hook-nosed and not much else. Later we met him again in our study of Shakespeare's play and felt he deserved all he got for causing so much pain in the translation of his boring war records. Our appreciation of Virgil in the Latin also left much to be desired. The opening lines on the coming of Aeneas to Carthage, 'a fated wanderer from the coasts of Troy to Italy and the shore of Lavinium' sounded promising, but as we struggled through the rest of it our deficiencies became only too apparent. A few, more resourceful than the rest, raided Smithfield once more and emerged triumphantly with *Kelly's Key To The Classics* with a full translation of the *Aeneid*. Each day the appropriate page was torn out and passed along beneath the desks where bored youths had stuttered in turn with the Latin text. The Christian Brother in charge must have smelt a rat at the sudden upsurge in literacy and grace of expression for he looked suspicious. But it was not until one smart Alec caused loud laughter by substituting 'holy pot' for 'sacred cauldron' that the short-lived conspiracy was revealed. Dear old Brother Maloney, better known as 'Slim Jim', a kindly soul ordinarily, darted behind the desk and snatched the offending page from his nerveless hands. The *Key To The Classics* was confiscated and mass punishment in the form of an extra half-hour of Aeneas's tiresome wanderings around the Mediterranean was prescribed.

In retrospect it is astonishing to realise that in those days we were receiving a sound secondary, or grammar, school education for the princely sum of one shilling per week! Many of the pupils came from under-privileged homes and could not afford even this modest fee. The Brothers turned a blind eye to their indebtedness and I never heard even a hint of their embarrassment. Yet from this class emerged men who afterwards carved out brilliant careers as doctors, churchmen, including a Cardinal (Bill Conway), barristers, journalists and senior civil servants. But it was tough going in those days for a Catholic in the competitive society of a work-starved Northern Ireland. Religious bigotry was almost an accepted way of life and many doors were closed to Catholics, however brilliant, because of the majority Unionist view that it was dangerous policy to permit the growing one-third minority to rise above their proper station in life as 'second-class citizens'. This was the officially sponsored policy from the top down. No bones were made about it. It was proclaimed from the house-tops by government politicians at every opportunity. Prime Minister Lord Craigavon laid it down that the Northern Parliament was a 'Protestant Parliament for a Protestant people'. Like the 'niggers' in the US south, the Catholic population, then representing about 34 per cent, did not come into the reckoning as 'people'.

Coming out of school those who had not elected for some of the professions tried their hand at the competitive exams for posts in the Civil Service. But this was an unusual obstacle race locally. While merit was usually the deciding factor for the Imperial Civil Service it was a very different ball-game for the local Northern Ireland Civil Service. You might be the most brilliant man of your year but there was the dreaded interview. This was the real hurdle. Unless someone of influence in Unionist politics could be persuaded to give you a 'leg-up' there was little hope of a Catholic boy or girl, however outstanding academically or in personality, surviving this so-called 'interview'. The unfortunate interviewees knew instinctively from the frozen faces of the panel that it was all over when the inevitable question was fired 'What school did you attend?' This became a kind of sick joke through the years and later in a superficial attempt at subtlety it was varied with 'What games do you play?' Those who replied 'Gaelic football' or 'Hurling', the games favoured by most Catholic schools, were usually assured in the finish 'We'll let you know' and that was the end of their hopes of a post. Clever Dicks who claimed to play 'Hockey' or 'Rugby' found the interview prolonged a little further until the panel probed out the truth about his or her religious persuasion.

Many years later, up at the Stormont Parliament Buildings, I discovered the identity of one of the leading interviewers. He was a local politician, a former shipyard worker, who rose from the role of a mob leader in York Street in the twenties to a post in Cabinet. What this ignoramus knew about the suitability of applicants for the Civil Service could be written on the back of a postage stamp, yet it was clear that his colleagues on the panel, usually senior civil servants from the ministeries concerned, must have taken their cue from this individual. These were the faceless men who sowed the dragon's teeth of the mass alienation which paved the way for the tragic events of the days to come. They sang dumb about this injustice because, after all, they had their own careers and promotions to consider under the regime. Those who tried and failed to penetrate the barbed wire defences of the Northern Ireland Civil Service gave up hope and accepted any humble job available. Some even became bookies' clerks and, ironically, wealthy men in their own right eventually, the silver lining to the dark cloud of rejection, perhaps.

There were no playing fields at St. Mary's. The school was surrounded by a mixture of commercial property and streets of kitchen-houses and broken-down shops. From nearby Barrack Street a local pork butcher periodically compelled the Brothers to close all the windows to exclude the nauseous smell of burning offal. At the weekends, however, we were expected to make an appearance in the broad acres of the Falls Park, three miles out in the suburbs, for Gaelic football and hurling practice. The upper reaches of the park beyond the tree-lined bowling-green, tennis courts and bandstand provided a lovely vista of the surrounding hills but the pitches were little better than corrugated muddy slopes. Would-be All-Ireland hurlers were severely handicapped by the impossible terrain in spite of Brother Murray's roaring encouragement 'Pull on it boy!' from the sidelines. The nearby swimming pool 'The Cooler' was certainly cool even on the hottest day as the children of the Falls splashed about in their hundreds in the ice-cold water from the mountain streams.

But our main diversion in sport was our intense interest in the fortunes of the local soccer team, Belfast Celtic, and the rivalry for championship honours with the ultra-Protestant Linfield team at Windsor Park. It was a Belfast version of the long-standing conflict between the Glasgow rivals, Glasgow Celtic and Rangers. Both teams outshone all others in the Irish League and the grim battle for supremacy was more like a re-enactment of the Battle of the Boyne. Riots were not infrequent. Referees were besieged in the dressing-rooms at times by angry partisans and occasionally police armoured cars were called in to quell disorders which broke out after a hard-fought tussle. The old joke was often repeated in the pubs on the few occasions that Celtic were downed by the 'Blues'. 'There'll be sore hearts in the Vatican tonight'. Celtic had no religious bar like Linfield and ironically frequently more than half the team were Protestants. But once they donned the green-and-white striped jerseys they became 'honorary Catholics' in the eyes of the fans. But to the Linfield support these players were 'Fenians' and 'traitors'.

Our heroes were Mickey Hamill, the owner of the 'Centre-Half Bar' who returned to Celtic from Manchester City and Jimmy Ferris, another returned veteran from the English league, a dazzling inside-forward with a bundle of tricks up his sleeve. Many times capped for Ireland was Celtic's famed goalkeeper, Elisha Scott, whose choice selection of oaths and advice to his team-mates, bellowed in a stentorian voice, could be heard on the grandstand by all including the priests present who feigned deafness. Elisha could be forgiven anyhow. After all he was a Protestant!

The 'Mahood-wing' was another Celtic by-word in those days with Stan and Jack Mahood running rings around the opposition. But the man we all feared on the Linfield side was 'Slip-it-to-Joe' Bambrick, another famed Irish International centre-forward who could run with the ball at his toe like a thoroughbred racehorse leaving the defenders puffing behind. Only wily old Elisha Scott was left to snatch the ball from his feet before Joe could slam it into the net. Those were the great days in Belfast when football was not so much a game as a battle of gladiators. Football was a kind of safety valve for the latent sectarian conflict bubbling beneath the surface. But oddly enough when an international game was staged in Belfast sectional feuds were forgotten for the afternoon. The crowd at Windsor Park roared 'Come on Ireland' against the common enemy, England, Scotland or Wales. When international football was extended to Europe an Italian team was mobbed by an angry crowd at Windsor Park. The newspapers reported 'Disgraceful Scenes' but the Italian newspapers came out with huge headlines in which the word 'Barbari' stood out. One Rome daily blamed Julius Caesar for failure to extend his civilising mission to Ireland!

What did we talk about on those long walks home from school in the late Twenties? All I can recall as an absorbing topic over many moons was the revived interest in the Great War and the wave of pacificism sweeping through intellectual society as the clouds of war gathered again in China and unrest began in Europe. German currency had collapsed and ordinary workers were reported to be carrying home their week's wages in wheelbarrows laden with millions of marks. Belfast bookmakers even distributed the useless

German high-denomination notes stamped with their names as advertisements to their clients. The craze for war films whetted our appetite and the cinemas snapped up *All Quiet On The Western Front*, *The Big Parade*, *Madamoiselle From Armentiers* and many others. We were fascinated by the pictures of trench warfare and all that we read about 'Big Bertha', the huge gun which fired shells into Paris from 75 miles away, the stories of raids across No Man's Land at night, the attacks at dawn on the 'Wipers Salient', the sappers on both sides burrowing beneath the Front to mine enemy positions, the poison gas and the first appearance of the tanks. Occasionally those of us who were interested tried to button-hole ex-servicemen about their war experiences but found them strangely reticent. They did not want to talk but when coaxed some told bizarre and unheroic stories about comrades driven crazy after days of bombardment and malingerers shooting themselves in the foot to escape from the horror of 'going over the top' to death. You could spot these veterans in the streets. They all looked alike, cadaverous, dull-eyed, unsmiling and silent. The sights they had seen were etched on their countenances, never to be forgotten, but rarely spoken about except in odd snatches of recall. Lloyd George, the 'Welsh Wizard', promised them 'Homes fit for heroes' but in peacetime that was forgotten. Most of them were unemployed. Some sold matches in the street while others reduced to penury begged under the placard 'ex-serviceman'. At the corner of Cornmarket in Belfast a distinguished looking ex-captain with a slight clipped moustache stood with a barrel organ seeking public support to ventilate some obscure injustice perpetrated by the War Office.

The heroes of yesterday were accorded little sympathy. Outside the GPO in Royal Avenue an ex-Navy man in a blue jersey, without legs, squatted his pathetic trunk on a leather pad in the rain, staring piteously, hour after hour, at passers-by, a few of whom threw the odd copper into his lap. Some said he had been blown up in an explosion on a battleship. Others commented 'What a terrible end.

He would be better dead.' After a few years the silent man on Royal Avenue, only half-a-man, had disappeared.

Years later during the 1939-45 war, I was standing in for a *Daily Mail* colleague, off ill, and was asked by the Manchester News Editor to interview the parents of a young soldier who was awarded the Military Medal during Montgomery's desert campaign. They lived in a tiny kitchen-house in a little street off the Shankill Road. After repeated knocks an old woman, frail and care-worn, admitted me to the humble and obviously impoverished home. Over the mantlepiece was a large framed photograph of a bemedalled soldier of the 1914 War in the uniform of a Highland regiment. The old woman dismissed my news of her son's award as of no account. 'Ah mister, what's the use of medals?' she said quietly, 'sure himself in there got medals too and look at him.' She pointed to a small inner room where an old grey-haired man lay coughing on a bed with a faded overcoat spread over him. Here was another of the heroes of yesterday, long forgotten by everyone except his poor old wife. I did not have much relish writing that story, and the picture of the old soldier has remained engraved on my mind ever since.

In the Stormont parliamentary dining room several years later I was introduced by an MP to a man in country tweeds, a surgeon from a County Down village near Belfast who, over the teacups, recalled his own chilling experiences of the Somme. He looked a typical country medico and nobody would have guessed that as the gory battle raged he had to spend hours and days in makeshift Red Cross tents amputating legs and arms of the unfortunate victims carried in on blood-stained stretchers, survivors of the deadly shell-fire, the holocaust into which they were sent in waves. These were Carson's Volunteers, recruited in the heady days of the Ulster Rebellion against Home Rule to fight for 'God and Ulster'. An army captain who served with them and who came back to serve as a police inspector in County Armagh told me that one of his most vivid memories was of Ulstermen cursing the name Carson as the full import of the Somme tragedy hit them. Here they were lying in the mud among the dead and dying far away from their native soil in a foreign land while the old rebel leader who once threatened to kick the Crown into the Boyne was ensconced in Whitehall as a member of the War Cabinet. My informant said he could never forget the weary survivor of one of the futile and deadly attacks which failed with heavy casualties, stumbling down into a dug-out and peeling off his mud-covered boot in the candlelight and hurling it at a faded picture of Carson pinned to a wooden prop. 'F—Carson!' he cried. That was the day the hero worship of the one-time Ulster leader died.

As the last few years of the Twenties rolled off the calendar and the end of our schooldays loomed up, we began to think about our future careers. Some of my friends took the easy option of studying for the Imperial Civil Service exams. In spite of the allurements of an easy-going existence, plenty of holidays, and a nice pension at the end, I resisted the temptation. A less easy-going and more exacting,and yet to me a more glamorous, if modestly paid, profession had been beckoning all the time, the old 'black art' of journalism. I had not then read Louis McNeice's funny *Bagpipe Music* and the lines 'No go the Civil Service ... Sit on your arse for fifty years and hang your hat on a pension' but I agreed with the sentiments. I had read every book the libraries could offer on journalism including Phillip Gibb's *Street Of Adventure*, the biographies of Northcliffe, Tom Clarke, TP O'Connor, HL Mencken, Theodore Dreisier and many others.

I cannot pinpoint when the idea first entered my mind but I suspect that the example of a favourite uncle, Patsy Magauran, my mother's elder brother, had a lot to do with it. He was then assistant editor of the *Irish News* and lived with us at Alameda Terrace. A tall, slim, handsome bachelor in his forties, bookish, reserved and with a keen sense of humour, he worked at night emerging from his book-lined bedroom on the to floor about 3 pm and then, some time after dinner at 7 pm, was off to the office. He carried a silver-topped walking stick and smoked a pipe and reminded me vaguely of Sherlock Holmes. Occasionally he called at the local National Club where he and his friends invented a kind of intellectual secret society which they named 'The Calathumpians'. It was designed to ward off bores who interrupted their discussions. Those who insisted were told that the first rule for initiation was to stand a full round of drinks. The joke persisted for years.Uncle Pat insisted on a supper of fresh sandwiches being delivered to the office nightly and soon I was pressed into service to perform this ritual. I was, of course, rewarded with a handsome tip for my nightly trip into town. This was my first insight into the mysteries of newspaper production. It was a sight to set alight the imagination of a teenager. Up the narrow stone stairway at the bottom of a long corridor I passed the 'Reporters Room' and 'Creed Room' where Kerryman Tim O'Connor's noisy teleprinter spewed out a never-ending tape of the world's news from the PA and Reuters. I passed through the Sub-Editors' department where men with green eye-shades stood at high desks or sat around a large table with thick pencils poised over wads of copy from correspondents, every now and again throwing pages into a huge wire waste-basket or thrusting the finished product into a small wooden hoist which rattled up to the compositors on the next floor. From a naked gas-bracket one sub-editor lit a piece of copy paper to start up his pipe. It was a scene of calm informality and steady application by men who knew their job well and, although working against the clock, could find time for a jar in the pub opposite and then quickly back to work to deal with more red envelopes of copy just collected from thePost Office by John, the nightmessenger.

Pat Magauran worked alone in the Editor's Room where the door leading to the subs remained permanently open. He sat at a desk cluttered with proofs and clippings from the Dublin and London papers, all ammunition for the editorial and leaderettes which he penned swiftly in the fast flowing hand of a man used to writing

31

thousands of words to an early deadline. From the upper floor came the rattle of linos and the thumps of metal type being hammered into the steel pages. The whole scene of bustle and activity in contrast with the quiet of the deserted city streets outside I found fascinating and I longed one day to be part of it.

By 4 am all the news from the far corners of the globe during the past 24 hours would be neatly trimmed, headlined, printed and packaged ready for distribution throughout the country by van, train, bus and bicycle. There were many more nocturnal visits to the *Irish News* and once or twice I caught a glimpse of the elderly editor, a Corkman named Tim McCarthy, a man in failing health but whose brilliant editorials were the subject of enduring admiration in Nationalist circles. The trips to Donegall Street ceased when my uncle left for London to take up a senior post as Sub-Editor in the old Fleet Street office of the *Irish Independent* but the picture of that bustling hive of activity remained with me for years and journalism became increasingly the object of my ambition.

Meantime on the death of Tim McCarthy, Uncle Pat was asked by the *Irish News* directors to come back as editor, but declined. A new editor was eventually found in England and was charged with the daunting task of building up the circulation of the paper. His name was Sydney Redwood and he proved to be a tough go-getter who had come through the mill with the Dundee-based Thomson newspaper group. In appearance he looked more like a Burmese with his yellow complexion, dark hair, prominent teeth and tortoise-shell spectacles. He had a loud bark and a no-nonsense manner. Some of those who incurred his wrath claimed that he had never recovered from seeing the film *The Front Page*. But he soon transformed the old paper into a smart up-and-coming daily with a rapidly increasing circulation. In doing so he shook up the easy-going staffs of all departments to near desperation.

A couple of introductions secured me an interview with this intimidating Englishman. I was then turned 17. He was brusque to the point of rudeness. My application for the post of junior reporter was disposed of very quickly. 'First go and learn shorthand and typing' he snapped, 'but don't expect a job here unless you can prove to me that you can write.' One way of doing that, he suggested, was to contribute gossip paragraphs to the paper's new popular feature 'Random Jottings' which he had introduced. For this I would be paid the princely sum of half-a-crown a paragraph. I took him at his word and duly enlisted for an intensive course of Pitman's shorthand, and typing. I bought a second-hand typewriter for £4, a heavy old Olivetti, and started out on the hard grind as a freelance journalist.

I was lucky for the first paragraph I submitted was accepted. No thrill ever exceeded the first sight of my paragraph in print the morning after I had handed it in to Redwood. We had moved by this time to the upper Donegall Road, a few hundred yards from Celtic Park, and my first essay in journalism was about the popularity of the neighbouring Bog Meadows as a nursery for famous footballers. The 'Bogs', an immense open space, stretched from Celtic Park to Windsor Park and southward to the far distant Stockman's Lane. Here on an evening hundreds of lads of all ages kicked football on improvised pitches. Sometimes a game would start with about half a dozen a side. But it was a free-for-all in which as many as twenty a side might join. Strollers of any age who felt they could kick a ball or demonstrate their talents at dribbling would take part.

During the day we jumped the drainage streams and penetrated deeper into the Bogs to the soggy high grasses and rushes where wild birds of all kinds found a haven. Occasionally we crossed the fences into the adjoining marshalling yards of the Great Northern Railway at Adelaide and watched wagons being shunted into position for the night goods trains South. Towns and railheads all over Ireland were chalked on their stained woodwork. We could only surmise what goods and commerce had been shifted from these faraway places to Belfast.

Recovering from my excitement at seeing my first journalistic effort in print, I set about the tough task of following through with more items. I roamed the city in search of subjects and people of interest, talked to oldsters about their memories, dug up old local histories, haunted the city reference libraries and succeeded in getting a lot of my contributions accepted. Some indeed ended up in the waste-paperbasket but I persevered for the best part of a year earning a modest £3 a month. But I was less interested in the money than in the thrill of authorship, seeing my copy in bold print at the breakfast table.

I don't know whether Redwood was impressed by this time that I could at least write a well-rounded paragraph or whether he became tired of my frequent appearances with copy but at last came a letter of invitation to come in for an interview. As I had hoped it turned out to be an offer of a job as junior reporter on a six months trial period at twenty-five shillings a week. I was delighted but at the same time uneasy about the stipulation 'on trial'. I was aware that others like me had been tried and having failed to make the grade had been told to seek their fortunes elsewhere.

THROUGH THE LOOKING-GLASS

THAT AUGUST NIGHT in 1929 when I walked up the familiar stone staircase and through the door of the Reporters' Room was my introduction to a fascinating other world beyond the looking-glass. I was an 'insider' at last, an observer of drama, tragedy and comedy in a city which is a byword among newsmen throughout the world, a city of saints and sinners where the sinners make more news than the saints, a city of contrasts, rough, tough and pathetic, church steeples and factory chimneys, killers, religious hypocrites, political rogues and endearing ordinary folk. Through time I learned that there was no real need to go to Fleet Street, London or Times Square, New York. Sooner or later they came to us and listened open-mouthed to the stories of the insiders.

In the Reporters' Room half a dozen men of varied ages were busy at their desks or around a big table strewn with newspapers, copy paper and gum bottles. They were too busy to take much notice of a new 18-year-old recruit, an innocent abroad, soon to be thrown in at the deep end to sink or swim. There were no new-fangled journalists' training courses in those days. It was a brutal case of the survival of the fittest. Redwood had warned me that I had six months to prove that I was a newspaperman.

Unlike many of my colleagues I had bypassed the drudgery of the usual apprenticeship on a country weekly. The *Irish News* was so short-staffed compared with its rivals, two morning papers and an evening, and I was assured, rather grimly I thought, that I would obtain more experience there in six months than I would get on most dailies in six years – if I survived.

They were right. It was hard going. A curt note 'Go and report this and that' and you were out on your own. No advice, no instruction. Ask for it and the Chief Reporter in charge, dear old Bob Hayes, would look at you amusedly and say 'Do your best'. He might suggest 'a couple of sticks', or 'half a column' but that was all. The Editor presented a tyrannical front but we respected him as a man who knew his job. No slipshod work missed his bespectacled brown eyes. We lived under the constant fear of the sack. Everyone was bawled out sooner or later. He was no respector of persons young or old. The yell 'This merits instant dismissal' was heard frequently from across his roll-top desk, reducing the negligent senior reporter, sub-editor or junior to desperation and afterwards to empty threat to sympathisers such as 'I'm getting out of this bloody office as soon as I can.'

My first job was 'Night-Town'. I was not a little shocked to be told that this entailed responsibility for covering all untoward happenings in the city between the hours of 7 pm and 3 am – fires, car crashes, arrests, murders, if any, and in short anything out of the ordinary not listed in the Diary of Engagements. My immediate predecessor on 'Night-Town' was Brian Riordan, a tall, good-looking young man who not long later surprised us all by going off to London, not to Fleet Street, but to join a religious order as a postulant for the priesthood.

Brian literally held my hand for a week to show me the ropes. Among other things this consisted of visiting or phoning the police, fire brigade and the city's three main hospitals at intervals during the night. But first came my introduction to my fellow journalists on the two morning papers. They proved to be a friendly lot. Brian seemed to be on good terms with our opposite numbers on the late night watch, often comparing notes on incidents. By mutual agreement the reporters kept themselves right. Scoops or exclusives were 'out' because of the general acceptance of the view that there was little credit for exclusives but a hell of a lot of trouble if you were 'stuck' by a rival paper. Occasionally a 'stinker' might depart from this gentleman's agreement but he would soon learn that it did not pay to let his colleagues down. They would combine to see that he missed something important and soon came to heel.

My first meeting with my new colleagues in the *Belfast Newsletter*, the dyed-in-the-wool Unionist paper, one of the oldest in these islands, was a pleasant experience. At ll pm the Reporters' Room was still crowded. Some were still awaiting their 'markings' for the next day as there had been a delay in completing the engagement book. An older journalist, a Scotsman named Ross, when told that I was a new Night-town man, grunted 'Every night is Night-Town in this bloody office'. There were no duty hours or rotas. A few men who had covered the courts in the morning were aggrieved at being marked for night engagements as well and I was shown a satirical poem pasted on the wall headed The Lonely Wives of Journalists. Pub closing time in Belfast at that time was 10 pm so meetings which lasted longer than 9.30 were expected to take the hint when the group of men at the Press table closed their notebooks and ostentatiously shouldered their way out to the nearest hostelry to enjoy a few pints before handing in their copy.

If wages and conditions on the Belfast papers were poor they must have been worse in some parts of England and Scotland. The *Whig* particularly seemed to be able to attract a fair proportion of English and Scots journalists to its staff over the years. Some stayed for years. Others made the mistake of stepping on the toes of the proprietors' political friends in the City Hall or the government and left quickly. One editor, an independent, outspoken Yorkshireman, attempted to lift the lid off the City Hall Unionist Party's monopoly and certain murky dealings, much to the joy of his staff and the enlightenment of his readers. Soon he too had perforce to pack his bags and leave to seek pastures new across the Irish Sea.

One-party rule and scandals went hand in hand at the City Hall down the years. Fortunes were said to have been made by property men from their inside knowledge of municipal planning. Rumours and reports of bribery and corruption surfaced every now and again but only the lesser fry were ever brought to book. The marble corridors of the City Hall were lined with portraits of whiskered old Lord Mayors who were rewarded with knighthoods if they succeeded in holding office for two terms. It took Buckingham Palace some years to awaken to the fact that this custom was leading to some ludicrous honours. The practice came to a stop suddenly when it was realised that this dubious arrangement had turned into a subject for wry amusement in Belfast.

Not all the members of the City Corporation toed the line, however. One fiery old maverick, Alderman Robert Pierce, with colourful touch of oratory, frequently indulged in a harangue against the ruling Unionist clique. One day they responded with a concerted walk-out in the middle of a long speech condemning 'Government maladministration'. That night the evening paper, the *Belfast Telegraph*, produced a contents bill which became a collector's piece. It read 'Alderman Pierce Empties Corporation Chamber'. Grinning newsboys were soon selling the bills to the highest bidder.

The Catholics, roughly a quarter of the population of the city, were represented by a small group of Nationalists and Labour city fathers. In a hopeless minority on all the ruling municipal committees they developed a precarious *modus vivendi* by a system of horse trading. This consisted of playing off one rival Unionist group against the other in the frequent squabbles over jobs for the boys. The return came in the shape of the crumbs which fell from the tables of greedy Unionists. One old-time Labour alderman, appealing for re-election at a Falls Road rally, was actually heard boasting, 'I got a gardener into the Falls Park', he claimed, 'and what's more', he added, 'he's there yet'.

In the civic pork-barrel the Catholics got the scrapings and they were expected to consider themselves lucky. But in so far as having influence on events in their native city they might as well not have existed and were generally regarded as 'white niggers', tolerated with a mixture of amusement and contempt. At one city council meeting I overheard a particularly scruffy member, believe it or not a barber by trade, remark to companion after some sensible proposal put forward by the redoubtable Gerry Fitt had been automatically voted down, 'Billy, you have to admit that if the other side proposed the erection of Heaven's pearly Gates in Royal Avenue we would oppose it'.

It was in these marble corridors of the magnificent City Hall that I came face to face with this naked and unashamed religious discrimination of which I had heard so much. The 'spoil system' as practised here meant 'grab all and keep the Micks out'. This was carried to such ludicrous ends in party jobbery that sooner or later the roof was bound to fall in, as it did years later. The sins of thefathers, the City Fathers and their ilk, were visited on their sons – but that is another story.

In the Reporters' Room of the *Irish News* we worked like galley slaves. It was all go from morning until late at night. No eight hours a day, no five day week in those days, and if you were lucky you got home on the last bus from town. Nobody questioned the fact that the show must go on. The big Diary of Engagements on the Chief Reporter's desk, completed most evenings about 8 pm, produced a new challenge for the next day. It could mean an early morning start with a first-class rail pass far into the country to cover a murder trial, a political demonstration with the possibility of a riot on the side or a hard slog at a country agricultural show in the summertime with the prospect of a lunch of lamb and mint sauce followed by strawberries and cream as provided by the good old Ulster Menu

Company in their big marquee. It could also mean a job in town, perhaps a High Court action, or a morning at the police courts where the luck of the draw might turn up a 'dirty case' which we judged too shocking for the delicate sensibilities of our readers. In that case we joined forces and repaired to the local YMCA for a game of snooker. Many of the cases in the courts went unreported in those days for reasons of good taste so that most of the population lived in blissful ignorance of what was going on in their own city. I confess that coming from a sheltered existence in a middle-class family my experiences in my first days of reporting in the courts came as an eye-opener. Here was the seamy side of life with a vengeance as, through the dock each day, there passed in procession the unfortunates, men and women who had fallen by the wayside, the prostitutes, perverts, small-time crooks and con-men. At first some of them looked confident and hopeful as they faced the case-hardened magistrates and then crestfallen and pathetic as sentence was pronounced. There was something infinitely sad about the scene as with the stamping of feet the were hustled by police through a side-door to the cells to await the arrival of the jail-van, the dreaded Black Maria, for the doleful journey to Belfast's grim old Crumlin Road Prison.

It was a new aspect of life for me. I was learning. One day I reported a case in which a restaurant proprietor, a fairly prominent officer in a certain very worthy religious organisation, was charged with operating a brothel in the upstairs of the Burlington Cafe in Great Victoria Street. There was copious evidence by the police that the mouth-watering spectacle of sausages and onions frying in the window of the Burlington was only half the story. A password to the manageress, a haunted-looking woman in her late forties, it transpired, sorted out the innocent in search of a meal from other clients 'in the know'. The evidence lasted most of the day as the police detailed the result of their 24 hours watch on the comings and goings of certain notorious damsels and their companions. In the end a heavy fine was imposed.

That night my quarter-of-a-column report about the fining of a proprietor of a 'disorderly house' in Great Victoria Street was too much for the religious susceptibilities of the sub-editor dealing with local copy, dear old Mick Foley. With a Cork brogue which you could cut with a knife Mick adminstered a sharp lesson to me when he stormed into the Reporters' Room grasping my copy. Pushing the offending story under my nose he began 'What I mean to say is – we can't report this. This is a bloody whore-house!

About this time Redwood decided to introduce new and brighter headlines. One was 'pyramid style' and I still recall Mick's brilliant headline of a case I covered at Downpatrick Assizes. Every element of the story was caught by his: 'Co. Down Shot Woman Tragedy Court Story Surprise'.

Subs on local copy had their lighter moments. A Hansard reporter who earlier had worked on the *Newsletter* told me that he once received a report of an Orange Order soiree from a local Grandmaster. It ended with a flourish, 'After sumptuous repast of pigs' feet and porter the proceedings concluded with the National Anthem'.

The late John Charlesson, editor of the Presbyterian weekly *The Witness* told the story of the obituary of an eminent churchman written by a clerical colleague in which he began his contribution with the words: Rev —— —— who has just died was for the past forty years a watcher on Zion's Hill.' A smart Alec c o m p o s i t o r changed 'watcher' to 'watchman' and a Bible-ignorant proof-reader went a step further and corrected 'Zion's Hills' to 'at Sion Mills'. When the proof came down to the busy Editor with scores of other proofs awaiting his attention he tut-tutted about the clergyman who presumed everyone knew the location of Sion Mills and inserted 'Co. Tyrone'! The finished product shook the late divine's congregation with the revelation that for the previous forty years he had led a double life as a 'watchman at Sion Mills, Co. Tyrone.'

When The Witness succumbed to the newsprint shortage during World War II the noted Ulster-born essayist, the late Robert Lynd, wrote its obituary. His piece in the *New Statesman* was entitled 'A Watcher on Zion's Hills'.

Many a time we blamed the subs for ruining our literary gems but more often than not they saved us from ourselves. They had much to withstand and developed a healthy suspicion of the contributions which came in from correspondents who lived on *linage*. Some were brilliant in conjuring up silly-season stories. My old friend Herbie Beatty of Dungannon was credited with starting up a 'gold rush' to a local river and when a local councillor complained that the new council houses were so cramped that they could not get a coffin down the stairs, Herbie arranged a follow-up with pictures of a councillor in a coffin jammed half-way down the staircase. Bob Brady of the *Daily Express* in Belfast used to amuse us with the story of the *Daily Mirror* man sent all the way from Fleet Street to investigate a local correspondent's report about 'The talking dog of Aughnacloy'. He arrived at a small farmhouse in County Tyrone on a Sunday morning and awakened the owner of the dog for an interview. Outside he heard 'Bark, bark, bark' from the wonder canine. 'There it is now,' said the farmer. 'What is it saying?' asked the reporter. 'Can't you hear it?' the farmer replied. 'It's saying "Get up! Get up! Time to go to church"'

As the only Catholic daily in the north the *Irish News* gave full coverage to the various religious occasions. For these events an old-time reporter, an almost legendary figure, the late Billy Duggan was in great demand. Billy, a County Clare man, invariably wore a red rose in his buttonhole and carried a walking stick. Stout, flush-faced, with a bristling moustache, he combined natural piety with a vocabulary of strange oaths and a gift for alliteration. Once he boasted that in an encounter with the Editor Tim McCarthy he had uttered 'A Clare man's curse to the Corkman' and the editor went white in the face! We never discovered the nature of this nerve-shattering malediction. A confirmed tee-totaller, Billy's earlier journalistic career was interrupted by the 1914-18 War. He gave up the devil drink, according to his story, when some kind friends decided that the army would be his salvation. They delivered the body to the Army Recruiting Office at the Grand Central Hotel after one wild night of carousing and Billy woke up next morning to find himself enlisted in the Mechanical Transport Corps. His stories about nincompoop officers were rich. Officer: 'What were you in civil life, my man?' Recruit: 'I was an agricultural labourer.' Officer: Right, go in and take charge of the books in the office.' When it came to Billy's turn he confessed that he was 'A journalist by profession.' Officer: 'A journalist, hey? Right, go in and clean out those stables.' His war service consisted of driving a traction engine around Cheltenham and his comrades were mostly Cockneys. Some were Pearlies from the Old Kent Road. One of them told him in the mess of his first visit to Church for the baptism of his first-born son. 'In comes this old geezer in a white nightshirt and begins to pour icy water over the poor little bleeder's head. Cor, it was proper cruel, it was.'

His extensive vocabulary was enriched by the few years he spent in the Army. 'Son-of-a-bitch' was his almost affectionate term for all and sundry, including men with dog collars. Bossy curates who tried to bounce him were 'clerical errors' and he dismissed subs who interfered with his flowery descriptive pieces, adorned with old-time journalese such as 'Red-letter days', 'sacred edifices', 'felicitations ad multos annos', 'coffins raised on catafalques', 'raging infernos', etc, etc, as 'Morons, not even threatened with intelligence'. A pushful local Senator who owned a rag-store called at the office and complained that Billy had cut his speech to ribbons. He was cut down to size and left. Misquoting the poet, Billy, with a wicked grin, remarked in a loud voice, 'You may paint the vase if you will but the scent of the rags hangs on still.'

The stories about Duggan were legion. His picture appeared

alongside Carson and the other 'Ulster Rebels' when they gathered at Belfast City Hall and pricking their fingers signed the anti-Home Rule Covenant in blood. That was in 1912. Many years later a puckish photographer took a picture of Lord Carson lighting Billy's cigar as they sat in a brake at the opening of the Silent Valley Water Scheme in the Mourne Mountains.Always on the spot for the big moment he often boasted how he scooped the Dublin scribes in their own front garden at the Eucharistic Congress in Dublin. The then Editor of the *Irish Independent* the late T R Harrington, was checking over photographs to go with the prelim of the immense Congress when he came upon one of G K Chesterton being interviewed at the gangway on his arrival by mail-boat for the event. He recognised Billy Duggan right away and had him traced to his hotel. Later he admitted that the "Indo" had been scooped on the Chesterton interview and prevailed on Billy to give them the story. Billy had a great admiration for T R who had built up the sales of the *Independent* to dizzy heights by various means, one of which was to cover every local item of news county by county in 'Provincial Brevities'. By scouring the local papers for hard news, often in three line pars, nothing was missed. The story goes that Harrington even took a bundle of provincial newspapers with him when on holiday. As he lay on the sands at Morecambe Bay, clipping paragraphs from papers and placing them in a large envelope for posting to Dublin it was said that he got into trouble for 'creating litter' on the beach! When Duggan heard the story in Dublin he commented 'Harrington must be a bloody cliptomaniac.'

SCENES IN COURT

THE POLICE COURTS were a welcome diversion from Night-Town. I was lucky. Nothing seemed to happen out of the ordinary during my monthly stint on late night duty. But on the very night that a newly-appointed junior from Omagh, County Tyrone, took my place on Town, the luxury liner Bermuda which was back at Workman and Clark's shipyard for a refit, caught fire. He went to the scene but never returned with the story. Apparently he was so appalled at the sight of the immense liner blazing from stem to stern that he stood rooted to the dockside watching the ineffectual efforts of the firemen to save the ship. A Senior Sub, Paddy Kelly, was sent to the docks to look for him but failed and ended up doing the story himself. There was more than one story as it happened. A late night reveller in a car attracted by the blaze in the sky drove down by Corporation Square and with his eyes fixed on the blazing liner drove straight into the harbour. A small schooner from Wales with a cargo of slates was tied up at the docks and the shocked reveller was lucky to be fished out of the water by a seaman who managed to stick a boat-hook in the seat of his pants. The reporter escaped censure. The Subs never told Redwood and the man concerned lived on to advance his career in Dublin.

The Police Courts at this time were the scene of a ludicrous campaign against illegal betting. As a result of pressure by the Presbyterian Church the authorities periodically raided the bookies, the majority of whom were Catholics, though not all. Money and betting slips were seized and the bookies prosecuted. Some were tipped off in advance so not much was lost in cash. Local JPs used to sit with the Resident Magistrate to decide such cases and the bookies became so incensed eventually that they organised their friends among the JPs to pack the Bench. At times the overflow from the Bench was such that you could hardly get into the Press seats. The anti-betting JPs voted for heavy fines while the bookies' friends sometimes won the day with a majority in favour of a fine of two shillings and sixpence. They became known as 'half-crown magistrates'. To make matters worse the bookies did not answer to their own names but used to send their junior clerks to appear for them. Occasionally I recognised an old school pupil answering to the name of some wealthy bookmaker and yet nobody batted an eyelid! Several years were to pass before this hypocrisy ended with the legalising of betting shops.

In the adjoining Summons Court the public gallery was usually crowded for the 'abusive language' cases in which rival solicitors put on a kind of running entertainment for the benefit of their clients. In the Solicitors' and Press Room across the corridor they mingled happily together around a glowing coal fire but as soon as they entered court they traded verbal abuse back and forth like ping-pong. It was a great show and the audience reponded with merriment as the squabbling neighbours were put through the hoops in the witness box to the continuous roars of 'Silence in Court' from the Clerk, Ben Lambe. It was a window into low life in Belfast. 'She called me a h—, yer worship.' The misspelling was never corrected by the weary RM. Nobody ever told them that it was 'wh—'. When the woman who had issued a cross-summons was asked why they had come to blows she replied, 'I lost my temper when she called me an oul mermaid.' Invariably it all ended in a draw with the

Magistrate putting both parties under a rule of bail to keep the peace for twelve months. Looking sadder and wiser both parties left the court surrounded by sympathisers recalling how Barney Campbell had 'put that old virago in her box' while the contesting solicitors resumed their friendly gossip around the fire.

Some of the solicitors were characters. There was one hoity-toity little man who looked like Mr Pickwick but whose clients were the lowest of the low. A man of uncertain temper, addicted to the bottle, he was noted for quarrelling with Magistrates in high flown language, often quoting German proverbs in the original in an attempt to overawe with erudition the man on the Bench whom he treated with disdain. His 'managing clerk' was a small, shifty individual nicknamed 'The Mouse' with the gift for assembling a steady flow of shady clients for his peppery boss whom we shall call 'Johnny'. They had no office outside of public house snugs and when police court attendants were asked directions to Johnny's 'business address' they were told 'First lamp-post around the corner'. To engage Johnny in your defence was to invite a sentence of six months' imprisonment. His tactics were to insult all around him, police, prosecutors and magistrates. Sometimes he was ordered out of court escorted by police while his bewildered clients got the book thrown at them.

Having, as it were, cut my teeth in the lower courts, I was thrown in one day at the deep end in the High Court among the wigs and gowns of the barristers, KCs and their Lordships, the judges. My assignment was to cover a Chancery Court case involving the million pound will of the Gallaher family, the tobacco tycoons. In those days the beautiful Royal Courts of Justice and the Stormont Parliament Buildings were in the course of erection. The High Court was accommodated, meantime, in the rather grim surroundings of the County Antrim Courthouse on the Crumlin Road, directly facing the even grimmer century-old Belfast Prison, the scene of many a grisly hanging during its chequered history. A tunnel from the Prison led under the main road across to the dock of the Crown Court.

Finding the Chancery Court in the maze of corridors was a problem. The first person I met was a man in wig and gown who courteously led me to a door marked 'Dining Room'. He was Edmond Warnock who years later became Northern Ireland Attorney General and Minister of Home Affairs. Warnock was one of the few politicians left who ranked as a first-rate orator. His was a colourful career and in the 1914-18 War he had miraculously escaped death after being shot down from an artillery observation balloon on the Western Front. I discoverd all that later. Warnock said, 'This is the Chancery Court' and ushered me into a long room with two fireplaces on either side around which a number of barristers stood warming their backsides, listening intently to the proceedings at a long table the length of the room from which a number of senior counsel addressed Mr Justice Wilson who sat at the head of the table. They spoke in almost conversational tones difficult to hear. I joined a small knot of reporters crushed behind a half-moon table strewn with documents. Nobody seemed to know what was going on except a sweating *Belfast Telegraph* reporter whose evening paper was devoting nearly a whole page per night on the abstruse legal arguments. The scene was a quaint one. The blazing coal fires and the regimental drums hanging on the high walls over the mantlepieces somehow reminded me of Charles Dickens's description of the Chancery Court in *Bleak House* as the interminable Jarndyce v Jarndyce case rumbled on year after year. Every time the door opened and another counsel came in there was the unmistakable smell of frying herrings wafting in from the luncheon room where the caretaker provided a makeshift meal for those barristers who could stomach it.

Mr Justice Wilson, a quiet, studious man, by chance turned up as the presiding judge at the first murder trial I reported. Through some mishap the judge designated for the Assizes at Downpatrick, County Down, was unable to appear and Judge Wilson, a Chancery judge with little experience of criminal cases, and a known opponent of capital punishment, found himself saddled with the trial of two itinerants, Kennedy and Morrison, charged with the murder of an old lady. They had robbed a recluse at her home near Dromara, stealing a bag of gold sovereigns and tied, gagged and bound her so cruelly that she died. During the evidence Morrison's father who ran a lodging house at Dromore, County Down, told the jury that he had put the pair up for the night there after the crime. You could have heard a pin drop when he admitted that his lodging house was located at the ominous-sounding 'Gallows Lane'.

Both men were found guilty and all eyes turned towards the judge as his attendant approached him with the dreaded Black Cap which he was supposed to wear while he pronounced the death sentence. Then something happened. The judge appeared to have taken a weak turn. There was a buzz of dismay as he was escorted off the Bench and into his private chambers. As the minutes ticked away the rumour spread that the judge was reluctant to impose the death sentence.

What happened inside was never revealed but after about five minutes the animated conversation around the court was stilled when the judge, looking considerably shaken, reappeared. Then in a quivering voice he addressed the two men in dock in the archaic words prescribed for the imposition of the death sentence. His voice was husky with emotion as he pronounced the time and place ... 'the Belfast Prison ... there to be hanged by the neck until you are dead. And may the Lord have mercy on your souls.' The two men were handcuffed together and ushered through a crowd out and to our amazement placed on an open police tender and driven through the streets of the town to the railway station for the journey to Belfast in a locked compartment of the local train which we joined a few minutes later with our copy. I remember the feeling of shock and horror I felt at witnessing this drama for the first time. In later years I was to hear this dread sentence imposed at least about ten times but the feeling of sickness about the stomach never left me each time. Worst of all was the night six young Republicans were sentenced to death in Belfast for the shooting of a police constable. The piteous cries of the mothers and sisters rang out as they were rushed away through the Crumlin Road tunnel to the death cells. Kennedy and Morrison escaped the gallows and so did five of the Republicans. One, Tom Williams, a youth of eighteen, bravely took responsibility for the incident although it was said that he did not fire the fatal shot. He was hanged amidst distressing early morning scenes outside the jail. So were several others before the whole paraphernalia of scaffolds, ropes and hangmen were swept away. I often thought that if the hangers and floggers down the years were forced to participate in these ghastly exercises they would be cured of their unchristian appetite for revenge. To read Charles Dickens's description of 'the last public execution in England' even today is a salutary reminder of why these scenes had to be enacted in secret in the intervening years.

Marked to cover an execution an old-time *Telegraph* reporter, Joe Porter, in the absence of inside information invariably drawing on his imagination, wrote 'After a hearty breakfast the prisoner walked steadily to the scaffold.' But through the years we heard different stories of agonising scenes in the last minutes of the hangman's victims.

The son of a head-warder told me of the strain endured by friendly prison officers deputed to stay by the side of the condemned man, playing endless games of cards or draughts, until the final awful moment.

In the condemned cell in Belfast Prison there was a large ugly press or wardrobe behind which was a secret door leading directly to the scaffold. The warders knew what lay behind it but it was not until the morning of the execution that the unfortunate man to be hanged realised its sinister significance. When the time came it was pulled aside and the fatal door unlocked as he was escorted the few yards to his doom.

Once I was asked if I wanted to view the body of a man who had just been hanged. I had been marked to cover the inquest after the execution of a man named Dornan who had murdered two women in a County Antrim bog. Being inexperienced I did not realise that the custom then was simply to ring the Coroner for details afterwards. When I presented myself at the entrance to the Belfast Prison and told the jailers my business I was admitted inside after much unlocking and locking of heavy doors. The Coroner was a Dr Graham and present as his 'assistant' I was surprised to find a well-known and enterprising local journalist, Jimmy Robinson, better known as 'Peter' Robinson, of the *Daily Mail*. Robinson was under the mistaken impression that the Press was barred at such inquests and persuaded kindly old Dr Graham to take him along.

My surprise was nothing to Robinson's to see this junior reporter calmly walking into the inquest he had gone to such lengths to report exclusively in person! After brief evidence by the prison authorities that the death sentence had been carried out and by the prison doctor that he had examined the body and found 'life extinct', the Coroner and police officer announced that they would view the body. Before adjourning to an adjoining room for this grisly duty Dr Graham turned to myself and Robinson and asked, 'Do you wish to view the body?' We both looked aghast and shook our heads. The Coroner then left minus his 'assistant'. They returned in a few minutes and I thought the police officer looked decidedly shaken. Needless to say I was glad when the heavy outer door of the jail closed behind me. I never attended another prison inquest. Years later I heard it said that poor Dornan should never have been hanged. By the more humane standards of law in later times he would have been confined for mental treatment.

Robinson boasted that he was present at an event that proved to be a turning point in Irish history. This was the occasion when Padraic Pearse gave the famous oration at the grave of Irish patriot O'Donovan Rossa. In a few years Pearse, poet and dreamer, led the 1916 Rebellion and was executed. Peter told us that as he crushed up to the graveside to take a shorthand note of Pearse's speech he found himself standing shoulder to shoulder with a man whom he later identified as the famous Michael Collins. Collins was almost unknown then but in a few years he became a legendary figure, the most wanted man in Ireland as leader of the Irish guerrilla war against the British, later to die tragically in an ambush after the Treaty which he told Churchill would prove to be his 'death warrant'. It is often a reporter's oppportunity to brush with figures of destiny. Such meetings may even become foot-notes to history.

Peter learned early to take politician's denials with more than a pinch of salt. He was asked by the *Independent* to go to the home of Mr John Dillon, MP, who succeeded to the leadership of the old Irish Nationalist Party on the death of John Redmond. Dillon lived then in Dublin's Mountjoy Square. When Robinson asked the maid if he could see Mr Dillon for an interview she returned to say that Mr Dillon was 'not in'. Meantime Robinson had spotted the famous man reading some papers in the front sitting room. When he drew the maid's attention to this fact she went inside again but returned and said 'Mr Dillon is not in to the *Irish Independent*.' Unknown to Robinson, Mr Dillon had taken umbrage at something the *Independent* had written about him.

From the *Independent* Robinson returned North to join the *Belfast Telegraph*. He used to recall ruefully how the *Independent* dismissed his description of 'The battle of the Mourne Mountains' involving a shooting incident between the IRA and the police. A leader in the Independent sent Robinson to his dictionary. The 'battle' according to the editorial writer could only be described as 'highly apocryphal'.

But Robinson had reason to thank the *Independent* for saving his life in another escapade. In the early days of the North-South separation the Belfast Government decided to send a platoon of 'B' Specials by rail to Enniskillen. There were two rail links to Enniskillen by the old GNR line in those days, one via Omagh and the other crossing the Border into the then Free State through the town of Clones. Through a blunder by the Transport Officer, a Major McCallum, later a Belfast RM, they were sent by the wrong route and the train was riddled with bullets at Clones by the local Republican guards. Robinson was sent in the car of Sir Robert Baird, proprietor of the *Telegraph*, to investigate this incident and the kidnapping of forty prominent Unionists who were held as hostages against the murderous activities of the Specials. Robinson was arrested on arrival as a suspected 'Ulster spy'. The late Maurice Linnane, then Assistant Chief Reporter of the Independent told me the rest of the story.

One afternoon he received a phone call from Monaghan inquiring if the *Irish Independent* had ever employed a man named 'James Robinson on its editorial staff. Remembering Robinson as 'Peter Robinson' Linnane at first replied 'No' but then as the caller was about to ring off he was reminded by his deputy, the late Billy Smith, an ex-*Irish News* man, that they had indeed employed Robinson as a young reporter a few years before. The caller then identified himself as General Eoin O'Duffy, the Army Officer in charge of that sector of the Border, and added grimly, 'It's just as well you remembered. We were going to shoot him as a spy.'

None of us made any fortunes in journalism but looking back money could not buy the richness of the experiences gained, the laughs, the human tragedies, the satisfaction of recording the history of our times, the inside knowledge, the revelations behind the scenes of the foibles and failings of the great, the easy entry into parliaments, palaces, lordly mansions and humble homes. Outside the office you were a different person, a 'gentleman of the Press' with special seats up front at luncheons, dinners and an occasional 'banquet', with sundry big-wigs of Church and State being very civil, slipping copies of their speeches with the usual whisper 'Give it a good show'.

Afterwards we anticipated the butchery of the Subs by trimming these effusions down to size. This was the power of the pen, or, more often, the power of the blue pencil. Was it 'power without responsibility' as Prime Minister Stanley Baldwin alleged of the newspaper bosses – 'The prerogative of the harlot in all ages'? We did not stop to think.

In the divided city of Belfast, Catholic and Protestant, our papers served the different communities and, if the editorials were any guide, were consistently at each other's throats. This was far from the truth. Among working journalists in Belfast there was a great spirit of comradeship, good humour and a measure of helpfulness. For me this was a ripening and enlivening experience. Politicians, Orangemen and religious bigots might hurl abuse at each other but it passed over our heads. We reported it and accepted it as an unfortunate part of a game in which we had no part other than as 'recording angels', some might say 'devils'. We had our own ideas about the idiocy of it all. The Fourth Estate could 'show up' the people responsible but it was the voters who 'put them in'.

When a Church of Ireland Dean and Orangeman claimed that St Patrick did not accept the 'yoke of Rome' a Catholic ecclesiastic was stung to accuse him of belonging to a church 'founded by a lustful monarch'. This kind of ecclesiastic tennis made the headlines but did little to heal the wounds of a fragmented society and no doubt played its own part in the build-up to the tragedy which came later.

My promotion to parliamentary reporting came unexpectedly with a brief note from Bob Hayes to present myself at the temporary headquarters of the Northern Ireland parliament at College Green at 2.30 pm. This was before the Stormont Parliament Buildings were opened. The government had leased, in the meantime, the gloomy old Assembly's College of the Presbyterian Church at the rear of Queen's University. My entrance pass was signed by the Sergeant-at-Arms, Brigadier H G Young, a retired old military gent attired in court dress with a ceremonial sword dangling against his spindly legs which were encased in long silk stockings. The attendants wore tuxedos and looked most impressive, belying the truth that they were paid as mere messengers.

The speeches of the 'Honourable members', the 'Right Honourable members' (Cabinet), and the 'Honourable and gallant members' (retired army officers) were as musty as the museum-like atmosphere of the place. The government front bench was headed by Lord Craigavon, grey, sombre, face-hewn-out-of-granite, a Boer-war military officer turned politician by his mentor Edward Carson and now Prime Minister of a Home Rule Parliament. He was flanked by an elderly grey-bearded Finance Minister, H M Pollock, a retired shipping magnate, and on the other side by another business tycoon, the millionaire linen thread manufacturer James Milne Barbour, who offered his services as an unpaid Minister of Commerce. A suave, gentlemanly type with a long moustache stretching from cheek to cheek, Milne Barbour, the spitting image of King Alfonso of Spain, looked out of place in such dour company. A side-whiskered limping Sir Edward Archdale, an ex-Admiral and country squire (Minister of Agriculture), the adenoidal John Millar Andrews, Comber linen boss, and a buck-toothed white moustached solicitor, Sir Dawson Bates (Minister of Home Affairs) completed the Front Bench.

The attendance of MPs was poor and as one speaker droned on the Cabinet sat like graven images. One day Joe Devlin, MP wandered in from Westminster. There was an immediate air of excitement as the seats filled up quickly, members and ministers coming hurriedly from the tea-room. Soon the atmosphere was electrified by a passionate address enlivened by the wit and humour of a great orator. Did I detect a flicker of a smile crossing the flushed face of Craigavon as Joe poked fun at the Government which he said, amidst laughter, presented a 'picture of masterly inactivity' while the recent Budget of the grey-bearded Pollock was ridiculed as a 'Saturnalia of finance'.

While nearly everybody enjoyed these occasional jousts by Joe Devlin, not so the rather humourless Deputy Speaker and Chairman of Ways and Means, Tom Moles. Moles, a willowy individual with a straggly moustache, a glittering glass eye and red nose, combined the editorship of the *Belfast Telegraph*, the deputy speakership and a seat for a Belfast constituency at Westminster. For these he drew three salaries but how he managed the three jobs was a bit of a mystery. Moles was an unashamed government hack who in return for access to tit-bits of Government information steered his evening paper along orthodox party lines, adroitly suppressing the voices of opposition to his masters. His appearances in the chair in the House of Commons reminded me of the activities of an over-zealous referee continually blowing the whistle. Speakers were reduced to frustration by his continual interruptions. His interpretation of what was 'in order' and what was 'out of order' in the end resulted in angry MPs cutting short their remarks and sitting down in fury.

One afternoon he dared to take on Devlin. In the middle of his speech came the familiar 'Order! Order!' which, some said, should be 'Border! Border!' in view of the Unionist preoccupation with the frontier. Devlin listened with rising indignation to a lecturette by Moles and his favourite observation that Devlin's speech was not 'germane' to the debate. A practised speaker in the British Commons for a generation Devlin was having none of this nonsense in a tin-pot 'subordinate Parliament' but Moles was adamant. At last Devlin grasped his papers in fury and walked out followed by the entire Nationalist Party. In a statement they said that if they were to be prevented from raising matters they wished to raise it was not much use bothering to attend the Northern Parliament. Devlin never returned. The place was never the same and even Unionists regretted the loss. Some more forthright than others blamed that 'bloody fool Moles'.

The proximity of the Assembly's College to the Queen's University Students Union led some boisterous spirits there to enliven the opening of a new session of Parliament with a bit of horse-play. The opening was modelled on the Westminster practice with the

Northern Ireland Governor, the Duke of Abercorn, a gouty old toper with a whiskey-voice, reading the Queen's Speech. MPs wearing top hats and swallow-tailed coats used to arrive at the gates in the humble tram which stopped outside. On this occasion they had to run the gauntlet of jeering laughing students armed with billiard cues. Shouting 'Top hat! Top hat!' they tipped off the silk hats as they hurried up to the gates. Angry MPs called in the police and an excitable Head Constable ordered a baton charge. Students fleeing down Botanic Avenue followed by baton-wielding police provided the press with a welcome diversion from another dull opening session. The Queen's Speech delivered by the Duke, as if his mouth was full of marbles, got short shrift. The headlines were all about baton charges and arrests of students. The Vice-Chancellor of the University, the strait-laced Sir Richard Livingstone, dubbed 'Sir Ricardo Dedbrick' in the students' Rag-mag *Pro Tanto Quid* was aghast and severe punishment was imposed on the offenders.

TRUTH IN THE NEWS

SMARTING OVER A row with Redwood I picked up a copy of the *Dundalk Examiner* one night in the office and read an interview with Eamon de Valera about his intention of launching a new Dublin daily, the *Irish Press*. The row was over the coverage of an attack by mobs at Portadown, Lurgan and Lisburn on pilgrims returning by train from the Eucharistic Congress in Dublin. A parish priest had complained that the report written by Paddy Donaghy and myself had omitted to mention that the windows in his parochial hall had been smashed! Although we had done what we thought was an excellent job on the story Redwood hauled us over the coals with the usual threats of the sack. We were incensed and once again thoughts of escape rose in our minds.

In the interview Dev spoke of the 'truth in the news' and his search for the best newspapermen he could find. This appealed to me instantly. Here was my chance. Very quickly I sent off my application including a few clippings of stories which had been front-paged. One of them was about the Eucharistic Congress riots. A few days later I received two replies. One was from Frank Gallagher, the newly-nominated editor of the *Irish Press*, regretting that there were no vacancies. The other delivered in the same post was from the news editor, Bob Egan, requesting me to come to Dublin immediately for an interview!

I was supposed to be on Night-Town but a friendly sub named O'Higgins came to the rescue and covered for me. I took French Leave at midnight and walked home through the sleeping city, hoping nothing out of the ordinary would occur, otherwise Redwood would find out and I would be for the high jump.

In some trepidation because of the contradictory letters, I left by the early morning train for Dublin. At Burgh Quay I was quite surprised to find workmen and plasterers still working on the converted theatre which was to be launched in a few weeks as a newspaper office. The interview with Bob Egan lasted only a few minutes. Obviously the clippings had clinched my application and I was then ushered into the presence of Frank Gallagher. I had modestly applied for the job as Editorial Assistant at the Belfast office and was rather taken aback to learn that I was assisting nobody and that in fact I was to be the *Irish Press's* first Staff Reporter covering the North. Their office was a former bookie's in Garfield Street just a few yards off Royal Avenue and the salary was to be four times what I was getting for slaving morning to night on the *News*. I kept quiet about my mere eighteen months' experience.

Shaking hands, Frank Gallagher hoped I would give the new paper first-class coverage, adding 'For example, if Joe Devlin, the Nationalist leader says something important we will expect you to be on his doorstep for an interview the next day'. On the way out Bob Egan confessed that although the first issue of the *Press* was due in a fortnight on Saturday 5 September, they had forgotten to appoint any local correspondents in the North. I was astounded but recovered quickly and assured him that there was no problem there. I thought to myself 'All the *Irish News* corrs are in for a pleasant surprise.'

After all this excitement I decided to cool off, spending the early afternoon in the Metropole Cinema in O'Connell Street where they were showing Charlie Chaplin in *Modern Times*. I arrived back in

Belfast by the evening train in time for, but in no mood for, the 7 o'clock 'Night-Town' stint. It's hard to keep a secret in a newspaper office and the news of my sudden flight to Dublin must have got around by bush telegraph for the Chief Reporter asked outright in the corridor 'Well James, did you get it?' He congratulated me on my promotion to the new national daily. It was years later that I heard that he had applied for the job! He was very much my senior and it was a mystery to me why I was so lucky. If I had known I would never have applied. Perhaps he asked for too much.

When the office was empty later that night I copied down the names of every *Irish New* correspondent in the Chief Reporter's book. They were located in every town throughout the North. I posted the list off to Bob Egan who promptly appointed them all correspondents of the *Irish Press*. I was amused to hear many of the newsmen concerned in later years telling how astonished they were to get letters and books of press telegraph passes intimating that they had been appointed fully-fledged correspondents – a profitable sideline – 'without even applying'.

They were all good corrs and I had no reason to regret the larceny. Some News Editors have trouble with less experienced corrs and I always recall with amusement the late John Parker's story about the County Antrim correspondent who missed the death of an important Ulster politician. Parker was then News Editor of the *Northern Whig* and when the rival *Newsletter* came out with the late news that the local worthy had died in hospital at 3.00 am Parker wrote him a reprimand. He did not bargain for the retort which he received promptly from the elderly corr. 'Dear Mr Parker', he wrote, 'I have been your correspondent in this district for twenty years but if you think I am going to wait around for the angel of death to flap his wings at 3.00 am for three-halfpence a line you have got another think coming!' Parker kept the letter in his desk for years.

In Dublin the staff of the *Irish Press*, many of whom were veterans of the Civil War, took time to get into their stride. The first issues were rather flat and W T Cosgrave was asked in the Dail if he intended to 'suppress this Republican paper'. 'No', replied Cosgrave tartly, 'by the look of the first issues it will suppress itself'. He was wrong. The widespread enthusiasm aroused by Dev's big bid for political power together with Bob Egan's professionalism as News Editor soon built the paper up into a lively production.

My first big story for the *Irish Press* was the 'Turk Murder', a crime which was afterwards written up in the American pulp magazines because of its bizarre circumstances.

The story began with the discovery of a naked foreigner's body lying in a ditch near Carrickfergus, County Antrim. A farmer driving along a lonely road was puzzled when his horse shied and refused to budge further as it came level with the ditch. Jumping from his cart the farmer spotted the body lying behind the ditch. The man was tall with semitic features and a bathing cap covered a bullet wound through his head. For weeks the police were baffled. Nobody could identify the victim whose picture was circulated far and wide. One theory was that he had been dumped from a Greek ship. Believing that he was a Jew the Jewish community undertook to bury the unknown man.

The first break for the police investigators, District Inspector Lewis and Head Constable Slack, came with the finding one morning of a heap of slashed clothing in a doorway in Church Lane and next came the news that some circus folk identified the murdered man from a picture which the police inserted in the 'World's Fair', a theatrical publication. He was a Turk named Achmet Musa who had come to Belfast with a Jewish former New York cameraman, Eddie Cullens, to promote a circus act, an ancient Turk named Zara Agha, who they claimed was the 'oldest man in the world'. Cullens was arrested dramatically as he was stepping into his car at Hyde Park in London and brought to Belfast for his trial.

The police claimed that while staying at a lodging house at Tomb

Street near the Belfast docks they quarrelled over a prostitute with whom they had been associating and that Cullens shot the Turk through the head and dumped the body. The bathing cap was traced to the girl. Cullens, a small dapper figure in a grey flannel suit with the delicate hands of a woman, the very opposite of the popular conception of a murderer, was found guilty and hanged at Belfast Prison. He was defended by a popular local Jewish KC, Bernard Fox, later a judge, who after the trial tried to have the sentence commuted and told me that he was convinced that there had been a 'miscarriage of justice' in the case.

Even more exciting times were on the way. An All-Ireland railway strike was accompanied by bombs, shootings and derailments, as blackleg labour, some including Boy Scouts, was tried by the rail companies. The three unions involved set up headquarters in Belfast bringing an influx of Fleet Street men, the veteran Freddie Chant, Labour correspondent of the PA, Sean Fielding of the *Daily Mail* and Morley Richards, then with the PA, and later the News Editor of the *Daily Express*. The strike was a prolonged and bitter struggle and while the Union bosses were deploring the violent incidents which occurred they were unaware of the fact that one of their volunteer drivers was in fact using a Dublin NUR official's car for a few private 'jobs' of his own. A character whom we nicknamed 'Scarface' – he said he had received a 'gun-beating' from the Free State soldiers during the Civil War – claimed that he had thrown bombs at the Midland Railway and the GNR. Charlie McDonnell of the *Irish Independent*, who wore a bowler hat, pin-striped suit and spats, to the amusement of the strikers, said 'Scarface' had told him that he was 'one of Frank Aiken's right-hand men during the Troubles'. Although this individual sometimes appeared in the background at press conferences in the old Royal Avenue Hotel, sitting smirking and winking as his boss condemned 'deplorable incidents', we decided to steer clear of him just in case!

The Fleet Street men were very much at sea in the strange

surroundings of a violent city like Belfast and depended on our local knowledge of affairs. One who arrived from London on the Heysham mail boat told me that he admired the view that morning coming up Belfast Lough, only he pronounced it 'Luff'! Another putting through his early morning call to the P A from bed in the Grand Central Hotel, after a heavy night, upset his breakfast tray and when the copy-taker asked what was the crash, blandly claimed that the telephone kiosk he was in had just been stoned! The same man was in trouble when his night call to London got mixed up with a BBC trunk line relaying dance music. A suspicious Night News Desk man accused him of taking time off at a dance hall and told him he was not being paid to show off his foxtrot in Belfast. He refused to believe that it was a crossed line. 'I can hear the music in the background quite clearly over here', he insisted. 'Pull yourself together and get back on the job', he snorted and put the phone down on the luckless reporter.

The Fleet Street correspondents were clearly master hands in the compilation of expense dockets – popularly known in the trade as 'swindle sheets'. I came upon two of them in their hotel bar rubbing invoices from a local taxi company into the carpet. 'If they are a bit grubby it makes them look more authentic', explained one when I raised my eyebrows at this odd behaviour.

In London apparently they would not dream of travelling a hundred yards without hiring a 'high-powered car', or calling a cab, or so they insisted to the paper's accountants. There are legends about expense dockets such as 'hire of tug' and other exercises of the imagination. Billy Duggan once successfully claimed for a brand new overcoat from the *Irish News*. Reporting an election candidate on a brake in Sandy Row someone threw a fruit-bag of human excrement and it landed fair and square on Billy's back. 'I stood up, threw off the coat and left it there,' said Billy. 'I was disgusted.'

Election brakes were a hazard for reporters. I once reported a Unionist candidate, Dr H P Lowe, on board his brake which traversed the side streets of Belfast's Dock Ward. The following night I was asked to undertake the same duty for his Labour opponent, Harry Midgley. His horse-drawn election brake covered the same streets. All went well until it turned into Lancaster Street. Immediately there was a commotion as Midgley began to speak. A red-haired girl in a shawl screamed obscenities, pointing to the brake and shouted, 'I saw him last night with Lowe. He's a f——g turn-coat!' The crowd took up the cry and there was pandemonium until a puzzled Harry Midgley told the driver to whip up the horse and flee the scene. The crowd surged after us with the red-haired girl leading the way still screaming 'turn-coat!' I did not tell Midgley that it was me she had spotted. By the irony of fate many years later, Midgley did in fact turn his coat, defecting to the Unionist Party and ending up as a member of the Brookeborough Cabinet.

Dr Lowe, an outspoken character who later became City Coroner for Belfast, was another maverick Unionist who did not conform. Small, pale-faced and sporting a Charlie Chaplin moustache, he used to hit out in all directions. The story is told of his brother Cecil, a dapper little man who took an 'assistant' with him when he went canvassing down York Street for the doctor. Replying to his knock on the door a shipyard worker, smoking a pipe, glared as Cecil began 'I am here to solicit your vote for my brother, Dr H P Lowe ...' The man took the pipe from his mouth, spat on the doorstep and exclaimed 'F— Dr Lowe!' Turning to his assistant who had his notebook and pencil poised, Cecil remarked coolly 'Put him down as doubtful.'

THE UNWILLING PRINCE

EDWARD, PRINCE OF Wales, ill-fated heir to the throne came to Belfast on 16 November, 1932 in what could only be described as a surly mood after a blazing row with his father, George V. The Ulster Unionists felt that the opening of the big, newly-completed white Parliament Buildings at Stormont should be graced by the presence of a Royal personage. King George who had opened the first session of the Northern Parliament in the Belfast City Hall away back on 22 June, 1921 with an appeal to all Irishmen to stretch out 'the hand of forbearance and conciliation, to forgive and forget, and to join in making for the land they love a new era of peace, contentment and goodwill' decided that it would be inappropriate to preach again to the unconverted. He decided to send the Prince of Wales instead but the Prince showed no enthusiasm for the task and it leaked out later that a heated argument at Buckingham Palace ended with the King ordering the heir to the throne to go to Belfast.

The sky was dark and overcast when the Prince and his retinue stepped ashore from the Liverpool steamer at Donegall Quay and drove past the drooping Union Jacks and thin cheers of the crowds lining the streets. Grim-faced 'B' Specials had been mobilised to assist the police and behind it all was the sombre understanding in the rest of Ireland that Royalty had been enlisted to 'put the cornerstone on the Partition of Ireland' at Stormont.

In Belfast itself the occasion could not have been more untimely, contrasting with the gloom of an unemployment crisis which had exploded only a few weeks before in riots, hunger marches and a mace-throwing incident at the City Hall. About a hundred thousand workers in the North were thrown out of employment by the depression. Grass was growing on the slipways of Harland & Wolff's great shipyard. Orders for ocean-going liners had dried up and I stood in Workman & Clark's 'wee yard' on the north side of the Lagan and saw the last remaining relics of a shipyard which had turned out luxury liners being auctioned off to salvage dealers. The chimneys of the linen mills in the west of the city no longer smoked and it seemed that Belfast had landed on hard times. Neither the Westminster Government nor the subordinate Northern Ireland administration of sectarian politicians appeared to be fully aware of the tragedy that was unfolding for a great mass of the population.

I saw naked poverty in the streets, hungry children lining up at the bakeries for so-called 'cutting loaves', the stale bread returned by the roundsmen, while others clamoured at the pork shops for 'griskins' and bacon clippings, or at the butchers for marrow-bones to make soup. Some, too proud to seek help from bodies like the St Vincent de Paul Society, slowly starved behind closed doors in suburban streets while unemployed husbands, shabby genteel clerks or insurance agents thrown on the scrap heap, tried to eke out a living selling shoe polish and laces from door to door in a distant part of the city where they would not be recognised. The full impact of the hard times came when unemployment benefit was exhausted and the workless came face to face with the real poverty of trying to live on 'Outdoor Relief' which could be as low as six to eight shillings a week for a married man. For this miserly pittance there was the humiliation of the dreaded 'Means Test', an inspector calling at the home and informing the unfortunate applicants that there could be no money unless some such item as a gramophone or a cherished old piano was sold first. Between the pawn-shop and the ODR inspectors only the most basic sticks of furniture were left in these impoverished homes.

The government left the administration of this iniquitous system to their Boards of Guardians, usually small-time third-grade politicians who normally had charge of the city workhouse, a relic of the days of Oliver Twist. In Belfast, with a few exceptions, this body consisted of hard-headed, unfeeling, local traders, rent agents, tick-men and even moneylenders. In their eyes to be out of work meant that you were a shiftless layabout and those who agitated for better conditions communists'.

Under the Outdoor Relief schemes men scarcely capable of lifting a heavy shovel were forced to dig roads or similar type of hard labour. I saw Harry C— who had lost his job when an assurance company collapsed, working on road repairs near St Mary's Catholic Church, his thin arms and blue veins bared as he tried to wield a sledgehammer. Sweat stood out on his face as he gasped with the unaccustomed exertion. Harry had been a great man at organising amateur dramatics and he used to call at our office for a chat about the stage and players he had directed. He turned away, ashamed, as I passed. I felt for him. Harry was in his late fifties and not long afterwards I heard that he had died.

A sub-committee of the Guardians dealing with the ODR system showed little sympathy to the applicants who were subjected to a kind of third-degree about their private lives. One of them, a black-haired woman member, a fat, meaty-faced harridan became notorious throughout the city for her hostility, particularly to those with large families. Her insulting remarks about their sex lives were humiliating in the extreme and were a byword at the time. Two members of the Guardians, James Collins and Harry Diamond, later a Stormont MP, fought hard to introduce a little humanity into their dealing with the unhappy workless but their voice was drowned out by the mean parsimonious skinflints surrounding them. Careless of the misery they were causing they doled out the pennies and shillings as if they were their own. It would have been easier to extract blood from a stone. I sat in on some of these stormy meetings when complaints from concerned organisations were cast aside and marked as Read.

Hunger marches were beginning in England and spreading to Belfast and Derry. One felt that an explosion of anger was imminent. A fellow feeling of sheer desperation brought the Catholic and Protestant unemployed together in Belfast. This was a danger signal to the Unionist Establishment which relied on the old sectarian green and orange divisions to maintain their long-term monopoly of power. The workers looking round for a band to lead their demonstrations faced a problem. Most of the bands marched for Orangeman's Day on the Twelfth of July and could only play sectarian tunes like 'The Sash' and 'Derry's Walls'. At last a band was found which had added to its repertoire the current hit, 'Yes, We Have No Bananas' and this became the marching song of the united Catholic and Protestant unemployed.

Sir Dawson Bates, Minister of Home Affairs who controlled the Royal Ulster Constabulary and the 'B' Specials as if they were the private army of the Unionist Party, was quick to sense the political menace of this historic turning point – 'the October Revolution of 1932' some optimists of the Left dubbed it. He ordered police baton charges when the pathetic, shabbily-dressed half-starved legions of unemployed from the Shankill and Falls attempted one night to march along Royal Avenue. They were dispersed brutally and among those arrested was Captain Jack White, son of a British general of the Boer War, who had come up from Dublin to show his Socialist solidarity with the Belfast workless. The following morning I saw this distinguished looking man standing in the dock of the Belfast Custody Court with a blood-stained bandage around his head.

With the notable exception of Jack Beattie, the Independent Labour

68

MP, the unemployed workers were shunned by most of the established political parties including the local Labourites. But almost from nowhere there suddenly appeared from their own ranks a leader who quickly dominated the scene, a small, thin-faced, almost cadaverous spare figure, a kind of workers' Robespierre, with a powerful voice and a commanding presence. His name was Tommy Geehan. Some said he was a Communist and others whispered that he had once been in the IRA. From an undisciplined mob he turned the ODR workers into what threatened to be an effective force to be reckoned with. With a mere gesture of a raised hand he could still to silence a wild and angry tunult.

I saw him in action at demonstrations at St Mary's Hall and the Protestant North Belfast Mission which the Church authorities, with more vision and charity than was displayed by the powers-that-be, had lent out for the unemployed's meetings. There were rumours that Geehan would be arrested but he seemed to enjoy a charmed life. The truth was that the authorities knew that any such wrong move on their part in the heightened tension of the times with thousands of hungry and angry men on the loose would tear the city apart.

Geehan and his trusted collaborators formulated their demands and decided to lay siege to the Belfast Workhouse on the Lisburn Road, the meeting place of the Board of Guardians. The gates were locked but an immense throng lay down on the road outside blocking all south-bound traffic. The frightened Guardians, by now realising that they had opened Pandora's Box, sat tight, waiting fearfully for the whirlwind which was soon to sweep them into oblivion.

There were cheers at Customs House Steps – Belfast's 'Speakers Corner' – when a demonstration was told that there had been unemployed riots in Birkenhead. Late at night I stood at North Street and saw the arrival at the Bakers Hall of a contingent of scarecrows, a Hunger March from Derry, with tattered banners, exhausted and starving after the long hike across the bleak Sperrins and down the

Glenshane Pass. There was confusion and an air of excitement as locals tried to arrange food and shake-down accommodation for the Derry men.

The local Unionist press was playing down the agitation and respectable citizens viewed the whole campaign with disdain but anyone reporting the mounting anger of the people in the little streets of the city could feel the tension building up to breaking point. The government, led by Lord Craigavon, and a tame Cabinet of local squires and a few linen 'lords' was too intent on its preparations for the opening of its palatial new Parliament Buildings at Stormont, far out in the Stormont suburbs, away from the strife of the city, to bother about the demands of a rabble of unemployed malcontents. The Prince of Wales was coming and a munificent British Treasury had provided several millions to provide a permanent 'home' for the legislature and new 'Royal Courts of Justice'. After twelve years of temporary accommodation and uncertainty John Bull had decided to put the 'cornerstone' on Partition. Against the background of unemployment and poverty no expense was spared to provide lavish and luxurious trappings for a ramshackle statelet carved out of the old province of Ulster to provide a permanent travesty of British democracy, a one-party state of six counties.

It was the legacy of the Welsh bully boy, Lloyd George, who after the Treaty of Versailles left behind a lot of equally ramshackle statelets and geographical absurdities to provide the seeds of interminable European conflicts. A quick head-count and hey presto, the lines were drawn across the map of Ireland eliminating 'dear old Donegal' and two other counties to provide the headless chicken which became Protestant-dominated, two-to-one, Northern Ireland. The Ulster counties which might have provided a fairer head-count of Catholics were arbitrarily excluded and became known to dismayed Unionists there as the 'betrayed counties'. An old schoolmaster at the time told us 'Always remember DCM – Donegal, Cavan and Monaghan'. Those who remember still grit their teeth to hear British politicians talk loosely about the Ulster 'Province'.

Having vacated the old Parliament at College Green at the end of its lease from the Presbyterian College – a 'formal sitting' of the Commons was arranged in temporary accommodation in the Robing Room of Belfast's City Hall. This was intended to be a two-minute affair but, as it happened, it provided a flash-point which made embarrassing headlines. During the proceedings the Independent Labour MP, Jack Beattie, tried to focus attention on the rapidly deteriorating situation with thousands of unemployed agitating for bread in the streets. He was shushed to silence by the Speaker whereupon he ran forward and with a roar, 'Then we have no use for this thing', seized the big gilded Parliamentary mace. We were accommodated at a small Press table on the same level as the members and I remember gazing, fascinated, as Beattie hurled the heavy instrument across the carpet in our direction. It slithered across the floor and hit me on the heel. Years later I achieved a kind of notoriety over the incident. A BBC producer of a programme on which I appeared said 'I hear you are the journalist who received a broken leg when an MP here threw the mace!'

Amidst uproar the elderly Sergeant-at-Arms, Brigadier Young, attired in his court dress with a silver sword, tottered over to the Press table and retrieved the mace from where it lay at our feet. He replaced it on the table of the Commons but Beattie, thoroughly aroused by the shouts of 'Shame' and 'Order, order', grasped it again and this time threw it under the table. There followed the ludicrous spectacle of the old Sergeant-at-Arms and Lord Craigavon both groping under the green-baize table to clutch the battered mace. The *Daily Express* the next day in a splash front page recalled Oliver Cromwell's order to the Commons 'Remove that bauble' alongside Beattie's 'Take this thing away'. Beattie was suspended and his always tenuous connection with the rather spineless Northern Ireland Labour Party ended with 'expulsion'.

It was the Home Affairs Minister, Dawson Bates, buck-toothed, white moustache stained yellow from chain smoking, a waspish solicitor, with a taste for the bottle, who finally lit the fuse which exploded in the 1932 unemployment riots. Bates, who had been the local right-hand man of Edward Carson back in 1912 was a little spindly-legged individual with bent shoulders whose appearance belied his reputation as the 'strong man' of the Cabinet. He was the Kremlin's Beria in local politics by virtue of his almost dicatatorial powers over police, Specials, prisons, local courts and law and order. Armed with the 1922 Civil Authorities (Special Powers) Act, Bates merely had to sign his name to a piece of paper to intern anyone, hold persons for questioning, ban meetings, inquests, newspapers and gramophone records, seize property and motor vehicles and 'exclude' individuals to remote areas of the North, a disguised form of deportation. In later years it was said that the South African apartheid administration was green with envy at these special powers. When Geehan and his committee arranged to hold a city-wide 'day of protest' demonstration Bates decided to smash the agitation. A proclamation banning all meetings and demonstrations with the familiar signature 'Given under my hand this day of October 1932 – Richard Dawson Bates' was hurriedly issued and reinforcements of armed police brought in to reinforce it.

For some reason which I cannot recall I walked from my office up the Shankill Road to see what would happen in the heart of Orange and Protestant Belfast. I was accompanied by a senior colleague from the *Irish Independent*, Mick Harkin, lately returned from New York. With his spectacles and expensive-looking tweed overcoat and felt hat, Mick had the impressive air of a country doctor. Crowds of unemployed shipyard workers were gathering at the street corners and you could feel the tension in the air as the hour for the demonstrations approached. At the corner of Agnes Street when I stopped to speak to a large group of angry men, Harkin was concerned when I told them that we were from the Dublin papers. He was unaware of the hostility which had arisen against the local

Unionist press and particularly the *Belfast Telegraph*. We were received with open arms. 'Well for you you're not from Baird's Ha'penny Liar,' one growled. 'Building bloody ships on the roof,' guffawed another, referring to Tom Moles's propensity for announcing new ship orders 'on the way' for Belfast, orders which never came. As we talked a stout, red-faced woman, hair unkempt, with a black shawl around her shoulders came running breathlessly across the road. 'They're kicking the sh— out of the peelers on the Falls', she shrieked, 'Are youse goin' to let them down?'

That was the match which set the flames alight on the Shankill that afternoon. There was a yell and the crowd broke loose setting fire to equipment, a watchman's hut and barriers at a road repair scheme, while others seized pick-axes to smash windows of food shops and the looting began, women and children running off with what they could grasp, loaves of bread, sides of bacon and clothes from drapers' shops. Soon the cry was heard, 'Here's the peelers!' An armoured police wagon with wire cage protection against bombs and missiles came at speed up the hill. As it swung into Agnes Street the rioters and onlookers fled. The police leaped out armed with rifles. We ran too. Several doors were slammed in our faces but eventually we forced back the door of a small shirt factory owned by the Faulkner family and ran upstairs to where a crowd of terrified girl stitchers were huddled. They did not know who we were and did not ask. Harkin jumped on a bench and pulled down a window sash to gain a view of what was happening outside. We took a risk because there was a sound of gunfire and shrill cries from outside. We saw about a score of workers running up Agnes Street towards the Crumlin Road pursued from a distance by the police. But what astounded both of us was the fact that some of the workers produced revolvers and, stepping into doorways for cover, fired on the oncoming police. Then the loud reports of the police rifles were heard.

We escaped from the factory on to the Shankill Road where

pandemonium reigned between the shouts of the mobs, the sound of breaking glass and the bells of the fire engines. More police appeared and there was a hoarse warning from behind us, 'Holy God – a baton charge!' There is only one thing to do in a baton charge – run like hell. No use brandishing a Press Card. That's an invitation for a split skull. We could hear the crack of batons landing on the heads of unfortunates who were left behind, the yells of pain and the curses of the victims. We followed a fleeing group into a butcher's shop whose windows had been smashed to bits. As more and more terrified citizens crushed in we found ourselves pressed into the few remaining sides of beef left in the shop. The din outside eventually subsided and we ventured out to view the scene of devastation with looters still clattering over the broken glass into the side steeets with goups of children clutching their booty.

Back to the office and an open line to the evening paper which was devoting an entire front page to 'Conditions approaching a revolution in Belfast'. From the Falls Road came reports of more riots and one man, an unfortunate flower seller, killed and several wounded when the police opened fire on demonstrators and onlookers alike. From one end of the Lower Falls to the other there was a scene of devastation – fires, shops invaded and looted, windows of linen mills shattered, a bus overturned and the old familiar ammunition, the smooth 'kidney-pavers' from the side streets torn up to throw at the police. From East Belfast there was a very different story. There the ODR workers were cowed by a local Unionist boss, a publican, who organised an Orange drummer to parade up and down Templemore Avenue beating a Lambeg drum as a warning to the shipyard workers to toe the line. It worked and thereafter we heard how Ballymacarrett had let their unemployed colleagues down.

While newsmen from Fleet Street poured in to report on the revolt the scared government rapidly revised the miserly relief rates upwards. The Board of Guardians was disgraced and a Bill prepared for its later dissolution. Bates imposed a curfew and that night West Belfast was in darkness, all street lighting having been smashed. F W Memory, correspondent of the *Daily Mail* gave us a laugh. He reported hearing a 'husky-voiced Russian' agitator urging on a mob in the Falls Road. But there were no Russians, with or without snow on their boots, just husky-voiced Falls Road men.

In the aftermath of the riots the opening of the new Stormont Parliament was hardly a joyous occasion. The Prince of Wales, with attendant women friends, looked bored, whether with the occasion or the dull, humourless local politicians who fawned on him, one could not say. Dressed in the uniform of a Rear-Admiral with a long sword which kept getting in his way he slowlyascended the long flight of steps to the entrance of the 'Parliament-on-the-hill' or 'White elephant' as critics later dubbed the place. Loyal cheers were acknowledged every step of the way as grim old Craigavon, scowling as usual, followed one step behind. Inside the marble Central Hall the pink-faced Prince read the inauguration speech in a sepulchral voice. The heir to the throne, so soon to be exiled after a brief reign, having not yet met his 'fate' in the person of an American divorcee, Mrs Simpson, looked ill at ease. His embarrassment was not relieved when a waitress passing the balcony overlooking the dais slipped and sent a tray packed with crockery crashing along the corridor. As plates and cups rolled noisily along the Prince of Wales winced and dowdy old dowagers seated on the balcony hissed to amused newsmen that 'the stupid woman should be sacked'. The local organisers of the Royal Visit typically had omitted Catholic institutions from his itinerary but, at the Prince's insistence, hurriedly arranged a call to the Mater Hospital where he met the nuns and doctors in charge. The academics at Queen's University were none too pleased either when he left them in the lurch, preferring to talk to a group of students.

The *Daily Mail's* distinguished Special Correspondent, G Ward Price, who usually accompanied the Prince on his world travels, was incensed when a fussy commissionaire refused him admittance as he followed the Prince into a York Street tobacco factory. 'I don't care who you are, if you have no invitation you are not getting in here', he snorted. Price got his own back in his report. He wrote that the Prince also visited a tobacco factory owned by manufacturers of 'cut plug'.

Unwittingly Edward blotted his copy-book that night when he issued forth from Government House, Hillsborough after dinner and was persuaded by the Duke of Abercorn's aide-de-camp, Commander Oscar Henderson, to speak to Orange drummers performing outside. Obligingly he allowed them to strap a big 'Lambeg' drum over his shoulders and he went down the village street whacking the drum, not realising its anti-Papist significance. Henderson tipped off his family's newspaper and the *Newsletter* scooped us all with the dubious announcement that the heir to the throne had ended his visit by beating an Orange drum. The drum was subsequently sold in Canada at a high price to some Toronto Orange zealots. In case this should develop into a racket, or because of its sectarian connotations, Buckingham Palace afterwards saw to it that other Royal visitors to Hillsborough refused similar invitations.

Meantime the Outdoor Relief workers' campaign had ended and Tommy Geehan disappeared as quickly as he had first appeared on the scene and the Catholic and Protestant workers lost a leader who had welded them together for a time into a force which had shaken the apparently immovable political establishment. Ten years later I got a glimpse of him in overalls sipping a pint in the Monico Bar in Rosemary Street with two workmates. The war was on at the time and I was told he, like many of his fellows, was working at the shipyard. From the lofty heights as a 'man of the moment' he slipped back into the ranks of the ordinary individual in the street, a forgotten man.

Unemployment continued to grow so the Unionist politicians

a further rapprochement between the two sections of the working-class. The Orange sectarian card proved once again the trump card to play. Jobless Protestants were told by politicians on Orange platforms that Catholics were taking their jobs. A Cabinet Minister, John Millar Andrews apologised to a Twelfth of July Orange demonstration for the fact that a Catholic ex-serviceman had been given a job as a door porter at Stormont and assured them that the post was only 'temporary'!

Sir Basil Brooke, a hitherto impoverished local squire from County Fermanagh, suddenly leapt into prominence with a series of anti-Catholic speeches on local Orange platforms. These were given considerable prominence in the Unionist press. He invented a new term for Catholic Nationalists – 'Disloyalists' and this caught on with other speakers. No exaggeration was too great for this propaganda campaign. The trickle of domestic servants who crossed the border from the South in answer to adverts offering six or seven shillings a week, 'live in' as a domestic drudge in middle-class Protestant homes, and the handful of boys who took up lower paid jobs as bar assistants, was depicted from the platforms as an 'invasion of disloyalists' and a 'plot to vote Ulster into the Free State'.

In an unscripted speech Sir Basil told a small Orange gathering at Newtownbutler that Catholics were 'disloyal' and wanted 'to see Ulster go to hell'. 'For my part I would not have one of them about my place', he declared and advised other employers to do the same. Although he later revelled in the description 'Boycott Brooke' and with sardonic humour named one of his prize bulls 'Boycott Brooke', Sir Basil lived to rue this speech which followed him all around the world. It might never have seen the light of day, however, had not a local correspondent by the name of Sherry from Newbliss, County Monaghan slipped over the border to cover the meeting. He took a full shorthand note of Brooke's remarks and saw to it that they got the fullest publicity in Dublin and elsewhere.

Brooke's sectarian outbursts set ablaze once more all the old fires of bigotry and even employers who in their heart of hearts disagreed with the fantastic canard that Catholics were taking the bread from Protestant mouths, meekly adopted the unwritten rule 'No Catholic Need Apply'.

DIVIDE AND RULE

IT IS IMPOSSIBLE to exaggerate the bitterness which the naked policy of discrimination brought in its train over subsequent years. Cynical old Craigavon, the Prime Minister, looking around for an up-and-coming politician who would follow in his footsteps and contemplating his own fading popularity, noted Brooke's rising star in Orangeism and promoted him, in spite of his inexperience, as Minister of Agriculture. Other politicians took their cue and vied with each other in bigoted speeches which were given wide publicity. A virulent anti-Catholic organisation called the Ulster Protestant League was formed and granted facilities at the Ulster Unionist party headquarters in Glengall Street to whip up the campaign in working-class Protestant areas with sectarian bands and demonstrations provoking confrontations and riots in sensitive areas almost nightly. The end result came with the sectarian riots of July 1935, with bombing, shooting and burning designed, it was claimed, to drive Catholic deep-sea dockers from their homes in the Corporation Street area of dockland. Many people were killed, more wounded, and others forced to flee their homes but the plot to take over the jobs at the deep-sea docks failed. City Coroner, T E Alexander, commenting on the deaths of the victims put the blame fairly and squarely on the unchristian utterances of the government politicians in the two years' campaign to divide and rule.

Although the British Army was called in during the worst phase of the conflict and set up barricades in the streets between York Street and Corporation Street to give some protection to the small Catholic enclave around St Joseph's Parish Church, shades of the so-called 'Peace Lines' years later, the British government maintained its ostrich policy on 'Ulster'. A high-powered deputation backed by influential opinion in Britain was sent to London to ask Prime Minister Stanley Baldwin to institute a public inquiry into the cause of the Belfast riots. Like several of his successors Baldwin refused to 'interfere' and the so-called 'convention' not to interfere in the 'internal affairs' of Northern Ireland – until it was blown up in 1969 – enabled Tory and Labour governments alike at Westminster to wash their hands of the many scandals perpetrated by the subordinate Parliament at Stormont. In the British press the troubles in 'Ulster' got short shrift and for the most part took their places alongside the short paragraphs from Reuter reporting 'communal conflicts' in other parts of the Empire, India and Africa, without giving any indication of what they were all about. They were part of the 'white man's burden', to be endured patiently as the price for their efforts to give inferior peoples the benefit of British rule. In 'Ulster' the languid cynicism of Prime Ministers and Home Secretaries at Westminster who, in theory, were responsible for the overseeing of Northern Ireland affairs, saw to it that the genuine grievances of the minority were swept under the carpet for nearly 50 years.

Whether by wink or nod the 'Ulster' government politicians acted as if they had *carte blanche* to do what they liked within certain financial constraints and while there were murmurs from time to time about an illiberal regime in the British 'province' across the Irish Sea, the governments in London seemed content to turn the Nelson eye to what was happening under the sheltering folds of the Union Jack in the oldest colony, or, as it has been suggested, the 'last colony'.

The ill-conceived Nationalist Party policy of abstention and non-recognition, a policy dictated from the outside by so-called Republicans, did nothing to deter the ruling clique, and in fact helped considerably to prevent the exposure of Unionist misrule. Speeches and meetings at obscure venues throughout the country, if not banned as 'likely to lead to a breach of the peace', only secured meagre publicity while focal points of publicity at Westminster and, to a lesser extent, Stormont, were boycotted. Abstention became the road to extinction for some of the politicians concerned. Not for the first time the Republican abstention policy played neatly into the hands of the Unionists. Nature abhors a vacuum and soon the Catholic population, fed up with the nonsense of 'Don't recognise them and they will go away' started to turn to Labour – Irish Labour – in preference to the moribund Nationalists. But the jibe 'Green Tories' did not rest easisly on the shoulders of estimable MPs like Cahir Healy who, even up to an advanced age, fought like a Trojan for his people in County Fermanagh.

Cahir, a quiet-spoken man of literary tastes and a poet of merit, was one of the most respected politicians of his generation, and he and Joe Stewart, the humorous Dungannon publican, defied the abstentionists by going to Westminster year in and year out to try to lift the veil on happenings in what Geoffrey Bing's expose later described as 'John Bull's Other Island'. They were continually sniped at by the 'head-in-the-sands' exponents of a fruitless boycott policy. Joe Stewart, in a typical aside about these years, told me how one party convention had been persuaded to vote for abstention by a young man who got up and threatened the unnerved delegates with a gun. 'A few years later when the War broke out I saw the same waster walking down a street in Dungannon dressed in RAF uniform' he said and groaned 'God, the things we have to suffer in politics!

Cahir, who was interned in the early Twenties on the prison ship *Argenta*, years later, at my persuasion, wrote his experiences in a series of articles for the *Sunday Independent*. He met many of the famous figures in both Irish and British politics but unfortunately never wrote his life story. I was always intrigued by his account of how Winston Churchill, during the days when he was out of favour with the Tories used to enter the House of Commons tea-room and looking all around the tables would spot Cahir and Joe Stewart and then come over and ask if he could join them. 'Churchill was being shunned at the time and it looked as if his career as a politician was finished. We used to chat about the old days and about Joe Devlin', Cahir recalled. 'We never imagined that he would make a comeback and actually become Prime Minister'. By an odd turn of the wheel of fortune when Churchill became war-time Premier in 10 Downing Street, Cahir Healy found himself interned for the second time in his career, this time in Brixton Prison, London. It was immediately after Dunkirk when panic set in with rumours of a Fifth Column and defeatist talk provoking the authorities to take desperate measures. All sorts of people were under suspicion including the Duke of Windsor. In Cahir Healy's case his dramatic arrest under Regulation 18b came swiftly after he had posted a letter to the late Canon Maguire, a Newtownbutler parish priest who was then active in Nationalist politics. Defeat for Britain seemed imminent and an editorial in the *Daily Mail* suggested some kind of a deal whereby Britain would retain its 'essential possessions'. Cahir in his letter asked the priest for his opinion whether in the event of a British defeat the German Minister in Dublin, Hempel, should be sounded about the future of the Nationalist minority in the North. The letter was intercepted and Herbert Morrison, the Labour Home Secretary in Churchill's Cabinet, ordered Cahir Healy's arrest. Whether by coincidence or not Morrision was paying an official visit to Northern Ireland at the time.

A cocky individual who seemed to be revelling in his new– found authority, Morrison was wined and dined by the local Unionists who found his right-wing ultra-Brit attitude to their liking. Old John

Andrews, who had succeeded to the Stormont premiership on the death of Craigavon, told a luncheon party in Morrison's honour at the Belfast Reform Club that he could imagine Mr Morrison one day heading the Twelfth of July Orange procession along Royal Avenue! Instead of being affronted at such a dubious honour for a Socialist, Morrison was delighted!

At a news conference later Morrison bored us with his unctuous and servile adulation for what he described as the 'gracious hospitality of their Graces, the Duke and Duchess of Abercorn' who entertained him at Government House during his stay. As he seemed to have nothing else to say I asked him if during his visit he had made any effort to contact the representatives of the Nationalist minority in Northern Ireland. The query seemed to hit a raw nerve. He glared at me through his spectacles and his tone changed to anger. Pounding the table he roared that if he had not met them it was not his fault. They had made no attempt to meet him! Healy's arrest had not been announced at this time and perhaps it was the knowledge that he had just signed his deportation order that led to the bluster. I formed the opinion that the man was a small-time bully, elevated by the exigencies of war to the position of a dictatorial Jack-in-office. I was told afterwards that while poor old Cahir Healy was whisked off to London by Scotland Yard men, Morrison was seen off by his Unionist hosts with a gift of a case of Bushmills whiskey.

On arrival at Brixton Cahir Healy noted with wry amusement that inside the gates the War-time Savings Movement had pasted up their well-known poster 'Lend to defend the right to be free'. On his release a few years later he told me that his fellow internees included Oswald Mosley, a British Tory MP, an admiral and a relation of the Duke of Abercorn, the Northern Ireland Governor. Cahir had a healthy respect for the British Secret Service. As an example of its ruthlessness he recalled the case of one fellow internee who before the war was sent to Romania in the double role as an oil executive of an Anglo-Romanian company and a secret service agent. His function was 'if the balloon went up in the Balkans' to superintend the sabotage of the oil wells before the Nazis got there. Whether he did or did not is not clear, but later he arrived back in England. He was astonished and pleased that both his salaries continued as before and took to drinking around the London night-clubs. In his cups he began to boast of his well-paid sinecure. But that was his undoing. He told Healy that one morning he was awakened in his West End flat by two Special Branch men who read over an order from the Home Secretary for his detention in Brixton Prison.

Much water was to flow down the Lagan before all that happened. While still with the *Irish Press* I added to my income my freelance work as Belfast correspondent of the *Manchester Guardian* and the *Glasgow Bulletin*, a popular Scottish tabloid owned by the *Glasgow Herald*. These connections proved invaluable both journalistically and financially. Representing the prestigious *Guardian* was a particular feather in my cap and opened a lot of doors which otherwise would have been closed. Meeting people like Patrick Monkhouse, News Editor of the *Guardian* and their famous Parliamentary Correspondent, Harry Boardman were experiences to be relished. Boardman who had been through the Irish troubles of the Twenties was described as having the great gift of conveying both the atmosphere and content of the debates in the Commons. He arrived in Belfast one Saturday morning to report a Northern Ireland General Election which he later described as Craigavon's 'Smash and Grab Election'. I was flattered when this seasoned newspaperman phoned early while I was still in bed, told me his mission and asked 'What do you advise me to do today?' Thinking swiftly, I said 'If I were you I would start off by going to a football match'. I could hear him chuckling at the other end. 'Right', he said, 'Tell me more' I told him that if he wanted to see some of the background of the politico-religious conflict in the North he could not do better than go to see the battle between Belfast Celtic and

Linfield that afternoon.

There was high tension in West Belfast that afternoon as thousands of spectators travelled to Celtic Park. Police reinforcements were brought in as fans from the Falls, Shankill, Sandy Row and many other areas crowded into the enclosure to witness yet another historic encounter between green and orange. My advice must have been inspired for the *Guardian* ran Boardman's piece on football and politics in Belfast across two columns on the front page. From his seat on the reserved stand Boardman described brilliantly how he saw the whole Irish problem in miniature at a football match! When Celtic scored the crowd at the upper end of the big unreserved stand opposite sang the Irish National Anthem, 'A Soldier's Song' and waved tricolours while Linfield fans boohed and cat-called. When the 'Blues' equalised the 'Loyalists' sang 'God Save the King' and 'the Sash' and waved Union Jacks.

'Suddenly', said Boardman, 'I saw the crowd on the stand part like the Red Sea before Moses as black-uniformed Royal Ulster Constabulary men cut through the fighting mob flailing them with truncheons'. It was a memorable report of a memorable afternoon, setting the scene for the stormy election campaign which followed. Boardman was delighted and thanked me for the tip-off. On the strength of it we took the day off for a car tour of the Antrim Coast Road and I remember his admiration for the beauty of the scene as we rounded the white cliffs with cotton wool clouds sailing across a blue sky reflecting in the blue waters of the North Channel. 'The cloud effects in Ireland are like nowhere else that I know', he said.

Earlier on the newly-fangled staff of the *Irish Press* blundered badly, deciding to defy convention by producing a paper on Boxing Day. Having announced the decision they took fright when they discovered, too late, that all the news agency services providing world news would be closed for the Christmas holiday. Messages were rushed out to all outlying correspondents and staffmen to send every scrap of news they could dig up to fill the paper. But that

Christmas there was a complete famine of news. Nothing was happening anywhere to disturb the peace of Christmas. Belfast, uncharacteristically, was as quiet as the grave. In desperation I lifted a brief paragraph from the Christmas Eve's *Telegraph* about dredging operations in the Milewater River at Belfast docks where an ancient Irish elk's horns were recovered from the mud. I rewrote the piece and sent it by rail-letter to Dublin thinking, 'Well, that's one for the waste-paper basket.' I was wrong. The news supply in Dublin and the rest of Ireland was as empty as Old Mother Hubbard's cupboard. My piece actually made the front page along with a minor motor accident at Burgh Quay! What was worse, to my embarrassment the contents bills of the *Irish Press* outside the newsagents' shops were emblazoned with the news 'Ancient Irish Elk's Horns Found In Belfast'.

You live and learn. Round about that time I had two experiences which illustrated the danger and sometimes far-reaching effects of indulging in political speculation. 'Dev's paper' was described by some Unionists as the 'Gunman's Gazette' with ex-IRA men like Sean MacBride, later a distinguished former elder statesman and holder of the Nobel and Lenin prize for peace, working as sub-editors. I recall the suave *Irish Press* motoring correspondent, the late Harold Brown, when I was introduced as the new Irish Press man in Belfast at the Ulster TT Race, asking 'Who did you shoot?' Years later I told this story to ex-President O'Dalaigh who also worked at Burgh Quay in the early days. He enjoyed the joke better than I did at the time.

One quiet evening in Garfield Street, the circulation manager, Pat McCann, once town-clerk of Keady, told me that he had been present at an informal gathering at which the tentative notion came up that Mr de Valera should be proposed as an agreed candidate representing all shades of Nationalist opinion in South Down in the 1933 General Election. I wrote a speculative paragraph not realising what a hubbub it would create. I was somewhat disturbed when at

Sackville Street, Dublin in the aftermath of the 1916 Rising. One of the author's earliest memories is of surveying the devastation on a family trip to the capital.

Irish News Library

Sir James Craig, later Viscount Craigavon,
Northern Ireland Prime Minister 1921–40.

Irish News Library

'Wee Joe' Devlin (1871–1934)
leader of the Nationalist Party in the Northern Ireland Parliament.

Courtesy of Mrs Sheila Hennessey

A controversial picture: the purchase of this Dutch painting by the Unionist Cabinet unleashed a major controversy at Stormont in the early 1930s.

Courtesy of the Public Record Office of Northern Ireland

James Kelly enjoys a joke with Cardinal D'Alton, Primate of All-Ireland and fellow journalists in 1957.

James Kelly collection

Brian Faulkner,
on his accession as Prime Minister, 1971.

Irish News Library

11 o'clock that night I received an urgent call from Dublin asking for further details. Apparently my message had been phoned to Mr de Valera by Joe Dennigan, the political correspondent. Joe asked who was behind the move and said that Dev had told them to let the story run. I told him that the people who had discussed it included Dr Eddie McEntee, brother of Mr Sean McEntee, later Minister for Finance in Dublin. 'Good,' said Joe, 'who else?' I remembered that McCann had mentioned Mr Frank Martin, a well-known Belfast solicitor and Joe Cosgrove, a local King Street publican. 'That's good enough for us,' said Joe. Next morning the *Irish Press* ran the story as a big scoop. The fat was in the fire for the local sitting MP, John Henry Coillins. He had not even been consulted about standing down in favour of Dev. The men who had idly toyed with the idea in the first place were both shocked and pleased. McCann who had let the cat out of the bag went into hiding for a day or two. Other papers were incredulous and some issued denials as Dev kept his usual enigmatic silence.

Arriving home late the following night I became aware of someone following me from the bus stop. I had just reaced the gate of my home when an out-of-breath Special Branch detective, Sergeant Morton, caught up with me. Briefly he confessed that his department, which was supposed to keep abreast of important political happenings, had been caught out on this one. 'There was hell to pay this morning when your story marked in blue pencil arrived in the Branch from the IG (Inspector General) with the query 'Why were we not told about this?' he said. In my story I had suggested that an 'envoy' from the North would probably be contacting Mr de Valera about the proposal. I confessed that I did not know who he was or when he was going to Dublin but when pressed I said that more than likely he would be travelling by train. This piece of misinformation had comic consequences.

The following Sunday morning detectives turned up at Great Victoria Street Station of the GNR in Belfast to check on travellers going South. They drew a blank but finally fastened on a local pork merchant by the name of Paddy Gilliland, who at one time had a connection with the Gaelic Athletic Association. Paddy had a hard time convincing the detectives that his mission was non-political and that he was merely travelling to Cavan to buy pigs!

Later I learned that the 'envoy' was in fact Sean McKeown, the veteran GAA correspondent of the *Irish News* and Dublin papers. Sean saw Dev privately. Later through his connection as a representative of Clonard Mineral Water Company in the area he was able to persuade the delegates and the local MP at a Castlewellan Convention that the election of Dev for South Down would be a great gift for the frustrated and isolated Northern Nationalists. At first the delegates were inclined to stay with the sitting member and I saw my story going up in smoke. McKeown then argued passionately that it would be a terrible slur on Mr de Valera if the nationally-minded Convention for South Down appeared to reject him. A vote was taken and recorded as 'unanimous' in favour of Dev. The *Irish News* reporter, Paddy Donaghy and myself had been admitted by some oversight. We joined in the show of hands. It was a good job it was not a narrow majority or we would have been in trouble. As it happens one delegate from Strangford wrote in challenging the 'unanimous' record. He claimed he had voted against!

Dev was elected with a 7,404 vote. He was opposed by a local Republican, T G McGrath, who received only 622 votes and lost his deposit. Bonfires blazed on the hillsides and Nationalists conjured up all sorts of exciting possibilities such as Dev's dramatic entrance at Stormont to confront Craigavon in his den. Stormont provided a letter-rack marked 'E de Valera' into which order papers were placed religiously each day for years but much to our chagrin Dev never turned up. In the end it proved one of the many useless 'gestures to the North' from Dublin. Dev who was once arrested and jailed for defying an exclusion order disappointed the Nationalists with his somewhat aloof attitude on coming to power in the South. Meantime very quietly Bates had withdrawn his exclusion order. Most exclusion orders banned Communists and left-wingers to the rural district area of Clogher, County Tyrone, and Republicans to the rural district of Limavady. In Dev's case, oddly enough, he was excluded from all areas in the North except the county of Antrim. We used to wonder idly what would happen supposing all the Communists and Republicans so named instead of clearing out took up residence in Clogher and Limavady instead!

The other rueful result of political speculation concerned Ramsay MacDonald, Prime Minister in the so-called National Government in Britain in 1931, and how I unwittingly brought his holiday at Mountstewart, County Down to a sudden end. Ramsay, once the darling of the Labour Party, had deserted his old comrades with Snowden and the pathetic Jimmy Thomas, to join in a coalition with their arch enemies, the Tories and the National Liberals, to impose savage economy cuts such as reducing the unemployment benefit and other unpopular measures. It was said that vanity was MacDonald's downfall. Some blamed it on the influence of high Society hostesses such as Lady Londonderry who flattered the Scots-born ex-Labour leader shamelessly. Ramsay, it was reported, even swaggered around in her salon dressed in full court dress to gain her approval, a sharp contrast with the old Keir Hardie cloth-cap days. The flattery paid off for her husband Lord Londonderry, an arrogant toffee-nosed snob and mine-owner, known in London society as 'Cheeky Charlie' became Air Minister in the Coalition, a considerable step up for a man who had been once an indifferent Minister of Education in Northern Ireland. Londonderry once insulted the Editor of the *Irish News*', the late Robert Kirkwood, at his ancestral home at Mountstewart with the remark 'My home is not open to the *Irish News*' when Kirkwood called for an interview. His parting shot as he showed Bob to the door was typical. 'My name is pronounced Londondree, not London-derry' he said. Bob used to tell the story of how he was thrown out of Mountstewart with relish as an illustration of the bad manners of one who claimed to be a 'noble lord'. Nobody was sorry when later on 'Cheeky Charlie' got his come-uppance, narrowly escaping internment for his pro-German book *Ourselves and Germany* and his friendship with the Nazi bosses, Goering and Ribbentrop.

Late one evening a newsflash announced that Prime Minister Ramsay MacDonald was flying with Lord Londonderry, the Air Minister, to Mountstewart, County Down. Nothing more. Prime Ministers rarely go to Northern Ireland without some purpose in view and I realised this was a story which would need developing. I phoned the police at Portaferry, County Down and they confirmed that two flying boats were just then droning up Strangford Lough. Then I phoned Mountstewart where the butler told me what they were serving for dinner. He added that he could see their guest, Mr MacDonald coming ashore at a small jetty close to the Mountstewart entrance gates. At the GPO where I was handing in my story to be telegraphed to Dublin I met an knowledgeable friend who suggested that MacDonald's visit might have something to do with the moves then being made at the Ottawa Imperial Conference to bring the disastrous Anglo-Irish Economic War to an end. I added this piece of speculation to my story. I visualised the whole thing ending up as a a fat paragraph but the report of MacDonald's surprise appearance in County Down combined with the magic reference to Ottawa where senior Irish Ministers Lemass and Ryan were negotiating on tariffs, set alight the subs room in Dublin. The story and speculation were splashed all over the front page the next morning much to my surprise and not a little misgiving. The 'Message from Ottawa' had done the trick. I was awakened with a telegram from the News Editor congratulating me on the 'scoop' and ordering me to follow the British Premier's movements closely in case there was a fast car dash to Dublin!

By this time I had begun to believe that something big was afoot and travelled down the Ards Peninsula to the Mountstewart estate.

At the entrance gates I arrived in time to see two Belfast press photographers being ejected but walked past without talking to them. A short distance further along the road I noticed a small entrance and turnstile marked 'Admission to Mountstewart gardens: one shilling (proceeds in aid of Queen's Institute of District Nursing)'. I recalled attending a meeting of the institute at the Royal Victoria Hospital where Lady Londonderry created a stir among the senior medicos present by sitting up front on a stage with scarlet snakes tattooed on her sheer stockinged legs.

I placed my shilling in the slot and passed in unnoticed to the Italian Gardens. Just who should then issue forth from inside of the stately home but Ramsay MacDonald himself, dressed in his country tweeds and plus fours. He carried a book under his arm and clearly was in no hurry to rush off to Dublin to meet de Valera or anybody else. For a moment I hesitated whether to reveal myself and ask for an interview but quickly made up my mind that this might have unexpected consequences for right behind him came Lady Mairi Stewart, one of Londonderry's younger daughters, hanging on to the leads of a flock of pretty ferocious-looking large hounds. She took the Prime Minister to a quiet spot in the gardens where he settled down on a stone seat absorbed in his book. I watched them for a few minutes from behind a clump of bushes and decided that it was time to beat a retreat. The 'Message from Ottawa' was clearly a non-event. Unfortunately that was not the end of the story.

Reeve, the *Daily Mail* staffman in Dublin set Fleet Street aflame with a follow-up story on the MacDonald visit quoting Mr de Valera's 'Government organ' the *Irish Press* about the 'message from Ottawa revelation'. Meantime back at Mountstewart Mr MacDonald's peace was shattered as newspapers and newsagencies maintained a barrage of phone inquiries, demanding interviews about his projected 'negotiations' with Mr de Valera. The *News Chronicle* in a leader headed 'Prime Minister's Duplicity' said that before leaving for Mountstewart, Mr MacDonald's office had sent a private message to the London newspapers through the Press Association stating that his visit had no political significance and was merely a holiday. 'But,' said the *Chronicle*, 'Mr de Valera's *Press* has revealed the true purport of his visit.' Poor Ramsay must have wondered what hit him. Nobody would believe him. Finally it was announced that the Prime Minister was cutting short his visit to Mountstewart and was returning to London immediately. The real story never got out 'How A Junior Reporter Ruined A Prime Minister's Holiday'.

There was, however, another revelation about the Ottawa Conference. It was told by Lady Brooke, later Lady Brookeborough, a few months later. Her husband, Sir Basil Brooke was one of the delegates in his job as Northern Ireland Minister of Agriculture. According to Lady Brooke, Sir Basil when travelling to Ottawa in a special express train filled with Commonwealth diplomats, Ministers and civil servants had occasion to visit the 'wash room' where he pulled the 'wrong chain'. It was the communication cord and the express ground to a halt with brakes squealing and passengers thrown from their seats. Sir Basil fled back to his seat while railway officials ran along the track checking the compartments for an emergency. The mystery remained unsolved and the train resumed its journey. Later on the *Irish News*, in an editorial attacking the Minister of Agriculture, referred to 'Sir Basil Brooke, who is chiefly noted for his train-stopping exploits in Canada!'

THE POPE AND KING WILLIAM

P ART OF OUR job was to report on the activities of the
Northern Parliament at Stormont. It was an easy job for with
the main Nationalist Party in disarray over its abstention
policy there was little in the way of opposition to the complacent
ruling Unionist Party. An atmosphere of low comedy hung over the
place as a makeshift opposition provided by two Shankill Road
Independent Unionists, Tommy Henderson and John W Nixon, and
three other MPs kept the pot boiling. The other three were Jack
Beattie, the Labour MP, and two BelfastNationalists who disagreed
with abstention, a KC, the late T J Campbell who later became a
Judge, and an elderly publican, benign old Alderman Dick Byrne.
Henderson, a painter by trade, was the arch-comedian of Stormont.
A rubicund talkative little man who was no respecter of persons,
high or low, Tommy could switch from high-flown oratory to broad
comedy in a twinkling.

When Craigavon entertained guests and invited them along to
the 'Distinguished Strangers Gallery' to see the Northern Ireland
parliament in action this was usually the signal for Tommy
Henderson, with a copious wink directed to the press gallery, to
come forward to the despatch box with some outlandish story to
shame the Government about the sanitary deficiencies of Troopers

Lane in the constituency of a Government Minister, Mr G B Hanna, KC. Other variations on the same theme dealt with Millisle, County Down. Here, according to him, the 'unfortunate inhabitants are compelled to use a sanitary bucket with a stick over it while wasps are buzzing around like hornets'. As his lordship the Prime Minister was hurriedly ushering his guests out to the tea-room, Tommy would hurl his final blast at the retreating Premier and his shocked guests, 'You don't care about these poor people. Why should you? You can exercise the functions of nature in the lap of luxury!'

The City Hall vestibule was a great centre of political lobbying and here pressmen on the look-out for local scandals and gossip used to meet local political know-alls after the municipal committee meetings had concluded about noon. One morning someone remarked that the one-party Unionist dictatorship at Stormont would never be removed except by a revolution or a *coup d'etat*. Tommy Henderson was all ears. Producing a packet of cigarettes he asked me to write down the pronunciation of *coup d'etat* remarking 'I must use that at Stormont one of these days'. In fact, the opportunity came that very afternoon. In the middle of a speech of denunciation of the useless government Tommy suddenly stopped and produced the cigarette packet. Ignoring the cat-calls about 'No smoking here!' he suddenly launched forth declaring that nothing short of a *coup d'etat* would shift Craigavon's immovable Government. Lieutenant-Colonel Alec Gordon, a Junior Minister, shouted 'What does that mean, Tommy?' Looking scornfully at the interrupter Tommy replied, 'Well, I am surprised that a Greek scholar like you doesn't know what *coup d'etat* means'. That brought the house down.

The growth of bureaucracy in the shape of innumerable boards for this and that – a Pigs Board, an Egg Board and even a Cap and Hat Board was a particular target for the ridicule of the 'Honourable Member for Shankill'. His famous sally in the Commons that bureaucracy had multiplied to such an extent that it had become 'like the testicles of an octopus spread all over the Province' brought another explosion of mirth. The story spread far and wide and years later I heard the then Prime Minister, John Andrews, pointing out Henderson to a visiting British Cabinet Minister as the author of the famous 'octopus' story.

A special edition of *Hansard* was printed to accommodate Tommy Henderson's celebrated record nine and a half hours non-stop speech to an exhausted and astounded Stormont Commons. Once again it had its origin in the City Hall vestibule where Henderson stood on the circular mat chatting to a number of idle Pressmen with nothing apparently to do but plan a bit of mischief. I mentioned that I had seen the film *Mr Smith Goes To Washington* at the Hippodrome the previous night and retailed how James Stewart in the title role had held up Government business by a remarkable filibuster. This started a conversation about filibusters in general. Tommy was listening with interest, his agile mind working overtime. We passed it off as an idle boast when he suddenly announced that when the Appropriation Bill, or the Consolidated Fund Bill, I have forgotten which, came up in the Stormont Commons the next day he would make history with the longest speech ever heard there or in any other parliament. The debate on these measures permitted a speaker to roam over an endless range of matters and it was clear that the redoubtable Tommy meant business when he appeared that afternoon armed with an array of blue books, bound volumes of Hansard and the Book of Estimates. Nobody realised what they were in for when he was called somewhere around 7 pm and amidst ironical cheers threw his formidable collection of books and papers on the table and began one of the most hilarious and far-ranging speeches we had ever heard.

Even to talk nonsense for nine hours would be a considerable achievement but to keep within the rules of order and avoid being ordered to sit down on the grounds of 'tediousness' was a remarkable performance. It was a speech of wit, invective and broad humour, with imaginative forays into low comedy, as, for example, he spotted the item 'Stormont hen relaying station' on the Ministry of Agriculture estimates and went on to picture at length the absurdity of white-coated civil servants chasing hens with toilet tissue in their outstretched hands! The speech went on for hours. MPs left for tea or went to the bar and came back to find Tommy still going strong on glasses of water and acid drops placed on the table at intervals by Labour MP Jack Beattie, who acted as his mentor with an occasional aside to keep the fun going.

At 1.30 am the bearded Minister of Finance, the elderly H M Pollock, who had to pilot the legislation through to ensure the supply of Government funds, fell fast asleep and slipped down prone on the bench. Pointing to the inert elder statesman opposite Tommy said he had just been reading in the newspapers about a Dr Voronoff who had discovered how a person could be rejuvenated by monkey glands. 'When I look at the Minister of Finance,' he said, 'I think that nothing short of something out of an elephant would do the trick.'

Meantime exhausted local newspapermen had given up the ghost and contented themselves with phoning their newspapers with stop-press communiques '2.30 am Mr Henderson still talking'. It all ended somewhere around 4 am when weary Ministers and MPs crawled out to their cars. Tommy, who lived on the Lisburn Road as he often boasted, 'Next door to the Workhouse', was refused a lift home but eventually got there as dawn was breaking in an *Irish News* delivery van.

Arriving half an hour late at Stormont one afternoon I went in through the swing doors of the main entrance and walked straight into an unusual commotion. A group of Glasgow Protestant extremists led by the editor of a bigoted Orange publication 'The Vanguard' had obtained tickets for the public gallery provided by the Woodvale MP, John W Nixon, the virulent maverick anti-Government ex-police inspector. Unknown to Nixon they had come prepared to protest against the 'King William picture' hanging in the lobby outside the Members Room. The picture had been the subject of much controversy among Orangemen who claimed that it was an 'insult' to their Order.

Dame Dehra Parker, later Minister of Education and a personal friend of Lord Craigavon, had persuaded him to purchase the historic picture but it must have been 'sight unseen'! While some of the more broadminded Unionists joked that the picture belied their reputation for bigotry the more orthodox among them were shocked for the 17th century Dutch artist had included an allegorical picture of the Pope in a cloud above William giving him benediction. Worst still, holding the reins of William's inevitable white charger was a Franciscan friar with rosary beads wrapped around his brown habit at his waist! The fury of local Orangemen knew no bounds. There were protest meetings and Nixon and others declaimed at the insult to King William, of 'glorious pious, and immortal memory' and to all true-blue Orangemen.

For a time it seemed that the reputation of the Government was at stake. Were there traitors in the camp or what dark conspiracy was afoot to besmirch the memory of the man whose picture adorned a thousand Orange banners and street gables riding gallantly against the papist cowardly King James across the beautiful River Boyne? Historians came to the rescue pointing out that the Vatican had been illuminated when the news reached Rome of William's victory at the Boyne but the Orangemen would have none of that kind of talk. Under every picture of King Billy on the walls throughout Belfast for generations was written 'To hell with the Pope'. They even scrawled it in chalk on the plates of the ill-fated Titanic soon to be ripped open by an iceberg in the North Atlantic. In Belfast history fights a losing battle against mythology.

One of the perpetrators of this mythology, Mr Ratcliff, editor of *The Vanguard* had come to avenge the insult. Before travelling out to Stormont he and his wife had called at Woolworths and purchased a short kitchen knife and a tin of red paint. Passing the offending picture with his followers Ratcliff lunged at the picture with the knife and threw the tin of paint over it. The knife landed on the hapless friar tearing a jagged hole while the paint left a red smear across the canvas. In the uproar which followed Ratcliff and his wife were seized by attendants and later removed by police to a small dungeon-like room at the rear of Stormont Castle. An embarrassed Premier, Lord Craigavon met us in the lobby but refused to comment on the incident saying that it would be improper as the matter was now 'sub-judice'. A Belfast Resident Magistrate, Major McCallum was sent for and later that evening we all crowded into the tiny room where Ratcliff was charged and remanded for the offence and later convicted.

Although the picture was 'restored' it never graced the wall in the Stormont lobby again but was said to have been displayed in the private room of a senior permanent secretary out of sight of the vulgar herd. An MP who saw it there subsequently told me that an odd feature of the work of restoration was that the friar's Rosary beads had been removed. Were they trying to suggest that he was an Episcopalian?

Years later an art expert at the Ulster Museum at Stranmillis blew the last traces of the controversy up in smoke reporting after considerable research that the figure mounted on the white horse was not William of Orange at all but an obscure German princeling leading his troops in a Continental campaign.

So ended the curious episode of the 'Pope and King William' picture. Like many other Stormont controversies it contained all the elements of farce. While it rocked the Craigavon Government for a while it at least sent some of the younger generation back to the more reliable historians to sort out the myths of history. T W Moody and F X Martin in their *Course of Irish History* dispelled some of the dangerous historical anti-Pope propaganda of the Orange Order when they pointed out that the Holy Roman Emperor and the Catholic King of Spain were 'William's allies and the Pope himself was no friend of Louis XIV, the patron of King James'. Furthermore, 'in a military sense the Boyne was not a decisive victory; the Irish losses were small and *Te Deums* were sung in the Catholic cathedrals for the victory.' Unfortunately a lot of water had to flow down the Boyne and much blood had to be spattered about before the debunking of the school history books began.

WEE JOE AND CARSON

A GREAT WAVE of emotion swept over Ireland the night in 1934 when Joe Devlin, MP, the then almost legendary Nationalist leader, died after a trying illness at the age of 63. I have never seen so many people weep so unashamedly as they did at his funeral up the Falls Road to Milltown Cemetery. The cortege was immense, friend and foe walked side by side behind the coffin of a man who had become a beloved figure, 'Wee Joe' the darling of the poor mill-girls who for years followed his election brake singing lustily 'Joe Devlin for the West' and 'We'll send him up the river with his ya-ya-ya'.

It was said that all Ireland was united for the day of Joe's last journey along that familiar dusty road which he had traversed for a whole generation from boyhood to the days of his election triumphs. Dev, whom he defeated in the famous 1918 election in Belfast, sent his eldest son, Vivion, while Cabinet Ministers from Dublin and Stormont walked side by side. In the weeping crowds thronging the footpaths as the procession walked silently to the graveyard were many of the children and young women whom he sent to the seaside on the Joe Devlin annual excursion, for he was a man with a generous heart. I still remember the sadness in his eyes the night we reported to him that a child had been killed falling from the train bringing the children back from the outing to Newcastle, County Down. Joe's advocacy of better conditions for the sweated labour in the big linen mills was as much appreciated in the Shankill as in the Falls. One Shankill Road man who confessed that he cried at Joe's funeral was Tommy Henderson, MP. He said it was a nostalgic moment for him when he passed Northumberland Street on the Falls Road and recalled that as a boy he had once thrown stones at Joe Devlin's election brake as it passed by. Like many other opponents of the old days the passage of the years had brought understanding and indeed affection for his generous spirit and passionate devotion to the poor.

Once while still with the *Irish News* I was sent to interview the man we all regarded with awe, not unmixed with fear, because of Duggan's stories about how particular 'Joe' was about reports of his speeches. Duggan, not the best of shorthand writers, used to groan publicly when Devlin, who was a director of the paper, would ring up to check on the reports of his speeches.

Mr Devlin lived at that time at Ard Righ, a rather grand mansion beyond Fortwilliam on the Antrim Road overlooking Belfast Lough. It was once the home of Francis Joseph Biggar, a famous figure in the Irish-Ireland movement who entertained Sir Roger Casement, Bulmer Hobson, Cahal O'Byrne and many others. I recall the trepidation with which I approached the residence. But I need not have worried: Joe 'interviewed' me, asking kindly about my job, my hopes and my background. I found him a most courteous gentleman and left sailing on air, resolving in future to take Billy Duggan's stories with a pinch of salt.

Later on when I wrote a descriptive piece about one of his excursions for poor children to the seaside I was told that he had gone to the trouble of telephoning his congratulations to the Directors of the *Irish News* adding that he had been very touched by what I had written. I felt good about that because what I had written was written from the heart. Craigavon, his old antagonist for thirty years, was genuinely distressed at his death and was moved to write a generous tribute. 'He and I, in opposite political camps, fought for our respective parties for over thirty years, and necessarily, at times, with keen enmity. But throughout that time I have never entertained anything but admiration for his personal character. I know that he represented the views of a large following of our citizens. Although always in opposition, no bitterness ever tainted his private life, in which he was a sportsman and a kindly gentleman. His word was his bond.'

A year later, another figure from the past was buried in a great public funeral through the streets of Belfast but my feelings about Edward Carson, the Dublin-born lawyer who had stirred the Unionists of Ulster to the verge of rebellion away back in 1912, were very different. Here was a man who misused his gifts as an orator to incite hatred. Without Carson the modern history of Ireland might not have degenerated into tragedy. The man who dined with the Kaiser on the eve of the 1914 War and threatened to 'kick the crown into the Boyne' rather than accept the democratic decision of the 'Mother of Parliaments' on Home Rule had then wiped the dust of Belfast from his feet to turn somersault and accept high office in the Parliament he had derided. Although commemorated in a statue outside the 'Home Rule' Parliament at Stormont he had before his death become a forgotten man in the city where he had once spawned the acts of violence, the gun-running, the threatening words and the contempt for law and order which have plagued a whole generation ever since. The funeral was almost a military display with grim-faced 'B' Specials lining the streets and rifle-carrying police marching at the head of the cortege along Royal Avenue to St Anne's Cathedral where the old rebel was to be entombed as if the Belfast which he had abandoned for London was his home.

As the Thirties gradually faded the long shadows of another unthinkable War began to gather. Over the radio we could hear the ranting voice of a madman named Adolf Hitler and the dull baying 'Sieg Heil' of the many thousands of storm-troopers at Nuremberg.

In Belfast the wheels of industry began to move again. We had been told that the coffers were empty in Britain but when the sinews of war are required the coffers are replenished magically. This time there were no bands playing in the streets to lead men to the colours but a fatalistic feeling that forces were at work which would inevitably lead to the horrors of modern warfare, a sample of which we had seen in Spain and Abyssinia. We had heard a leading British Minister write off Hitler's rape of Czechoslovakia – 'a far-off country of which we know little' – and there was the temporary relief when the 'umbrella-man', poor old fuddy-duddy Chamberlain came back from meeting Hitler waving a piece of paper. The British Premier looked pathetic as he quoted Hotspur 'From this nettle danger we pluck this flower safety' amidst the cheers of the relieved crowds who had already begun digging trenches in London to shelter from the aerial bombing everyone dreaded.

I recall the lovely bitter-sweet summer of 1938 when there was so little to do that Paddy Scott and myself used to drive to Ballymaconnell beach near Bangor in the morning and endeavour to teach a visiting newsman from the *Irish Press*, Dublin, Brendan Malin, to swim. Brendan, a midlander to whom the sea was an unfamiliar element, made a gallant effort to master the art but failed. He must have swallowed pints of salt water as he struck out feverishly, legs and arms akimbo only to sink again and again. As we lay sunning ourselves on the beach looking out on the beautiful vista of Belfast Lough and the Antrim coast opposite we could see the colourful Manx ferries heading out for Douglas, Isle of Man and a few colliers sailing up to Belfast. It was an enchanting and peaceful scene and one we felt we must savour for in our innermost minds we feared the years of comparative peace were coming to an end. The 'Destiny Waltz' was echoing out again as the irresistible forces of Armageddon were gathering. Had we the gift of second sight we could have seen these quiet waters of the Lough crowded with shipping, battleships and troop carriers lying at anchor in a few years time poised for the Invasion of D-Day. I recalled that the earlier War of 1914-18 in my childhood was supposed to be the 'war-to-end-war' but here it was again in a more horrible form than ever. The unbelievable was happening and nobody was able to apply the brakes to stop the juggernaut.

IF THE BALLOON GOES UP

WORLD WAR II began dramatically enough for me on the Sunday evening of Chamberlain's declaration that Britain was at war with Germany. A telephone message from the United Press of America office in London came asking if I could obtain the passenger list of the liner *SS Athenia* which had just been torpedoed North-West of Donegal with the loss of 112 lives. The Anchor Line had an office in Belfast and the *Athenia* had called at Belfast Lough and taken on board a large number of Americans hurrying home because of the looming conflict. Because of the good offices of the local agent I was able to obtain the full Belfast passenger list. The UP, which catered for 1500 papers and radio stations throughout America and Canada, wanted the names and local addresses of every passenger they could obtain and I spent an hour on the phone dictating the details, realising that this would be important news to small towns throughout the States. The *Athenia* which was a frequent visitor to Belfast Lough carried a total of 1,400 passengers many of whom were picked up and taken into Galway.

Earlier I had been asked to become the UP correspondent in Belfast and had covered the IRA 'Declaration of War' on Britain which had appeared on posters throughout West Belfast. This was the prelude to the abortive bombing campaign in London, Manchester, Coventry and elsewhere. People gazed curiously at the 'ultimatum' calling on England to 'withdraw her armed forces' and adding that 'the hour has come for the supreme effort' to fight for Irish Independence but few took it seriously. It was signed by, among others, Sean Russell, later to die in a German submarine *en route* for Ireland, and Stephen Hayes, the IRA Chief of Staff, later sensationally charged by his erstwhile comrades as a kind of super-spy and informer for the de Valera Government.

The full rigour of wartime censorship particularly in the neutral South of Ireland took time to get into its stride and this enabled me to pull off a major scoop for the UP. At Scapa Flow the British Admiralty were shocked when an intrepid German submarine commander penetrated the outer defences of the anchorage, which were believed to be impregnable, and torpedoed the battleship HMS *Royal Oak*, with heavy loss of life. A veil was drawn over this major setback beyond a bare announcement. A tip-off by a friendly compositor who said he had talked to a survivor in Beagon's pub at the corner of the Springfield Road alerted me to the possibility of an eye-witness account of the disaster. I traced the man, an ordinary sailor, to a little kitchen-house not far from the pub. At first he was reluctant to talk saying that they had been sworn to secrecy about the affair but later when I told him that the story would not appear in any local or British paper (it would not have got past the censor anyhow) he opened up and gave me a graphic description of the scenes below decks on the night that the torpedo crashed into the doomed ship. He described the turmoil as sailors, some scalded from the burst boilers, fought their way up on deck and overboard into the oil-thick waters of Scapa Flow.

I sent the full story to Dublin by rail letter to be picked up by the UP man there and transmitted via Valencia radio to the New York office of the UP. The UP were delighted and told me that my interview had made the front pages in New York.

But the free and easy days were soon to come to an end. One night the Liverpool to Belfast ferry ran aground in a fog off the Point of Ayre, Isle of Man, and without thinking of the possible consequences I telephoned the story to the *Evening Herald* in Dublin. That evening I noticed that the evening paper, the *Belfast Telegraph* did not carry even a line of the story in its early or late editions. Then the realisation dawned on me that it had been killed by censor.

Liverpool at this time was being bombed regularly by the Luftwaffe and I had nightmares that my story in the *Herald* could have alerted the German Minister in Dublin to the fact that here was a sitting duck, a big cross-channel ferry providing an easy target for bombers. Fortunately nothing of the kind, in fact, happened but the *Telegraph* the following night came out with a long editorial entitled 'Anomalies of Censorship' complaining that while they submitted the Liverpool ferry story to the London censor and had it 'killed' on the spot their 'Dublin contemporary' had been enabled to give the full story for its readers!

I waited for the blow to fall but for a few weeks nothing happened. Then one night I received a telephone call from an official who introduced himself as Captain Hayden. Very politely he asked if I would mind telephoning him first before reporting any news item concerning the movements of ships or aircraft. He explained that this was an interim arrangement to 'assist' me pending the establishment of a Government Censorhip Office in Belfast.

Later a Censor and assistants were appointed to Belfast and established themselves in an upstairs office in Lombard Street. One of them, a Cornishman, had worked in a publisher's office before the war and he and his men whilst proving themselves very agreeable and courteous saw to it that there were no more scoops.

On Sunday evening, November 24, old Craigavon, then aged 70, passed away peacefully at Stormont Castle as he smoked his pipe and read a detective novel. It was said afterwards that Craigavon wanted the controversial upstart, Sir Basil Brooke of boycott fame, to succeed him but his time had not come as yet and trusty old John Millar Andrews, 69 year old son of a Comber linen bleaching firm, took up the reins as Deputy Premier and no questions were asked for some months. Andrews cut a poor figure and soon the criticisms started of the 'second-rate Prime Minister of a second-rate Government'. He made the ritual demand for the imposition of conscription but with a hefty slice of the Loyalist workers in either reserved occupations in the shipyards, aircraft and engineering firms, or the 'B' Specials, alias the Home Guard, there was not much objection except from the Nationalist population on whom the full brunt of conscription would inevitably fall. Andrews looked and sounded somewhat pathetic as a war-time Premier. He talked of prosecuting the War against a 'cruel and inhuman foe' only in his adenoidal tone it came out sounding like 'inhuban foe'.

In the Unionist establishment there had been scandals about inferior workmanship in the rickety street air-raid shelters, talk of rackets in black-out blinds and Home Affairs bossman, Sir Dawson Bates had been rocked by accusations from the redoubtable John W Nixon, MP, his old enemy, that he had used his influence to get a client of his solicitor's firm involved in bribery charges concerning a site at Rathmore for a TB sanitorium out of the jurisdiction to Canada in spite of war-time travel restrictions.

Early in 1941 I talked to Bertie Sayers, Editor of the *Belfast Telegraph* about the strange immunity of the port of Belfast from German air attack, while all the major ports of Britain were being bombed repeatedly. I think it was just about the time of the air raid on the Clydeside. I voiced the opinion then current that perhaps the Germans were influenced by Mr de Valera's policy of neutrality and his insistence that the whole country belonged to the Irish Nation. Bertie, an unswerving Unionist, grinned darkly and said, 'Touch wood. I hope you are right.' But I was wrong and so were all those who thought likewise, not least the Government and defence moguls. Belfast was about to suffer in its turn. With typical German precision

it was to be targeted in its correct order as fifth port in the United Kingdom.

A few weeks before the blow fell on the unsuspecting and ill-prepared northern capital there was the strange lapse by the censorship authorities in London over a visit to the city by the Australian Prime Minister, Menzies. He did the rounds of all the big industrial establishments and afterwards in a fulsome speech said, 'When I think of Belfast I think of your great shipyards, turning out aircraft carriers and warships for the war effort. Again when I think of Belfast I think of your great aircraft factory ...' etc. As I listened to the speech and took a note of it I thought to myself that this reference would never see the light of day. Amazingly the censor let it through and the people of Belfast were astonished to hear it coming across word for word on the six o'clock BBC news for all the world to hear, including 'Lord Haw-Haw', the German radio propagandist, to whom the whole country listened with fascination and dread. Some people blamed Menzies's 'big mouth' for the appalling and speedy aftermath but there is no record to suggest that the Germans took account of the Australian Premier's ill-timed boost for Belfast's war effort.

We had become familiar with the baleful wailing of the air raid sirens but most of the alerts had proved groundless. The previous September shipping had been attacked at the entrance to Belfast Lough and mines had been dropped. A few incendiaries had been dropped by a lone raider at the railway station and gas-works in Bangor but no damage was done. Then came the small raid of April 7-8 when six bombers, detached from a larger force which attacked Glasgow, swept in over the Belfast harbour area and dropping bombs from seven thousand feet just above the balloon barrage, set fire to a timber yard, damaged a large fuselage factory belonging to the shipyard and damaged a few terrace houses. One of the raiders, a Heinkel, was shot down by a Hurricane fighter which made contact near Downpatrick. It blew up at 1.30 am and the wreckage and crew fell into the sea.

None of these incidents dented the sense of complacency which the long immunity from what was happening in Britain had built up so we were totally unprepared for the shock and tragedy of Easter Tuesday, April 15-16 when a force of 180 bombers blitzed Belfast in the heaviest and most concentrated raid of the war. I have a vivid memory of walking home in the black-out from the trolley-bus stop at the end of the Glen Road when the sirens went at 11.40 pm. It was a mild night with only a small amount of white cloud and a light breeze. I had just reached the open fields at the city boundary when I heard the unfamiliar heavy 'bub-bub-bub' sound of aircraft approaching from the south-east. As the noise got closer my instinct that the menacing sound spelt danger was confirmed when suddenly a couple of anti-aircraft guns crashed into life. Quickening my pace I reached home to find that the family late night supper had been abandoned as the realisation dawned that we were, at last, about to experience an attack from the air with God knows what consequences.

We could hear more and more planes droning overhead and we waited with bated breath, wondering when some unknown airman would press the button releasing his deadly load of high explosives on the hapless victims below. Worst of all was the nerve-shattering sound of the anti-aircraft guns which seemed closer than we had realised. They sounded like iron fists pounding on the front door which rattled on its hinges and we looked anxiously at the windows as they too shook with each detonation. Soon there were other sounds from the city five miles away from our suburb. Every minute or two came the dull boom and echo of bombs landing on their targets, the din increasing in intensity as the attack was pressed home by new waves of bombers. Down there in the city people were being killed, homes destroyed and buildings levelled to the ground. We prayed for them and for ourselves for who knew when one of those aircraft homing in on the city might release its load out in the suburb and fly back to base?

Father Tommy Cunningham, curate of St Teresa's parish who lived next door, had gone out in his car and for hours on end we could hear the sound of his engine above the guns and bombs as he drove back and forth around the parish in the brave endeavour of rendering spiritual comfort to the victims if the misfortune of war brought death and destruction to the district. His bravery encouraged some of us to venture out eventually to gaze on a sight never to be forgotten. The Glen Road is on high ground flanking the western hills and below us lay the city now a sea of flames across the horizon. Ghostly flares cast a blinding white light as they floated like sinister candleabra tearing the dark veil of night apart revealing the spires, chimneys and high buildings waiting pathetically for their fate. Searchlights and the 'flaming onions' from the shipyard dockside aircraft carrier, HMS *Furious*, fortuitously in Belfast for repairs, ripped through the sky at the unseen targets but it seemed that the city was helpless as every so often there was another dull boom and we could see a cauldron of flame and smoke, as from a volcano, shoot upwards.

The defences seemed to peter out after about an hour. The bombers had the city at their mercy until about 3.00 am when people crowded out on to the road and gazed at the awesome sight of a city enveloped in a sea of flames. There was a stricken silence among the onlookers until one hoarse voice exclaimed, 'My God. That's Belfast finished.' After a few hours' sleep I prepared to drive into the city to try to pick up the pieces for a major news story for the Dublin *Evening Herald*. For a newspaperman the show must go on however appalled and stunned you might feel by happenings around you. I noticed wads of burnt paper lying in the back garden and on examining them I was surprised to find that they were invoices from a commercial concern at Prince's Dock, five miles away. Presumably they had been blown into the sky by a bomb-hit and wafted by a breeze to the Glen Road slopes.

Driving into the city was no easy matter with roads blocked by wreckage and warnings about unexploded or delayed action bombs. Miraculously my office in Donegall Street was intact but there was destruction all around the city. The scenes in York Street, the broad thoroughfare leading to the Midland Railway and the Docks, were harrowing. Crowds of people, the lame, halt and the blind, aged folk and children, were fleeing the city on foot or in lorries, vans or anything on wheels. Some carried bundles of belongings, some were tear-stained and grime-covered. They had only one ambition – to get out of Belfast, as far away as possible, they did not care where they landed. There was an urgency in their countenances which spelt fear of any repetition of the night of tragedy which they had experienced.

Behind them was the fearful back-drop of a huge mound of rubble and bricks which had been the giant York Street Flax Spinning Company's mill. It was reputed to be the world's biggest mill of its kind but, as bad luck would have it, a huge parachute mine had floated down on the building for a direct hit. The big mill toppled over, burying more than sixty tiny kitchen-houses in Sussex Street and Vere Street.

There had been immense destruction everywhere, rail stations, public buildings, churches, tram depots, banks, hospitals, cinemas and warehouses but the worst loss of life had been in the north and west of the city. By the light of the flares the first bombers to arrive over the city were believed to have mistaken the big reservoirs on the Antrim and Cavehill Roads for the docks and their marker bombs had attracted the worst bombing attacks on the residential neighbourhoods in that part of the city. More than 800 people were killed, over a thousand injured and 70,000 homeless crowded into schools and welfare centres, or took trains, buses or any vehicles available, throwing themselves on the mercy of the inhabitants of neighbouring towns and villages, or simply fleeing to Dublin, Bundoran or just anywhere. Anxious inquirers at these places were appalled at the stories told by the refugees. They lost nothing in the telling and in the midst of the tragedy we laughed at the story about the fat woman who was asked in Ballymena, 'But what did our anti-aircraft guns do?' She glared, 'Anti-aircraft guns, did you say? I could have done more damage with my arse!' Then there was the story about the man running up the Falls Road past the City Cemetery at the height of the raid. Nodding towards the tombstones glinting in the unearthly light of the flares he shouted to his companions, 'They don't know how lucky they are this night!'

Filing my story to the Evening Herald which had just gone tabloid was no easy job, with the telephone system in a mess and more and more wild stories and rumours to be checked out including one that the wreckage of a Nazi bomber was lying in Trinity Street. It took precious time to dash up there and find that the story was false. There was smoke and the smell of burning rags everywhere. The Censor's office in Lombard Street was damaged and he had set up in a room elsewhere and it had to be located. When I did find him in a building at the rear of the Ulster Hall I submitted my story in triplicate, as required, and received it back with all references to the deadly parachute mines deleted in blue pencil and likewise the reference to refugees fleeing the city. The Censor asked me what I thought of civilian morale after the raid. I have forgotten what I told him and often wondered what he reported back to the Ministry of Information in London.

Meantime a reporter and photographer from the Dublin office arrived to give me some assistance. The photographer had to be equipped with special permits to take pictures, otherwise he was liable to be arrested. I was told to bring him to Victoria Military Barracks for the purpose but, on arrival, found that it too had been bombed. In the end we located an over-burdened junior duty officer in a room with a blind flapping through a shattered window. He knew nothing about Press permits and eventually after a search of a voluminous file discovered a blank permit authorising photographs for architectural purposes! 'That's the best I can do for you', he said as he signed the paper. The photographer used this so-called 'permit' happily for the rest of the week unchecked by anyone. He also took the precaution each evening of taking the train to Dundalk leaving us to face whatever 'music' would ensue overnight.

Meantime the United Press of America had been early on the phone from London. The raid on Belfast was the big story of the day the European Manager told me and they wanted a good colour story for the States. 'You know the kind of thing,' he said, 'Paddy Murphy waving his shillelagh at the German planes and telling them to come down there and fight.' I laughed and made up my mind that I would never descend to that kind of Paddyism. Instead I sent them a story describing the fire engines from neutral Southern Ireland – from Dundalk, Drogheda, Dublin and Dun Laoghaire – with headlights blazing dashing through the night to the aid of stricken Belfast. I said this single act had done more to unite North and South than a generation of statesmen back to Gladstone. Two days later I was astonished to read this in a panel in the *Independent*. It appeared in a despatch from the New York correspondent of the London *Daily Telegraph* quoting the 'United Press correspondent in Belfast'!

In Belfast's hour of travail the hard-pressed Minister of Public Security, JC McDermott, had phoned Dublin for help and Mr de Valera, throwing diplomacy to the wind, issued orders from his home to set this mission of mercy in train. That afternoon McDermott, later to become the North's Lord Chief Justice, called in the press for an urgent conference in a temporary office in the city. He told us of his fears that unless fire-watchers and householders 'stayed put' there was the danger of a fire-bomb raid destroying what was left of the city. 'The headline I would like to see in the papers is "Stay Put",' he said. But apart from the more courageous ARP personnel there were few who took heed of his injunction that night. Even before the sirens went as darkness fell there was an immense evacuation of the densely-populated areas and even the suburbs, out into the open fields and ditches of Counties Antrim and Down.

There had been many stories of courage and bravery among ordinary people but rumours had spread that McDermott was one of the few Ministers and high officials who remained at their posts. Members of the government and civil dignatories had fled with their families to hotels at Newcastle, Portrush and Ballygally on the Antrim coast. Dublin firemen who called at the Belfast Fire Brigade headquarters said that the deputy, later promoted to Fire Chief, had taken over control. The English-born Fire Chief had suffered a nervous breakdown during the raid, taking refuge under a table.

At Amiens Street Station in Dublin, a Belfast city Alderman who held a top post in ARP was spotted among the refugees streaming along the platform from the packed train from Belfast still wearing his ARP helmet!

Gallows humour is never far from the surface in Belfast even in times of stress. A Shankill Road woman taken on a stretcher from a wrecked house spotted 'Dun Laoghaire' on the fire engine outside and said 'Oh God, that must have been a hell of a bomb!' A family which had taken refuge in a street shelter returned later in the afternoon to find that a dead horse had been blown through an upstairs window on to a bed.

While phoning the news-room in Dublin with the story of a Belfast doctor who worked through the night at the Mater Hospital not knowing that his wife had been killed when a bomb demolished his home on the Antrim Road, a message came in to cancel the story. Rescuers digging through the rubble had found his wife and servant alive and unharmed. They hid under a heavy mahogany dining-room table and were found under the table with a small electric heater switched on. Many other people were saved by taking cover under the stairs which often remained intact when tons of brickwork and plaster collapsed.

The reporter sent from Dublin to help me disappeared, and later, using his imagination filed a story recalling his youth in Belfast and adding, 'It hurts me to see the churches in which I once worshipped levelled to the ground.' Earlier in my evening paper story I had mentioned that not a single Catholic church had been hit so this piece of fiction never saw the light of day. In fact the immunity of the Catholic churches and the Falls area gave rise to a typical Orange myth that the Fenians had signalled the bombers with lights!

A Passionist Father at Ardoyne Monastery said the Blitz was better than a hundred revival missions. The queues outside the confessionals were never so large. Religious differences too were largely forgotten and grateful Orange families from the Shankill joined their Catholic counterparts in the safety of the crypts under the Redemptorists' Church of the Most Holy Redeemer at Clonard. With a few small raids and another big blitz with fire bombs a week later, when every military target in Belfast was put out of action – railways, bridges, power stations, engineering works, shipyards – people sheltering from the raids prayed as they had never prayed before. Family groups among the Catholics recited the Rosary as the bombs fell but in one household a girl leading the prayers was acutely embarrassed when she announed the first 'Joyful' mystery as 'The agony in the garden'.

In the meantime Paddy Scott, my *Irish Press* colleague and friend, had been blitzed out of his home at Rosemount Gardens on the Antrim Road and I was glad to arrange temporary accommodation for him at my parents' home on the Glen Road. When the second big raid was at its worst and we all wondered if we would survive this most determined attack the phone rang suddenly in the hallway. It was the *Irish Press* office in Dublin and Scott could not get the man at the other end off the phone quick enough telling him that there was a big air raid in progress. The reporter in Dublin was most intrigued. 'Is that the sound of bombs I hear in the background?' he asked. 'Yes, and for God's sake get off the line,' snapped Paddy. But the other man was relishing the whole thing. 'Fancy me sitting here in Burgh Quay listening to an air raid in Belfast ...' he ruminated but Paddy had enough. 'Go to hell', he shouted and hung up.

Another night there was a call from the *Irish Press*. A night-town man rang about 11.00 pm. 'I thought I would tell you that in Dublin here we have a report about the sound of planes heading for Belfast,' he told Scott, who like the rest of us was none too pleased with this tit-bit. We waited and waited that night but nothing happened. We could have killed that bearer of bad news.

We worked like Trojans covering the long and painful aftermath of the raids in a city where all ordinary life was in chaos. Around Donegall Street the smell of burning rags still hung in the atmosphere and every so often we could hear the rumble of dangerous buildings in North Street and Bridge Street being pulled down. A whole area of High Street, stores, cinemas and hotels had been laid waste and the place became known as Blitz Square. Amazingly the *Belfast Telegraph* had escaped the worst of the bombs and for several nights produced morning papers for the *Irish News* and *Newsletter* which were put out of action.

A surprise visitor turned up at the office one morning – the Honourable Frank Pakenham, later Lord Longford. He asked if he might have a chat with myself and Scott of the *Irish Press* over a coffee. We had difficulty in finding even a restaurant or hotel open. They had all been either blitzed or closed down. Eventually we found an upstairs room in the Cosmo Cafe in Garfield Street where Pakenham disclosed that he was over in Belfast from the Ministry of Information to speak to a number of people including the Marquis of Dufferin and Ava. We had a discussion about the local political situation and he seemed shocked at the continuing sectarian attitudes of the powers-that-be in the north but he then turned to the main purpose of his visit. I recall that he said something about Churchill being overheard in the Savoy Hotel emotionally attacking de Valera, almost sobbing about 'that bloody man' and 'to think of all I have done for Ireland'. This, of course, was in the context of Dev's refusal to allow the British Navy to have the use of the Irish Treaty ports.

Suddenly Pakenham put a straight question to us, 'What do you think would be the reaction if, instead of the British, the Americans asked for a lease of the ports?' I have forgotten what reply we gave but it was probably not encouraging. We ended on friendly terms as he hurried off to his other appointments.

Clearly back in London the feeling was growing that the German bombing of Belfast would alter public opinion in the South. There was further evidence of this from the Fleet Street newspapers with obvious evidence of official leaks suggesting that the situation in the North was becoming more favourable to the imposition of conscripition on the Six Counties. Resentment against the Germans, it was hinted, would now manifest itself in a general desire to join up! There was very little evidence of this back in Belfast or the North generally but as the propaganda campaign increased with even papers like the Liberal *News Chronicle* and others following the same line I talked our fears over with Scott at my home. We decided to communicate our suspicions to Senator Tom McLoughlin, a close friend of Cardinal MacRory, the Primate of All Ireland. The Senator lived close to the Cardinal in Armagh and seemed impressed by what we told him. A British Cabinet meeting was due to discuss the matter on the following Monday morning so the Senator agreed that as all other spokesmen on the Nationalist side seemed unaware of what was afoot, he should see the Cardinal urgently. The upshot was that the Primate issued a strong statement attacking any plan to revive the conscription controversy and quoted the famous 1918 declaration by the Irish Hierarchy in which they said the imposition of conscription on Irishmen would be 'resisted by every means in accordance with the law of God'.

Years later Harry Midgley, the Labour MP who later joined the Stormont government, told me that on the Sunday night before the Cabinet meeting he received an urgent phone call from a former Trade Union colleague who was private secretary to Herbert Morrison, the Home Secretary. He said Morrison was worried about

Gerry Fitt, (now Lord Fitt),
former SDLP leader and M.P. for West Belfast, 1981.

Irish News Library

The SDLP leader John Hume, MP, MEP addresses the SDLP Conference, November 1990.

Irish News Library

MEN BEHIND THE WIRE: Rev Ian Paisley, the DUP leader and Ken Maginnis, Unionist MP, confront the RUC outside Maryfield in opposition to the first meeting of the Intergovernmental Conference under the Anglo-Irish Agreement, November 1985.

Pacemaker Press International

Historic signing of the Anglo-Irish Agreement at Hillsborough, Co. Down, 15 November 1985.

Pictured from left: Peter Barry, Irish Minister for Foreign Affairs; Garret Fitzgerald, Taoiseach; Dick Spring, Tanaiste; Margaret Thatcher, British Prime Minister; and Tom King, Secretary of State for Northern Ireland.

Irish News Library

A MOMENT OF HISTORY: An historic handclasp between Gerry Adams, the Sinn Fein president, Taoiseach Albert Reynolds and SDLP leader, John Hume marks the announcement of the IRA ceasefire, September, 1994.

Pacemaker Press International

STORMONT,

BELFAST, 4.

21st. April, 1964.

Dear Sir,

   The Minister of Home Affairs has requested me to
acknowledge the receipt of your letter of 18th April,
1964, enclosing a copy of the pamphlet entitled
"Northern Ireland – The Plain Truth".

   This pamphlet is typical of the type of
scurrilous propaganda put out by a small section
of the community whose avowed intention it is to
overthrow the Constitution of Northern Ireland.   I
suggest that you, as an intelligent man, would be well
advised to ignore such nonsense.

                  Yours faithfully,

                  HRHigginbotham

                  Private Secretary

J.J. Keating, Esq.,
26 Ludlow Road,
Blacon,
Chester.

'Scurrilous Propaganda':
On the eve of the Civil Rights campaign the Unionist Government's
response to charges of discrimination and gerrymandering in Northern
Ireland was to smear its critics.

James Kelly collection

the possible consequences of conscription in Northern Ireland and wanted to get his opinion informally. Midgley told me, 'I was caught on the hop and then told him that I had just been reading a strong statement by Cardinal MacRory in the Sunday Independent on the subject.' Morrison's secretary asked him to read it over the phone to him. 'When I came to the part about "resistance by every means according to the law of God",' said Midgley, 'he asked me to wait while he got pen and paper so that he could report it back to Morrison.'

In my opinion that clinched the issue. When the Cabinet met the subject was played down by all the papers that had been playing it up as inevitable and there were unattributable reports that Churchill had muttered that conscription in Northern Ireland would 'cause more trouble than it was worth'. He was right. One could visualise the likely consequences with the 'B' Specials rounding up unwilling conscripts all over the North or pursuing them down to the Border. Needless to say the unwilling cannon fodder would not have been confined to the Nationalist population. While volunteer forces in the North were a mere trickle compared to the First World War, surprisingly those who did come forward were considerably augmented by young men from the South including deserters from the Irish Army looking for 'action'. It was somewhat ironic to see contingents of these new recruits passing down Donegall Street en route for the docks to the jeers of shipyard workers crowded on homeward bound trams on an evening. Wisely the Orange Order cancelled the annual Twelfth of July march through the city for the duration of the war.

It was said at the time that British Army officers quartered in the Grand Central Hotel might have had some caustic comments to make about this martial display of able-bodied loyalists marching behind the Union Jack along Royal Avenue with bands and big drums to celebrate an ancient battle when they might well be marching to a real war. There is a world of difference between flag waving in peace-time and flag waving in war-time. Local Orange grandmasters were stung into a public denial when a mischievious paragraph appeared in the *Irish Press* suggesting that a parade of some hundred Junior Orange Lodges included a large number of hairy-legged youths of military age! After that there were less marches of Junior Lodges.

YANKEE INVASION

Warned to be at Dufferin Dock Belfast on the morning of 26 January, 1942 for a 'big story' we already knew what to expect. This was to be the first landing of US troops in Europe and as we stood in the cold misty morning air watching the tenders packed with troops in full battle kit sail silently up to the dockside sheds, Robinson of the *Mail* remarked out of the blue, 'Ulster will never be the same again.'

The invasion by thousands of free-spending GIs – wrongly labelled in the local Press as 'doughboys' – certainly turned Presbyterian `Ulster' upside down in those first few months. The first night in Belfast was a kind of Bacchanalian orgy and we saw sights which gave point to Robinson's prophesy. It was the biggest booze-up ever seen in Belfast with reeling GIs and their 'colleens' staggering from pub to pub, singing, bottles of whiskey sticking out of their pockets, even invading hotels hitherto reserved for British officers. The latter were pushed aside by the nattily dressed Americans, their wallets bulging with dollars. The British no longer counted in these establishments and quietly faded from the scene. The 'Stars-and-Stripes' had taken over. In the upstairs lounge of Lavery's in Chichester Street, an American woman correspondent from Dallas, Texas, who had grown expansive on the local cocktails was giving away her jewellery to an embarrassed bar hostess, while from another end of the bar, a confused American voice was heard shouting 'Gimme another pint of that Bushmills beer'!

Earlier, after disembarking from the troopships following the long journey across the Atlantic from Halifax, they had been offered coffee and sandwiches but this was their night to howl and paint the town a lurid red.

The scene on their arrival was like a Holywood movie-set welcoming the Commander of the US Forces, Major General Russel P Hartle, while a band struck up the 'Star Spangled Banner' from a gaily decorated shed. I spoke to the first GI ashore. He turned out to be the son of a German pastry cook from near Chicago. I asked him why he had been selected for the honour of being the first American ashore. He replied, 'I wasn't. I just happened to be at the head of the gangway and was pushed.' The U P used my story about the first American soldier to set foot in Europe for World War II and he became famous, with bags of fan mail and even offers of marriage pursuing him to North Africa!

The *Independent* thought this historic event merited a double-column lead but Frank Aiken, the punctilious and too-fussy boss of the Censorship Department in Dublin killed all reference to the event in the Dublin press using instead a bald Associated Press telegram from Washington announcing the arrival of US troops in Northern Ireland. My chagrin was relieved a long time afterwards when Mick Rooney, later Editor of the *Indo* sent me a proof copy of my 'big story' which never saw the light of day.

As the US forces expanded, with the opening of naval and air bases and US generals flying in and out, I was kept busy by the U P, recording the activities of the personalities who came to see the forces on the ground. The public relations machinery of the US army was impressive and the facilities accorded the press made us green with envy. Colonel Arters, an ex-newsaperman from the deep South, laid on transport for what he called 'sorties', usually interviewing some top-brass Air Force General at the Toome, or Langford Lodge Airfields, with lunch and wine thrown in. Everything was made easy for us. None of these VIPs ever appeared without a portfolio of typescript details of their careers, family background and photographs for the assistance of the press. This was the American way of life and we revelled in it. At one such lunch I had my first taste of cheese-with-apple-pie and to my surprise the unfamiliar mixture was delicious.

The 'sorties' were not all so pleasant. The US forces were drawn from all sorts of individuals and included some violent characters. We were taken one morning to Castlewellan, County Down to cover a US court martial involving the murder of a deaf-mute girl in the gate lodge of Castlewellan Castle demesne where American troops were stationed. The trial took place in a village hall where the decorations for the Christmas pantomime were still in place. On the stage was a group of senior officers sitting at a table while to the right of the court sat the accused soldier between two guards. The realism we could have done without was provided by the blood-stained bed of the murder victim. It had been erected immediately in front of the Press table. The case lasted all day as the prosecuting and defending officers argued and the court responded with 'Objection overruled' or 'objection sustained' in the style we were accustomed to in American films. In the end it was the bizarre circumstances in which the murderer crept back in the moonlight to the gate lodge to retrieve his army boots from under the bed where the dead girl lay that nailed him. He was spotted this time by another GI who gave evidence of identification. The prisoner was convicted and sentenced to life imprisonment, presumably to be served back in a US Prison. I was glad to escape from that sordid scene and the sight of that rumpled blood-stained bed.

Before leaving the US Office in Linenhall Street for another 'sortie' Colonel Arters told us that while we were waiting for our transport he wanted to read a file of complaints which he had just received from the pentagon. The first was about a UP story which he said made it appear that the US forces in Belfast were 'cowering in barracks' on the day that Republican Tom Williams was hanged in Belfast Prison. I told him that I had merely mentioned that the troops had been confined to barracks on that morning so as not to get involved in any scenes following the execution. 'Oh I see', he said, 'I guess they blew up your story in New York but that's not your fault.'

We could hardly restrain our mirth when it came to the final rocket from the Pentagon. It concerned a picture front-paged in the *Belfast Telegraph* showing Princess Mary with her mouth open sinking her teeth into a doughnut at the canteen in the US Red Cross Club in the Belfast Plaza! The Princess Royal looked particularly horse-faced at this unguarded moment. Apparently the picture editor forgot the strict rule that Royalty must not be photographed while eating and used it. 'Who was responsible for this?' the Colonel demanded but we all feigned ignorance. We knew it was 'Big Herbie' McMullan, the popular veteran *Tele* cameraman. But if the Pentagon in the middle of one of the worst wars in history was going to spend its time witch-hunting on behalf of some Palace pip-squeak we were not going to join in.

The influx of so many free-spending strangers brought with it a varied assortment of local characters from far and near anxious to join in the spree. They ranged from black-marketeers, selling dubious 'whiskey' in the black-out to teenaged 'floosies' whom the 'Yanks' mistook for the Irish 'colleens' they had read about back home. Their foul language should have disillusioned them. The dance-halls were packed with jitter-bugging GIs and with petrol becoming scarce and only a few taxis operating on rubber tanks of gas suddenly there appeared the weird spectacle of ancient horse-drawn cabs and jaunting cars, resurrected from God knows where. These were much used by the Americans until a row started over the exorbitant prices charged culminating in a pitched battle in which a gang of angry jarveys with whips advanced into the Ulster Hall charging a number of protesting GIs right on to the dance floor. Another one of these worthies from out of town made some sort of legal history by being prosecuted for running a 'brothel on wheels'.

When the whiskey supplies started running out Americans were heard protesting about the stuff they were sold in the black-out by the harpies on the make. A joke current at the time spelt the danger of such transactions. One such bottle labelled 'Scotch' was sent to the public analyst who, the story goes, reported 'This horse's kidneys are out of order and need the attention of a vet.'

The appearance of American black troops in the camps brought its own problems and there was heavy censorship about what was whispered as the 'Battle of Antrim'. A dance-hall row with troops from the Southern states over a coloured soldier dancing with a white girl erupted into a prolonged confrontation which was only resolved when a black General was sent post haste to pacify the troops concerned.

When police were called to a rumpus in a York Street cafe an RUC sergeant hit a coloured soldier who had gone berserk. The baton landed on his head but he merely shook himself and said, 'I'll get you for dat' and producing a razor chased the policeman to the door slitting his raincoat clean across his back and cutting through the braces so that the policeman's trousers fell down. US military police arrived in the nick of time and wielding their long truncheons shouted to the police, 'Go for their ankles. No use hitting their skulls!' The US military police with their white helmets were the toughest I have ever come across. Nicknamed 'Dew-drops' they struck first and asked questions afterwards.

The manager of a city cinema told me that when they were locking up one night they found a US technician sound asleep in the cafe. They could not waken him as he seemed the worse for drink. So they phoned the Military post in 'Blitz Square' High Street and asked if someone would take charge of him. Within minutes a jeep pulled up outside and three American MPs dashed in brandishing clubs and rushed up the stairs. 'So this is the guy who is giving trouble', they yelled to the startled manager as they started to belabour the unfortunate technician. 'No, no trouble' said the manager, 'he was just sleeping', but they ignored him and hauling the inert form down the stairs threw him with a crash into the back of the jeep and made off.

Wartime marriages were not encouraged by the US authorities but inevitably there were many GI brides left behind when the troops were shipped off for the North African campaign. Some of the unions were happy and some not so happy. A parish priest in South Down told me that when he asked one prospective GI bridegroom to obtain 'a letter of freedom' from his priest at home indicating that he was free to marry, the soldier protested 'Father, I don't see what all the fuss is about. This is only one of those wartime marriages.' He was quickly shown the door.

The select band of citizens who had access to the troops' own weekly paper *The Stars And Stripes* which was printed by the *Telegraph* were shocked when the US authorities decided to tighten up discipline by printing a special supplement setting out a long list of addresses which were declared 'out of bounds' for US troops. What did surprise a lot of people was the evidence of the spread of these night 'salons' to the respectable neighbourhoods of Belfast. Robinson's prophesy was coming true!

THE LION OF PROGRESS

DURING THE WAR years the Stormont Parliament, which used to be called the Big White House on the Hill, was painted a drab black for fear of enemy action. Once a sneak German bomber laid a line of incendiary bombs up the processional way to the Carson statue but the building itself escaped damage. Stormont had become known as the 'Parliament of Threes'. It sat three days a week, three hours a day and three months a year. Just before the War I was elected Chairman of the Press Gallery, a job which largely consisted of keeping a watch-out for jealous civil servants encroaching on our accomodation and vetting visiting journalists. But each year when I attempted to relieve myself of these duties someone would move my re-election. I think it was Macmillan who said 'Why change horses when crossing the stream?' so I continued in the job for years.

Stormont was a free and easy place for newspapermen with a minimum of protocol. We could move around the lobbies unchallenged, speak to Members or Ministers in the Bar or dining rooms without any of the ceremony or fuss associated with Westminster or Leinster House, Dublin. Visiting Pressmen from Dublin and London were astonished at the facilities we enjoyed. We often wished that the good crack in the Bar between political opponents could have been transferred to the floor of the Commons where to maintain public attitudes the exchanges could appear so bitter.

There was a lot of laughter too. Tommy Henderson in his day provided a lot of fun. I still recall vividly his memorable threat to the Government about the risen people of 'Ulster'. Waving his finger at the front bench he declared, 'The day is coming when the lion of progress will march down Royal Avenue, hand in hand with the flood-gates of democracy!' Hammy McDowell of the Whig claimed to have heard even better mixed metaphors at Belfast City Council. He said that the fiery Alderman Pierce in a stirring peroration declared 'There is a fire raging in East Belfast. It's light is shining on the dome of heaven. If we don't stop the leak in this ship the plough of progress can't go forward.'

Crises were frequent at Stormont and during one I remember Jack Beattie, the Labour MP, likening the Unionist Government to 'a drowning man clutching at the crumbs that fall from the table'. Usually the Party Headquarters in Glengall Street, next door to the Grand Opera House, were able to stymie any threatened revolt in what, after all, was a kind of one-party dictatorship which lurched on from decade to decade content in the knowledge that no power on earth could dislodge the Protestant-Unionist grip on the reins of office, with the added satisfaction that British politicians, for the most part, whether Tory, Labour or Liberal, did not want to know what was going on in 'Loyal Ulster'.

Presiding over the Glengall Street power-house – once said by Beattie to resemble the Nazi 'Brown House' – were two individuals, Captain Herbie Dixon, the Government's Chief Whip and his assistant, Billy Douglas. Dixon, a race-horse owner, brought all the cunning of the racing stables to his job as 'Mr. Fixer' while Douglas who called him 'the Governor' became even more adept at the political tricks needed to keep the sometimes rowdy monolith of Unionism in line. Douglas holding court in Robinson's Bar in Great

Victoria Street, a stone's throw from his office, was reputed to be capable of organising anything from an election to the appointment of a dog-catcher, a JP, or even promotion in the police. Where there was danger of a Unionist MP losing an election Billy could arrange a split vote among the opposition. He thought he had devised a winning coup in West Belfast once against Jack Beattie by sponsoring a last minute 'Republican' candidate to split the Catholic vote. But the publican who offered to put up the money was unmasked as a Glengall Street under-cover man during the election campaign and the 'Republican', who was an unwitting party to the plot, lost his deposit.

Years later when I met him after a Radio Telefis Eireann confrontation in Dublin, Billy was in a reminiscent mood in the reception room. He confessed that the greatest mistake in his life was to send a young man named Ian K. Paisley packing when he came to Glengall Street seeking Unionist nomination for a vacant Stormont Senatorship. Paisley had been making a name for himself as a rabble-rouser in a local Dock election, appearing for the first time as 'election agent' in a hotly contested marginal seat. Douglas considered that some elderly wheel-horse Unionist had a greater claim for membership of the Senate than this young upstart who before many years rocked the whole Unionist edifice by founding not alone his own breakaway Free Presbyterian Church but also his own Democratic Unionist Party. Billy groaned audibly between drinks. 'When I think of the trouble we could have avoided it makes me want to weep,' he said.

But all that was water to flow under the bridge. While Dixon, later ennobled as Lord Glentoran, irreverently dubbed by reporters as 'Lord Football' after the East Belfast team of that name, and his chief lieutenant Douglas, were running the party machine, opposition candidates found the running so hard that elections were often a foregone conclusion with upwards of 20 to 27 Unionists returned unopposed out of a total of 52 seats!

Election trickery in one form or another, and particularly impersonation, has always been endemic in the North. Impersonation has been so rampant over the years that many of us were cynical about the so-called 'democratic process' and the claims of high turn-outs at successive elections. The intimidation of 'personation agents' in voting booths and the widespread belief that you must win, by fair means or foul, resulted in wholesale impersonation. Attempts to check the abuse on the spot were dangerous as witness the two Nationalist election agents who had to be rescued from a Sandy Row polling station in a police armoured car.

Then there was the scandal in the Victoria Division of Belfast where a titanic struggle between the sitting member, Sir Dawson Bates and a Progressive Independent resulted in such a flurry of votes and rumours of 'changing rooms' for impersonators that it was afterwards revealed that the ballot boxes were found to contain more votes than appeared on the Parliamentary register! Demands for an inquiry into this odd occurrence fell on deaf ears. Because so many dead electors rose and appeared in so many polling stations the political parties were forced to keep a record of death insertions in the newspapers for months preceding the elections.

I toured an election area on one polling day and was speaking to a Labour candidate when an election worker came up and told him that things were going well. 'Don't worry', he said. 'We have had the flying squad out since three o'clock.' The man was a trade union official and his contention was that if the 'other side' were at it they would beat them at their own game. In such circumstances we used to laugh at the claims of 'record turn-outs' at the count.

The British Labour Party sent over a high-powered London election agent from Transport House to help the Northern Ireland Labour Party at a General Election. The man was a first-class organiser, or had this reputation back in London, but he soon found that he was a mere amateur in the elective process as practised in Belfast. Every time we met him we could see the dawning realisation on his face that things were different, damned different, in this part of the UK. He lapsed from surprise to shock and finally admitted that he was appalled by what he had seen. Before leaving for London, a chastened man, I heard him so losing his British phlegm as to engage in an altercation with a Unionist Alderman. It was at the end of the count in the City Hall with the inevitable succession of Unionist 'victories'. 'Don't lecture me about democracy', he roared. 'I have seen it here. If you stuck a Union Jack up a baby's bum you would vote for it'.

The so-called 'Palace Revolution' which toppled the Andrews' government was planned and executed by Unionist lawyers in conjunction with Sir Basil Brooke. Andrews and his 'Old Guard' ministers were said to be clinging on like barnacles and were incapable of putting any real impetus into the War effort. Jack Beattie had won back the West Belfast seat at Westminter from the Unionists and the anti-Andrews faction made much play out of the defeat, with long letters attacking the Andrews administration appearing in the Newsletter headed 'The lesson of West Belfast'.

Both Paddy Scott and I were friendly with Beattie and at his request we did some speech-writing for him. We got a lot of fun out of these efforts, sailing into the Unionist moribund establishment with humour and sarcasm which we found went down well in the press. Beattie's attacks on the dictatorship of an immovable Government, in office more than twenty years, began to make the headlines. We had thoughtfully provided all the newspapers with carefully typed speeches in advance.

The Unionist MPs returned to Westminster were considered a joke. They were seldom heard and Henderson had described them as 'Ten Dummies'. The candidate selected for West Belfast was Lieutenant Colonel Knox Cunningham, a member of the 'Whig' Cunninghams. As a speaker he was pathetic and the only speech we heard from him was in the context of 'I ask Mr. Beattie where does he stand on the Union?' Beattie ignored this oft repeated query and took up the attack once more on the incompetent dictatorship of Glengall Street. In desperation the Unionists obtained a telegram from Churchill endorsing Cunningham but it was received on the anniversary of the day the Unionists had sought to tear Winston limb from limb in Belfast in 1912!

This was an amazing coincidence and we saw to it that Jack plugged it for all it was worth in his eve-of-the-poll rally in a packed St. Mary's Hall. The speech nearly brought down the roof and the next day Beattie won the election. His victory shook the Unionists and caused a minor sensation at Westminster, leading up to the formation of a large group of Labour MPs who called themselves 'The Friends of Ireland' including Geoffrey Bing, KC who was inspired later to produce his major indictment of the illiberal regime at Stormont entitled 'John Bull's Other Ireland'.

Andrews and the 'Old Guard' were in deep trouble but not even an uneasy vote of confidence secured at a stormy meeting at Glengall Street, could save them. Over that weekend the Marquis of Donegall in his column in the Sunday Despatch wrote that the 'Ulster Government is hanging on by its eye-lids.' He had been the guest of Dame Dehra Parker, MP, aunt of the powerful Chichester family, and we knew then that the plot to overthrow Andrews was still going on behind the scenes. Brooke then fired a torpedo into the engine room by offering his resignation. It was a shrewd and calculated move. Andrews tamely resigned and most of the 'Old Guard' went down with the sinking ship.

The ouside public played no part in these machinations and with the excuse of the war and a complacent Governor, the Duke of Abercorn at Government House, Hillsborough, there was no election. Abercorn, whose slurred speech at ceremonial occasions conveyed the impression that he was perpetually tipsy, always saw to it that his hosts were informed in advance that his favourite 'refreshment' was a brand of Scotch known as 'Cream of the Barley'.

A new government headed by Sir Basil, later Lord Brookeborough, was smuggled in and the public learned of its composition when the hi-jacking operation was completed with the appearance of the new Cabinet ministers on the lawn of Stormont Castle for a photo-call. Among the casualties were Lord Glentoran, the Chief Whip, long-time Boss at Glengall Street and Sir Dawson Bates, the so-called 'Iron Man' of Unionism.

One of the lawyers consulted about the composition of the new administration was Mr J.C. MacDermott, KC, a serious-minded politician whose probity was in stark contrast to the reputation of Glengall Street. At the time it was claimed that MacDermott, who later rose to become a Lord of Appeal and Northern Ireland Lord Chief Justice, had told the Cabinet makers that Bates must go. In fact he was quoted as saying, 'We could not touch that man with a forty-foot pole.' The last straw for Bates had been the accusation on the floor of Parliament by the old enemy, John W. Nixon, that he had smuggled out of the country to Canada an errant client accused of corruption and bribery. Bates with a quivering voice challenged him to repeat the accusation outside Parliament so that he would have his answer, presumably in a slander action. Nixon did just that at a public meeting in the Grosvenor Hall, having first invited Bates to be present. Bates backed down. There was no action. There were few tears shed over the departure of this ruthless politician and manipulator. With a stroke of the pen Bates could jail a political opponent without trial for years or run him out of the country with an 'exclusion order'. He could ban public meetings, inquests, gramophone records, seize vehicles and buildings, suppress local councils and gerrymander constituencies.

The department was supposed to have a private map-room where a civil servant devoted his time to producing surrealist outlines for constituencies. The object was to ensure that the rising Catholic population in places like Derry City would not endanger Unionist political control. The design of some of these voting patterns was fantastic. One of them reached out from Derry like an organ-stop to bring in a Protestant pocket of voters in order to prevent the Nationalist majority taking control of the city council.

Not surprisingly, Bates, always with his ears close to the ground, reacted with speed on hearing that a Catholic girl had been appointed as a telephone operator with links to his department. She was quickly transferred to another job and so the danger of leakage of guilty secrets was averted. The British Home Office was in close touch with the Ministry of Home Affairs over the years but it says much for the almost criminal absence of oversight by a succession of British Home Secretaries that the open chicanery practised by its subordinate regime in Northern Ireland went on unchecked for decades. Brooke was chosen as Prime Minister not just because he had been active as Minister of Commerce, the department mainly concerned with the 'War effort', but for another reason. There was his family connection with Alanbrooke, Chief of the Imperial General Staff, and also because of his supposed influence in Buckingham Palace. This had been much publicised when the Duke and Duchess of Gloucester accepted his invitation to spend their honeymoon at his Colebrooke, County Fermanagh estate. Since the Curragh Mutiny days Unionists always considered that it was a wise insurance policy to be 'in' with the 'big boys' who could pull strings in the British Establishment. Sir Basil, although anathema to Catholics because of his notorious utterances, was considered to have all the necessary qualifications to make him acceptable on both sides of the Irish Sea. Besides he was young and energetic and would provide a contrast to the fossilised left-overs from the Craigavon era.

This was how the argument ran at the time. But taking the longer view all it meant was that the needle was stuck in the anti-Catholic record for another twenty years. Elsewhere the old ideas were changing under stress of the horrors of modern warfare and the threat to Christian values but Northern Ireland found itself set in the rock-hard mould of the past with a sectarian-minded Government whose Prime Minister spoke only in the rhetoric of the 1920s.

Brookeborough could have taken the opportunity of the war to lead the Unionists away from their sterile siege mentality but preferred, like his predecessors, to play the old Orange card. A Stormont civil servant who had served as a captain in the First World War phoned me one night in high glee at the embarrassment of his political bosses at the news that an announcement was about to be made that a Catholic navyman had been awarded the Victoria Cross. Leading Seaman Magennis, one of three brothers from Belfast serving in the Royal Navy, operating from a midget submarine, had set off limpet mines under a Japanese cruiser in the Johore Straits disabling the vessel from intervening against the allied invasion of Malaya. 'How will Brookeborough square that with his line that to be a Catholic is to be a disloyalist?' he chortled. The same gentleman for devilment used to go round the Stormont wash-rooms harassing stay-at-home loyalists by writing in soap on the mirrors, 'Join Up Today'. After the war Magennis was given the lowly job of a telephone linesman as his reward and eventually became so hard up that he was forced to sell his decoration. He was the North's only VC in World War II.

In his subsequent travels around the world to Australia, the United States and Canada, Brookeborough was confronted with some of his sectarian utterances and particularly his 'Boycott Catholics' advice to employers. In Australia he must have been hard pressed for he was forced to lie. He claimed that the speeches resulted from a threat by Republicans to kidnap his children. But at the time he initiated this poisonous campaign all his children were grown to manhood and were absent in Britain furthering their education. In the end he left this sectarian mill-stone round the necks of his successors. Before he left office a few of his colleagues tried to mitigate the sectarian image of 'Ulster' Unionism but it was a thankless task and when the lunatic fringe of Orangeism took up battle stations against change, the Prime Minister did not raise a finger to help them.

The first casualty in war is said to be the truth. Propaganda is heard on all sides and with the censorship clamp-down the ordinary man in the street either swallows it all or becomes a disbelieving Thomas. During the war we listened with fascination to two voices coming out over the radio: Winston Churchill 'We'll fight them on the beaches and on the streets ...' and the renegade Galway man William Joyce, alias 'Lord Haw-haw', sardonically 'Germany calling' to Britons 'Ask the Admiralty where is the Ark Royal?'

During the war years Radio Eireann in Dublin toured the country with an extremely popular 'Question Time' feature conducted by the popular Joe Linnane, veteran Irish broadcaster and compere. Someone suggested that they should bring the show to Belfast but there were many difficulties in the way because of the war-time situation. Eventually these were ironed out with the authorities and with the help of the BBC the 'Question Time' programme was laid on for a Sunday night in the spacious St Mary's Hall.

A number of people were selected for the panel including a representative of the ordinary man-in-the-street, a well-known character named Fearon, then employed as a barber in the US Red Cross Club. Fearon, a little white-haired man, pale and intense-looking, waited patiently on the stage for his turn. Joe Linnane, pleased that the show had attracted such a huge audience, including a sizeable sprinkling of US officers and their lady friends, eventually thrust the microphone in front of your man and asked, 'Can you tell me the name of the world's greatest compiler of fairy tales?' Fearon blinked, looked around the hall, hesitated for a few seconds and blurted into the mike, 'Winston Churchill!' For a moment there was dead silence and then the hall rocked with laughter as poor Joe Linnane, realising the enormity of what had happened, tried vainly to make himself heard above the laughter, cheers and hand-clapping in which the US Army joined with evident delight.

The rest of the show was a disaster so far as Joe Linnane was concerned. Every time he approached Fearon there was renewed laughter. It was Fearon's night to howl. He was heard all over the country but fame can be short-lived. The following morning the broadcasting barber was called before the Director of the Red Closs Club who laughed as he recalled Fearon's big moment the night before. 'I'm real sorry', he said, 'but I am afraid we have to dismiss you from the staff.'

Some weeks later I met Fearon in Royal Avenue, standing in a doorway sheltering from the rain. He told me what had happened and then, astonishingly, added that he had written letters of protest about his treatment to Winston Churchill, Roosevelt and as an afterthought said he had also addressed a letter on the subject to Joe Stalin! He had received one reply – from Churchill's private secretary informing him that the Prime Minister knew nothing about the incident and was not responsible for his sacking! The next 'Question Time' after this diplomatic incident was held at a Curragh Turf Cutters Camp in County Kildare. One of the panel told me that just before they went on the air Joe Linnane warned them, 'By God, if anyone even mentions Hans Christian Andersen or Winston Churchill I'll slaughter him!'

The formidable John W. Nixon, M.P. for Woodvale, known on the Shankill as the 'DI' from his early days as District Inspector in the RUC, was no respecter of persons, and particularly of blue-blood friends of the Government like Lord Londonderry. Londonderry was lying low during the war years back at his County Down seat at Mountstewart. He had suffered an eclipse since the old days when at his London home he entertained the top dogs in society and politics. The reason was that he had made no secret of his pro-German sympathies and in 1938 was foolish enough to publish a Penguin special *Ourselves And Germany* whose cover carried the blurb 'Should Britain regard Germay as her potential enemy or seek her friendship? Lord Londonderry thinks we should adopt a policy of friendship with Hitler and a better understanding of Grrmany's aims.'

When many other lesser lights, including a Tory MP, a British Admiral and a relation of the Duke of Abercorn were interned at Brixton Prison because of their pro-German sympathies, Londonderry considered it judicious to retire to Mountstewart for the duration. But he did not reckon with the redoubtable stormy petrel from the Shankill, John W. Nixon, MP, a huge beefy man, sallow-faced with bags under his eyes and a stentorian voice. Nixon who wore a heavy frieze overcoat in the Commons insisted also on wearing a big sombrero hat as he sat glaring at the Government front bench. He was a sinister figure whose black patent leather notebook thrown on the table of the House with a crash invariably sent a shiver along the Government benches, for generally his information on local scandals and misconduct was on target, mostly gleaned from his police connections.

With all the talk about the 'enemy within' and the Fifth Column of pro-Germans in high places, Nixon enjoyed a field day about the activities of Lord Londonderry. Had this man not entertained Ribbentrop, the top Nazi plotter, at Mountstewart before the War and had actually been an honoured guest and friend of Marshal Goering whose planes had bombed Belfast? Had he not conversed with Herr Hitler himself? The inference of all this was that Londonderry should be locked up with all the rest.

The Stormont government, although it had kept clear of its former Education Minister for some years, was clearly embarrassed and played down Nixon's campaign. But the publicity must have worried his Lordship greatly. Tommy Henderson, Nixon's stable-mate from the Shankill, told me afterwards that he was surprised to get a message from Lord Londonderry to meet him for a chat in a private room at the Grand Central Hotel. Tommy was mystified as meetings with noblemen were hardly his cup of tea but he decided to go along. He told me that after a lot of preliminary sparring and general conversation Lord Londonderry got down to the real object of his tryst with the man from the Shankill. 'The old buffer was worried about the publicity he was getting about Ribbentrop and Goering and all that and wanted to know if I could tell him in confidence what Ministers were saying about him at Stormont', he said. Apparently Henderson was not very reassuring for Ministers were keeping their opinions close to their chests and there was little he could tell the noble lord. Stormont, in any case, would have little say in the matter. It was up to the War Cabinet in London and Herbert Morrison, the Home Secretary, in particular.

Obviously Londonderry still had friends in high places and he escaped further notice but he was lucky. In the appendix to his book is a letter from Hitler in Berlin, dated 10 April 1938, which would have been sufficient to put someone less influential behind bars for the duration. It read:

'Dear Lord Londonderry,

I have received with great interest your recent book *Ourselves And Germany*, which you have just sent me, with an inscription written in your own hand. I share with you the hope of a better understanding between our two countries which you have thus expressed.

Please accept my warmest thanks for this renewed and valued notice of my work, as well as for the appreciation shown in your book.

With best regards to Lady Londonderry and with friendly greetings,

Yours cordially,
Adolf Hitler.'

The question naturally arises: Did Hitler, Ribbentrop and Goering regard the Lord of Mountstewart as a fool or a dupe? The War Cabinet must have given him the benefit of the doubt. But he remained in the pages of Nixon's famous black book. Incidentally, on the first page of this dossier on the follies and scandals of Stormont we all knew from its frequent extraction, was a newspaper clipping dated about the mid-twenties headlining a speech by Lord Craigavon in which he declared: 'If Mr. Baldwin does not solve the unemployment problem I will.' Nixon would then throw the book down, bang the table with his fist and bellow, 'When he made that speech there were 40,000 unemployed. Now there are 100,000!'

If ever there was a thorn in the side of the Unionist Government, Nixon was it. He was cordially hated and the feeling was mutual. When Jack Beattie intervened dramatically one afternoon at Stormont to allege that two well-known Protestant gunmen who, he said, were in the pay of Captain Dixon, had been shadowing him around the Pottinger constituency, Nixon took the opportunity to throw petrol on the fire. His remarks so angered Dixon that he shouted across 'You'll not murder me, my boy!' This caused another shock-wave around the Commons because everyone knew what lay behind the allusion. Some years earlier Nixon had sued a London publisher of a book named *Nomad* written by a Derry-born soldier of fortune called Captain McGuinness. McGuinness as a mariner had run guns for the old IRA and later accompanied American Polar explorer Commander Byrd on his expeditions.

In the book describing his earlier exploits with the IRA during the early Twenties, McGuinness referred to the horrific 'McMahon murders', a deed which shocked the whole of Ireland in 1922. A number of uniformed men, believed to be 'B' Specials, burst into the Antrim Road home in Belfast of the Catholic McMahon family during curfew hours and murdered five of the family in cold blood, only one young boy escaping by hiding himself. The author claimed that the men were under the command of a Police District Inspector who, he added, was now a Stormont MP. Nixon instituted libel proceedings immediately. In public and in private he had vehemently denied any complicity in the deed although admitting that he had been in charge of police and Specials in that part of the city.

FRIENDLY NEUTRALITY

WHILE POLITICIANS KEPT blasting 'Eire's neutrality' right up to the end of the war we had plenty of evidence that it was an odd kind of 'neutrality' with stories of Irish Army officers paying clandestine visits to Newry in the North to arrange the transhipment of military supplies to the South, and the blind-eye turned to crashed UN and RAF planes in Southern territory.

I had more concrete evidence of what was going on behind the scenes when, an accredited war correspondent, I received an official letter marked 'Confidential' delivered by a despatch rider who requested my signature. I had received a number of similar notices usually referring to censored matters but this one was more than illuminating, to put it mildly. It blandly requested that there should be no reference in the Press to the forthcoming meeting in Northern Ireland between Major General McKenna, GOC, Irish Army and Lieut. General Cunningham, British GOC in the North!

Of course there was no possibility of this sensational news ever receiving the splash headlines it deserved for the censorship authorities in Belfast and Dublin appeared, from our experience, to be working at that time hand-in-glove. But I confess that it startled me at the time and made me realise that big things were afoot with rumours of the invasion of Europe flooding in on all sides, not to mention the dire possibility of a German counter-stroke in Ireland to throw the Allied landing into confusion.

Another straw in the wind that momentous events were coming up fast occurred when Peter Robinson, with a transparent air of mystery in his demeanour, called and asked me to cover for the *Daily Mail* during his absence on a mission to the South. His wife Sheelagh, however, let the cat out of the bag. It appeared that the *Mail* had got hold of a story that the Germans had landed by parachute an Irishman named O'Reilly who had agreed to contact the IRA with a view to arranging an internal uprising to coincide with the Allied invasion of Europe.

O'Reilly, who had been dropped close to his parents' home in County Clare, was quickly arrested by Irish security and brought to Dublin to be interrogated by worried Army officers anxious to probe the sinister implications of his mission. Meantime Robinson arrived at the O'Reillys home to be informed that Mr O'Reilly, Senior was out. By an extraordinary twist of fate, I was told that O'Reilly Senior, in 1916, then a young man, had been a member of the Royal Irish Constabulary involved in the arrest of Roger Casement when he landed from a German submarine on the coast of Kerry. Suspicions must have been aroused by Robinson's inquiries for later that night a Chief Superintendent of the Gardai arrived at his hotel. The name 'Robinson' only increased the police officer's suspicions and after further grilling about his mysterious appearance in County Clare, he told Peter 'We think you are spy!' Peter protested that he was simply a newspaperman in search of a story for the *Daily Mail*. The upshot of the interview was that he was put under house arrest in his hotel for the night before being sent to Dublin by train for further inquiries.

Robinson afterwards ruefully confessed that there was a guard at every station *en route* to check that he was still aboard. On arrival in Dublin he was taken to the Chief Censor's office and later taken to the office of Sir John Maffey, the British Minister, where he was given a severe lecture on the serious consequences of any publicity about the O'Reilly affair in relation to the impending Second Front and the possibility that the Germans might take further measures to ensure that their plans for an Irish uprising were not affected by the capture of their important agent.

Robinson returned to Belfast bloody but unbowed. For a man who had suffered many vicissitudes in his newspaper career, Peter was a cool customer, much admired by his colleagues. Under pressure by the Manchester News Desk to produce at least one good story per day he was often at his wits' end to make up the daily schedule demanded by a tyrannical News Editor. Peter had to be resourceful. Realising that General Montgomery was big news because of his successful Desert Campaign leading the Eighth Army, Peter struck up a kind of business friendship with the General's aged mother, Lady Montgomery, who revelled in the publicity Peter gave her. She lived at Moville, County Donegal, and had no telephone but, nothing daunted, she and Peter used the local village post office for exclusive interviews and comments on this and that. These usually made headlines in the *Mail* but their frequency became a subject of irritation to Monty and there were rumours that the irate general had threatened horse-whipping for this audacious reporter who was apparently exploiting the old dear.

While Robinson was absent on his spy mission to County Clare, I received a call from the *Mail's* sister paper in Fleet Street, the *Sunday Dispatch*, requesting a special article from Lady Montgomery for the following Sunday's Mother's Day. With the kind assistance of the Moville post-mistress I contacted Lady Montgomery who readily agreed to write the article along the lines suggested. Before ringing off she asked is she would be paid for her trouble, recalling that the *Belfast Telegraph* had paid her fifteen guineas for a recent article. I assured her that she would be paid at the 'usual rate'. I did not quote to her Dr Samuel Johnson's famous dictum 'The man (or woman) who writes for anything but money is a fool'. This was put to me once by a Stormont MP, a doctor by profession, in response to a request for a published interview. I told him that NUJ would fully endorse the views of the old Grub Street scribbler. When I reported back to the Editor of the *Dispatch* about Lady Montgomery's fifteen guineas fee, he laughed 'We are paying her £150' he said.

The sequel to all this came with a visit to the *Mail* office in Rosemary street one afternoon by Montgomery's brother who I believe was a chaplain to the forces. His message was that the General was fed up with the *Mail's* exploitation of his mum and that Robinson must cease 'pestering' her. Peter listened courageously to this message from the desert but calmly ignored it. Lady Montgomery was just as keen on the sudden fame as her famous son, and later wrote a book on her life story, probably inspired by her mentor in Belfast.

My relations with the Censors Office in Belfast were cordial but there were times when one felt somewhat frustrated with a big story on your hands but knowing that it would be suppressed. One afternoon while people were sunning themselves on the promenade at Bangor a dull-sounding explosion was heard from Whitehead on the opposite County Antrim side of Belfast Lough. Smoke could be seen coming from a freighter lying a few miles offshore as she settled down in the water. Almost immediately the alarms went off at the Admiralty pier at Bangor and we could see a fleet of small launches heading across the Lough in the direction of the sinking ship. Dead and injured seamen were soon streaming back to Bangor where ambulances were waiting to take them to hospital. The pier which had taken over by the Naval authorities at the beginning of the war was closed and no information was available about the urgent activity within. It later transpired that a ship, the SS *Troutpool* had been testing its compasses and had shut off its degaussing equipment for the purpose. In its manoeuvring it had activated a German magnetic mine which must lain on the shallow seabed for many months.

I was an eye-witness to all this drama but not a line could be printed about it for the duration of the war. That Saturday afternoon drama remained one of the unreported incidents of the war years although the superstructure of the *Troutpool* with its wreck buoy kept disappearing and re-appearing at low tide close to the main shipping lane for years afterwards.

The mining of Belfast Lough by long range German aircraft was also kept secret. The favourite time for one of incursions seemed to be around midnight on Saturdays. Several times while week-ending at Ballyholme, Bangor, one heard the sirens going for an alert and then the buzz-buzz of a marauding plane and a few salvoes from the coastal anti-aircraft guns and then silence followed by the all-clear. On Sunday morning there was the unusual spectacle of the big cross-channel ferries from Liverpool, Heysham and Glasgow hove to off the Copeland Islands at the Lough entrance while a small mine-sweeping launch with a superstructure like a large dog kennel cleared the channel. Few of the people who complained about their cross-channel Sunday papers not being available until the late afternoon realised that the cause was enemy action so close to home.

As D-day approached Belfast Lough presented an astonishing sight with more and more American battleships and British and even French cruisers taking up stations off Bangor. When General Eisenhower flew in amidst great secrecy on 19 May to inspect this vast armada there were no fewer than nine big battleships, twenty US destroyers and more than a hundred smaller vessels ready to sail off on 3 June down the Irish Sea to join the other armadas gathered for the descent on the Normandy beaches. On board one of the naval escort ships was a friend, Lieutenant Alfie Briggs, whose wife and family lived at Ballyholme, Bangor. He had been at sea for months on the north Atlantic convoy patrol and here he was within sight of his home but could not go ashore for all leave had been cancelled. 'It was one of the most frustrating moments of my life', he confessed to me years later.

145

Censorship became tighter with all kinds of distinguished personages flying in on inspection. When King George VI and Queen Elizabeth arrived there were D. Notices to the Press reminding them that their presence could not be publicised until their departure had been signalled. The Royal couple eventually departed from Larne in a destroyer. As they walked up the gangway to be piped on board the silence was broken by a guldering loyalist clinging to the roof of the dockside shed. 'Long live their Royal Highnesses!' he roared. Their majesties looked disgusted to be so down-graded by this idiot.

The telephone censorship became a nuisance to newsmen like myself who depended on the telephone almost a hundred per cent to put copy across. The lines kept fading in and out and dictation took twice as long as normal. The London line was even worse than the line to Dublin. When phoning a brief piece to the United Press of America on the Royal visit, the US newsman in London complained of the bad line and just could not get the place-name 'Larne' correctly. I remarked, 'The line is bad because of all these damned censors listening in.' Suddenly a fruity voice cut in 'Hello Belfast. There's only one censor.' and then addressing the United Press man said briskly, 'Hello London. The name is LARNE – L for Larry, A for Annie, R for Robert, N for Nelly, E for Edward'. My American friend gasped, 'Gee this is something'. I gasped too. I never made any remarks about censors after that.

COFFEE-HOUSE DIVERSIONS

IN A LIFETIME a newspaperman must write millions of words in articles and news-stories and in the nature of things most of them are gone and forgotten, although I often recalled the old time journalist who reminded me 'Don't forget that you are writing history', especially when I afterwards spied some well-known historian poring over the files of daily newspapers in Belfast's Linenhall Library. But I think the articles which gave me most satisfaction over the years did not appear in a newspaper at all but instead in the thick, glossy *Capuchin Annual* edited then by a remarkable Capuchin Friar, Fr Senan. This marvellous publication with its wealth of pictures and literary contributions from outstanding Irish writers, poets, journalists, politicians and artists, created a considerable stir during its heyday, particularly in the war years. It was responsible for the sensational expose – 'Orange Terror' which the Stormont Government stupidly banned, giving it an even greater worldwide publication. Through the good offices and influence of my friend, the late J J Campbell, MA, later Professor of Education at Queen's University, I wrote 'The Pogrom' and later 'Journalist's Diary' both of which apparently inspired Fr Senan to urge me to write a biographical memoir. Both articles were much quoted in several publications in subsequent years by authors interested in events such as the Unemployed Riots of 1932 and the Air Raids of 1941. Apparently the value of eye-witness accounts was much appreciated and I profited for the first time by the copyright fees!

The Linenhall Library became a happy hunting ground for me. For a few guineas one could become a member of what resembled a comfortable mellow gentleman's club with its rows of bookshelves, coal-fire burning in winter, comfortable armchairs and settees, news-rooms, its famous Irish Section and its smiling, helpful male and female librarians. It occupies a magnificent site overlooking Belfast City Hall in one of Belfast's loveliest thoroughfares, full of colour, life and bustle.

Here I came as a young reporter seeking background information for an *Irish News* 'special' on the need for a memorial to Ireland's patron saint, Patrick, at his landing place, Saul, overlooking the lovely island-studded Strangford Lough in County Down. Redwood had spotted an article in a Down and Connor antiquarian's journal and good newsman that he was he decided that it would make a front-page story. The Librarian, Mr Burgoyne, could not have been more helpful and the following morning the *Irish News* started the ball rolling to make up for the neglect of centuries with a proper monument to the man who banished the snakes from Ireland. According to Brendan Behan, they went to America and became Irish-American politicians!

On the strength of the news-story a steering committee was formed and the giant statue erected on the site has now become a place of national pilgrimage every St Patrick's Day. I mention this because I would like to pay tribute to the dear old Linenhall Library for the part it played in the build-up to this worthy venture and also for the many pleasant hours I spent down through the years doing research or just browsing in its pleasant atmosphere.

I met many of the *literati* of the North here at one time or other, among them the late Captain Denis Ireland, the genial Presbyterian United Irishman, successful writer and a man so respected in the

South that he was nominated as the first Northerner living there to be a member of the Irish Senate. Denis had a rich sense of humour and a wide circle of Protestant friends who rejoiced to be known as Irishmen as well as Ulstermen. He enjoyed some of my stories about the odd happenings at Stormont and the City Hall and once advised me to write an 'arse-ways book on Belfast'. I wonder would he say that this is it?

We used to leave the library, (which he often joked to Jimmy Vitty, our librarian friend, that it should be called 'the Sepulchre of Knowledge') and repair to Campbell's Cafe for morning coffee and a bit of crack. There was plenty of that for gathered at one time or other there would be a star-studded circle of local personalities. They included Joe Tomelty, William Conor, Dr Jim Ryan, Patrick Woods, John Boyd, David Kennedy, Jack Loudan, Jimmy Vitty, Markie Robinson, Sam Hanna Bell, John Hewitt and many others.

The conversation was lively, sometimes ribald, covering the theatre, the arts, politics and newspapers which was where I came in. Willy Conor often regaled us with his story about his first big exhibition of his famous Belfast pictures. Crowds gathered outside the Stranmillis Museum and Art Gallery as the distinguished visitors arrived in their limousines, including the Governor and the Duke and Duchess of Abercorn. Then on foot came William Conor, wearing his famous shallow black felt hat. He overheard a woman say, 'Who under God is that? Her male companion replied, 'Och, sure that's only an oul sh— called Conor!' Inside the distinguished company were gathered to honour Willy but outside it was typical uncaring don't-give-a-damn Belfast. Willy always laughed when Joe Tomelty would pretend to introduce me for the hundredth time, 'Jimmy, have you met an oul sh— named Willy Conor?'

Denis Ireland founded the Ulster Union Club whose aim was to invoke the spirit of the Presbyterian United Irishmen like Wolfe Tone and Henry Joy McCracken who first raised the banner of Republicanism at McArt's Fort on the historic Cavehill, Belfast in

1795. It was one of the odd quirks of history that the Presbyterians largely abandoned this heritage in later years and, for good or ill, passed it on to the Catholics. The explanation probably was that most of the Presbyterian activitists of that day were executed or fled persecution to America where they became the 'Scotch-Irish' of Washington's armies. The memory of those liberal-minded Presbyterian patriots was reviled and finally buried under the weight of the bigotry and anti-Catholic ranters like Dr Henry Cooke and his ilk down through the years. Like a hound sniffing political heresy in the wind, Sir Dawson Bates moved in swiftly to crush this modest effort to revive Protestant nationalism. He ordered the Special Branch or 'Crime Special' Department of the Royal Ulster Constabulary to raid the Ulster Union Club premises in Wellington Place, Belfast. They seized the membership files and police called and searched the homes of scores of respectable citizens all over Belfast. They included Presbyterian clergymen, teachers, university lecturers and others who were outraged by this ham-fisted attempt at intimidation. One young minister said that a particularly stupid detective gazed suspiciously at his bookcase and eventually seized the classic book about the Blasket Islands in County Kerry – *Twenty Years Agrowing* – because of its possible subversive content. The minister called him back and said, 'Should you not take this one also?' pointing to Alexander Dumas's *Twenty Years After*. The detective glanced through it and took it also!

Later a young Protestant who had joined the club concealing the fact that he was a member of the IRA was arrested and charged with the possession of a gun. Much was made of this arrest to smear a perfectly law-abiding and innocent organisation. Thus was the ever-watchful Sir Dawson Bates and his minions able to stifle and suppress the slightest movement in the Protestant community away from the orthodox Unionist Party oligarchy. We did not know it, nor did Sir Dawson and his political Special Branch men, but at that very moment was born a force which in years to come would rock the very foundations of that Party dictatorship, a menace from within the fold which threatened and still threatens to out-bigot the bigots.

I have mentioned Campbell's Cafe opposite the City Hall. It was so popular that the *habituees* occupied three floors. We preferred the quiet of the top floor but as we ascended the stairs most mornings we noticed two young men engaged in earnest conversation at a table close to the stairway. One was stout and pale-faced with a small Charlie Chaplin moustache. His companion was a burly man, heavy jowled, with bulging eyes and a loud Ballymena accent. The first man was Norman Porter, later to become an Independent MP at Stormont and founder of a virulent but tiny organisation rejoicing in the odd name of the National Union of Protestants. The other was a man whose star had not yet risen, the stormy petrel of extreme Protestantism, Ian K Paisley. Thereafter I saw the pair of them colloguing together like Siamese twins, watching and studying the antics of local politicians, sometimes in the public gallery at the City Hall or in the public gallery at Stormont. They kept turning up everywhere in Belfast where there was a debate or discussion in which the King Charles's head – or should it be King Billy's head – of sectarian conflict was likely to arise. One could sense that all this conspiratorial plotting and planning was leading somewhere but we never dreamed it would explode into the force which has now become notorious around the world as Paisleyism – a kind of throwback to the 17th century, the fires of Smithfield and the language of Cromwell.

Eventually the pair went their separate ways, Porter to Australia and Paisley on to greater things as the unchallenged Protestant Pope of the breakaway politico-religio of Free Presbyterianism, the thundering 'back street Savonarola' as he was dubbed by a Unionist Cabinet Minister. I did not realise it then but those coffee mornings must have been the modest beginning of a very small stream which before many years threatened to become a flood.

SLOW TRAIN TO GALWAY

A WEDDING IN WAR-TIME poses problems unheard of at normal times. Ours was no different. At the *Independent* office I met and fell in love with Eileen Shanahan then secretary in the Belfast office and later secretary to the N.I. office of Twentieth Century Fox film corporation. Eileen, a native of Co Meath and a lively and cheerful personality in her own right, has been a wife, a pal and mentor to me over the years and dare I say an unfailing source of inspiration. When a Belfast hotel proposed an austere meal of spam for the wedding reception we quickly decided to change our plans and have the marriage in Dublin where we could entertain our friends in style. It was a brilliant success. From the Ormond Hotel we rode across the quays in a limousine playing romantic background music to the Church of Saints Michael and John where the guests were gathered with Father Michael Grant.

After a champagne reception we stayed overnight in Dun Laoghaire before joining the early morning train from Dublin to Galway. Although Phoenix Park was stacked ten feet high with emergency stocks of coal and turf, an odd spectacle in that beautiful setting, journeys by train in those days were an adventure in which anything might happen. At times the locomotives, burning anything from wood blocks to sods of turf, would run out of steam far out in the midlands and might just sit there for hours waiting on a relief engine. A reporter, Paddy Donaghy, an old friend, told me about his experience on the night mail train to Cork. Sometime around midnight the train slowed to a halt far out in the country, miles from anywhere. Nothing happened for a long time and then suddenly Paddy noticed a trickle of passengers leaving the train and crossing the fields. Someone had found a country pub. Paddy joined the throng and found the pub with lights blazing and the sound of clinking glasses and merriment within. He said it turned into a great 'hooley' lasting far into the night until someone from the train came in to tell roistering passengers that it was time to go, for a relief engine had arrived to continue the journey to Cork.

When we arrived at the station in Dublin the scenes of bustle and confusion beggared description as hundreds of holiday-makers, families with children, nuns and priests, some with bags, some with bikes over their shoulders, stood poised along the platform ready to dive into the only train scheduled that day for the West of Ireland, Galway, Mayo, Sligo and stations *en route*. It was August Bank Holiday and it was obvious that the train would be packed to suffocation almost.

There were several false alarms as the Bray train steamed in, followed by a goods train, the passengers falling over their bags in the rush only to be waved back by drivers and porters shouting warnings. An Englishman with two lady friends who seemed to be enjoying this first taste of 'Irish comedy' remarked loudly, 'I would not be surprised if the next train is driven by Jimmy O'Dea.'

Anyway by superior agility and gamesmanship from years of experience of thrusting through mobs I managed to get my wife and myself into a First Class carriage before the corridors filled up with passengers and baggage. Approaching Athlone the doors were held ajar as hardened travellers on this route stood ready to leap on to the platform for the obstacle race to the refreshment room, there to grab the few sandwiches available, to be washed down with a

Guinness or a Miwadi Orange drink. It was every man and every woman for him or her self and when the guard's whistle rang out there was the sound of breaking glass as passengers dropped their drinks and bounded for the moving train to be helped aboard by their friends. Soon the train slowed to a fast walking pace and as we gazed out of the windows at the endless succession of bog and fields covered with daisies and heard the monotonous clunk-clunk over the sleepers, we wondered if we would ever make Galway that day. But we did. By late evening Athenry hove in sight and then the welcome first sight of Galway Bay in the twilight. It was then goodbye to all the friends we had made on the long journey westward and another scramble to retrieve luggage in the guard's van from a tangled mass of bikes, prams and fishing gear.

Friendly old Galway with its smell of peat fires, thronged Shop Street with its street musicians playing the 'Rose of Arranmore' on their banjos and accordians, and tawny-haired tinkers' women in plaid shawls alternatively cursing or uttering the blessings of God on those who refused or contributed to tin begging boxes, was no different from four years before when I last visited it. The Royal Hotel on Eyre Square, not yet knocked down to make way for Woolworths, received us with open arms and we noted with approval the number of Parish Priests in the dining room for the evening meal – always a four-star indication of good food and comfort hotel-wise in Ireland.

That summer must have been the hottest for years because the beaches were packed with sun-bathers and I actually suffered from sunstroke on Grattan beach. Petrol was rationed to the minimum so we hired bikes from a great old character named Egan who ran a bicycle shop in the shadow of the ancient Cathedral where legend has it Christopher Columbus attended Mass before his voyage of discovery to America. Egan regaled us with his stories of the days when he ran a local taxi service and used to invite us round for a drink in Taaffe's old-fashioned tavern with its sawdust floors and snugs like confession boxes. It was heaven speeding in the balmy air along the sunlit Galway Bay through Salthill and Barna to the Gaelic-speaking village of Spiddal where a massive pier sheltered an occasional solitary tiny fishing boat, or a couple of curraghs, and acted as windshield on a blustery day for the people resting on the adjoining spit of almost white sand.

'You cannot come to Galway without seeing the Aran Islands,' I told my wife. She readily agreed so we sailed off in the old SS *Dun Aengus* which delivered passengers and goods, including barrels of stout, by hazardous means to the curraghs which came out to meet her off the smaller Inishere and Inishmaan islands.

We thought we were going to witness a tragedy when one small barrel dropped on a curragh, holing it at the stern. Water gushed in but one of the oarsmen calmly stuffed a rag in the hole and rowed away towards the beach where a crowd of islanders and visitors watched the excitement offshore.

On arrival at Kilronan pier on Inishmore there was more excitement for, clearly, the appearance of the *Dun Aengus* thirty miles out as the bay opens on to the blue seas of the Atlantic Ocean was a major event. A handful of jaunting cars stood at the back of the crowds shouting invitations to cross the island to the towering, almost frightening, cliffs on the lip of the ancient Dun Aengus fort. We were beguiled with others to make the trip and soon were galloping along at a fast pace past the ancient memorials to the dead in stone, along the dusty winding road through the rocky 'fields' of Aran. The smooth-talking jarvey persuaded us that it would be foolish to rush back to the boat for the evening return sailing when there was so much to see and enjoy on this island of mystery where time seemed to have stood still from the dawn of history. A turf-boat could take us across to Connemara in the morning, he said, and there were plenty of buses to take us into Galway and even hotels if we wished to stay or have a meal. He even arranged accommodation in a small guest-house at Kilronan so we stayed overnight. Two Gaelic-speaking and rather surly Connemara men arrived but if they could speak no English they certainly knew the value of the pound sterling in any language and there followed some tough bargaining for the privelege of travelling back on their black-sailed hooker which had been delivering turf to Inishmore.

Unfortunately I enjoyed a hearty breakfast of bacon and eggs the next morning. I say 'unfortunately' for that journey across the North Sound to the tip of Connemara was like a nightmare. A young doctor and his wife who had been holidaying on the island joined us on the hooker, a dirty old scow littered with fragments of turf and smoke pouring from a small cabin at the rear. The doctor had been charged double what we paid and the Connemara men, thin, cadaverous, with aquiline noses which gave them an almost Spanish appearance, smoked their evil-smelling pipes and ignored us. The seas were choppy and a stiff breeze was blowing as we sailed out from the shelter of the pier. We had been told that the journey would only take about an hour but about half an hour out I began to suffer the unmistakeable pangs of sea-sickness.

A church on a distant hillside of Connemara became like a mirage as the hooker tacked back and forth in the wind gusts. I lay in the scuppers in agony with the sails swinging first this way then the other, narrowly missing my fevered brow, while spray and spume from the waves swept over me, giving momentary relief. The young doctor who earlier had expressed sympathy at my plight after a while lay beside me ashen-faced and sick. But the strangest thing was that the two women, who must have gone easy on the breakfast, hung on unaffected by *mal de mer*. The Connemara men looked scared as the old craft heeled over throwing the turf fragments over us and occasionally uttered a pious ejaculation in Gaelic but took no notice whatever of their passengers' plight. The ordeal in the accursed North Sound lasted more than three hours and I cursed that smooth-talking jarvey when I thought of the smooth passage I missed back to Galway in the reliable old *Dun Aengus*. Without a

156

word or even a nod the turf-boat pair landed us on a deserted small pier at the back-of-beyond where there was neither bus nor hotel. I believe it was Lettermullen and we were told that a hotel in the vicinity had been closed down for the duration of the war. A donkey and cart took us and our bags to a shop a few miles away from the pier which, in my imagination, was rocking from side to side like the motion of the old boat.

They say that after sea-sickness you feel better than you ever did before and I can testify that after the walk behind the cart on *terra firma* I felt in tip-top form although still wondering how we would extricate ourselves from this wilderness of a rock-strewn landscape. Sitting on the steps of the shop thus ruminating in the sunshine, salvation suddenly appeared from nowhere in the shape of a Great Southern Railways supply lorry. The driver, a humorous Dubliner, spoke of the Connemara folk as if they were an eccentric species. 'They'd moider you for a bag of money,' he remarked as he drove us over an unstable wooden bridge and claimed that the locals had once removed the deck of the bridge when a new dispensary doctor whom they regarded as an interloper was due to arrive in the area. 'Sure they regard themselves as separate from the rest of the country,' he laughed. 'When they were working on the Shannon Scheme they even said that they must come back to Ireland next year!' We bid goodbye to our cheerful friend from Dublin as he left us off at Spiddal, heading back for dear dirty Dublin by the Liffey, his home-town and none better. One result of that experience was to make me suspicious of soft answers, the other was to avoid boats of less than say ten thousand tons. As for turf-boats, wild horses would not drag me into one for even the shortest journey.

WESTMINSTER BLINKERS

U NDER THE GOVERNMENT of Ireland Act (1920), often referred to in the North as the 'Ulster Constitution', the British Home Office was supposed to supervise the affairs of the subordinate parliament in Belfast but the supervision over the years mostly consisted of turning a Nelson-like eye to the happenings in that corner of Ireland. A staff of seven minor civil servants in the general department of the Home Office dealing with such matters as London taxi-cabs, liquor licensing, state-owned pubs in Carlisle and British Summer Time was responsible for a sub-division handling the Channel Islands, the Isle of Man, the Charity Commission and Northern Ireland.

The briefings of Home Secretaries of their responsibilities in Northern Ireland were scanty and as late as December 1967 James Callaghan complained that Northern Ireland was not even mentioned when he opened his box purporting to set out the problems facing him on his appointment to the Home Office. He was not surprised for the subject, according to him, rarely if ever came before the British Cabinet. Visits to their domain across the Irish Sea by Home Secretaries were infrequent and when they did insist on coming they were largely what I called 'blinkers-tours' to see and hear no evil and, as far as the Stormont government could manage it, turned into quick junkets. Efforts by journalists like myself to elicit some response by the British ministers to the real problems of Northern Ireland were met with bland evasions at the occasional hurried press conference. When questions became tricky there was always the escape hatch of the 'Convention' preventing Her Majesty's Government from 'interfering' in the internal affairs of Northern Ireland or the intimation that the Home Secretary's time was limited, 'pressing engagements', etc. For the photographers there was the nonsense of presenting the Red Hand of Ulster tie and similar complimentary twaddle but never any serious effort to explore the causes of the seething cauldron of discontent building up year by year.

A group of us tried to corner these evasive ministers on Partition, discrimination and allied awkward questions and to a certain extent pin-pointed London's determination to evade its duty to bring to heel the bigoted regime in the Six Counties. These encounters got wide coverage in the North and Dublin but unfortunately the British press, with the exception of papers like the *Guardian*, ignored these first intimations of the fact that all was not lovely in the 'Ulster' garden.

Manny Shinwell came in the unlikely role of Defence Minister and we gave him a memorable roasting at the Lisburn Army Headquarters. He went on at great length about the provision of comfortable married quarters for the troops quartered in Northern Ireland but nobody bothered to take a note. There was an awkward pause and then I asked him if he had visited the Irish border. The local Army PRO groaned inwardly. He knew this was the beginning. The GOC too, knew, and looked at the ceiling. 'No, I have not', said Manny and then asked, 'Why is the border coloured red on the map?'

There was a barrage of questions after that and, wily politician that he was, Manny wriggled out of most of them but the question and answer session took up nearly a column in the *Evening Herald*.

I recall one of his replies. I asked him if he did not think that in the interest of military strategy that a united Irish defence force made more sense than having two armies divided by a border. The GOC sighed loudly, the PRO looked beseechingly at me and Manny pursed his lips. Then in his best Gorbals accent he retorted, 'Well, I am reckoned to be a pretty good administrator but strategy is not my strong point.' Everyone laughed and the General remarked impatiently, 'Surely gentlemen, we have had enough about the border for one morning.' Walking down the gravel path from the Army Conference Room the PRO confessed, 'I died a thousand deaths during that interview.'

Harold Macmillan came as Prime Minister at the invitation of Brookeborough to attend the Unionist Party's annual luncheon in the Ulster Hall. Someone overheard a waitress telling another ladling out the soup, 'They do this every year and get someone over from London to give them a wee injection!' Macmillan went through the ritual of sporting an 'Ulster tie' and made a speech which justified the waitress's comment.

The next morning we were informed that the Prime Minister had agreed to an interview at the Airport on his way back to London. When he sat down he looked at the BBC microphone which had been placed on the table and shouted peremptorily to an aide to fetch Brookeborough. When the latter appeared Macmillan, pointing to the mike, asked rather sharply, 'What's this? I did not give permission for a live interview.' Brookeborough whispered that the interview was not live but would be 'recorded'. While waiting Macmillan borrowed someone's bundle of morning papers. He went through the lot until he came to the *Daily Express* which he examined page by page, including Low's cartoon and the editorial. The rest of the papers he discarded. Obviously Supermac had a healthy regard for attitudes of the unpredictable Beaverbrook.

After some preliminary sparring we got down to the meatier interrogation about his Government's views on Irish politics and the baneful results of Partition. Cyprus was in the news at the time. Makarios, who had been reviled in the British Press as a devil incarnate had been brought back from exile in the Seychelles and offered an Independent Republic within the Commonwealth. I put the obvious question, 'If partition is not good enough for Cyprus why is your Government supporting partition in Ireland?' Old Mac glared at me and instead of answering threw the ball back at me. 'Have you ever been to Cyprus?' he asked. When I confessed that I had not he said, 'It's a rather different situation, you know.' He then gave us a brief lecture on the difference between the political background to Cyprus and the situation in Ireland, mentioning something about 'homogeneous populations'.

We reported every word of this and the story caused quite a stir, particularly in Dublin, where people felt that Supermac had a damned cheek speaking in these terms. This was not the end of it by any means. It so happened that Ed Murrow, the famous US radio and TV commentator, was conducting a hook-up programme between the United States, London and Dublin and to the surprise of the BBC, which was relaying the feature live, Macmillan's visit to Belfast came under scrutiny. All went well as Murrow with his inevitable cigarette smouldering between his fingers first talked to Noel Coward in London. Then he switched over to Dublin to speak about the theatre to the noted Irish actress, Siobhan McKenna. Siobhan, who had lived in Belfast as a young girl, took Ed's cue but instead of dilating on the state of the Irish theatre waded into Harold Macmillan. While Noel Coward looked on uneasily and Murrow grinned, Siobhan spoke indignantly of the people in the South being incensed at the nerve of Macmillan going over to Belfast to tell all and sundry that while Partition was good enough for Ireland, Britain was at pains to eliminate it on the Mediterranean island of Cyprus.

This breakthrough in the hidden censorship of anything critical about the Belfast regime caused an upheaval among the super-sensitive Unionists and the wires between Belfast and the London

BBC fairly sizzled with protests about 'anti-Ulster propaganda'. The supine BBC chiefs threw dust on their heads and grovelled to the Unionists. Ed Murrow's remaining programmes were cancelled. Lord Brookeborough, when asked for a comment, opined with unaccustomed humour that Siobhan McKenna should be 'spanked'!

We did not realise it at the time but this must have been one of the first shots in the battle to let the world know by television what was going on in what the *Sunday Times* later described as 'Britain's Ulster Slum'. It was a hard struggle. Ed Murrow was not the only victim of the cowardice of the BBC top brass. Another famous communicator, Alan Whicker, who came on the Northern Ireland scene in 1959 to do a short series for the BBC's 'Tonight' programme, was shocked by the uproar which the first of the series caused. To set the scene he did a few shots of Stormont, the Belfast City Hall, the graffiti on the walls of 'No Pope here' and 'Vote Sinn Fein', the armed police and an illegal betting shop. In retrospect it was an innocent enough little introduction to the 'Ulster scene' but the entire establishment of politicians, bishops and tourist chiefs blew up in a volcano of protest which nowadays sounds ludicrous. Whicker, in his book *Within Whicker's World*, commenting on the actions of the BBC in not alone cancelling but destroying the tapes of the following seven programmes, said Baverstock, his boss, and the BBC were 'thrown into a funk' by the 'massed ranks of hypocrisy'. 'It was not a glorious moment for the Corporation,' he added.

Later on when Rab Butler came to address the Ulster Unionist Council at its annual luncheon we had high hopes of getting some worthwhile views of the 'Ulster' imbroglio from the man who was said to be the frontline intellectual of the Convervative Party. For once he had agreed as Home Secretary to meet a Nationalist deputation and afterwards a 'press conference was laid on at the Ministry of Commerce office in Chichester Street. When Butler appeared the only newspapermen present were from the Dublin press and the *Irish News* and he must have wondered why he was receiving such an onslaught about the iniquities of his hosts, the failure of his own government to deal with the scandals of discrimination in Derry, Tyrone and Fermanagh, and the whole sad saga of misgovernment by an immovable dictatorship. During the interview when the Home Secretary was making heavy weather, Brian Faulkner, then Minister of Home Affairs, arrived to tell Butler's aides that the luncheon was already half an hour late and the people sitting at the tables in the Ulster Hall were becoming restive. The soup was getting cold. To his mind it was shocking that the Home Secretary was prepared to sit nodding his head in apparent agreement when Paddy Reynolds of the *Irish Press* suggested that a *prima facie* case had been made out for immediate action by the British Government to initiate reforms in Northern Ireland to deal with the long-standing grievances of the minority. Mr Faulkner wrung his hands and asked a local civil servant, 'Where are our reporters?', obviously meaning the Belfast Unionist press. It appeared that they too were back at the Ulster Hall waiting on their lunch and missing all the fun of this rare encounter with a powerful politician of the calibre of Butler.

In the end the strong impression he gave was that something would have to be done in reply to the points put with such strength at the two conferences with the Nationalists and the Press. After all this his prepared speech at the Ulster Hall was out of date and useless. Butler, unlike his predecessors, appeared prepared to listen sympathetically without the usual evasions and it seemed that at last a little daylight was getting through to one of the most powerful men in the Tory camp. The dismay of the Unionists that he had actually ruined their annual luncheon by sitting down with Nationalists to listen to their grievances was amusing. The odd sequel to this strange interlude was that there was no sequel.

Butler, who in addition to his many other offices over a long career, was Home Secretary from 1957 to 1962, a key position in which to exert his powerful influence on Northern Ireland affairs, but there is no record to show that he lifted his finger in the slightest degree to do anything about the genuine grievances which were impressed upon him with urgency during that visit. This was a vital moment when resolute action could have been taken to defuse the time-bomb which blew up a mere seven years later.

The Home Secretary went back to London. We all waited for results but there were none. An interview he gave at London Airport seemed at variance with the interview he gave us in Belfast. Was this an exercise in cynicism? Was this man, tipped to succeed Supermac as Premier, just putting on an act, being 'all things to all men'? In the end he did not succeed Macmillan, whom he had cynically described in an interview with George Gale of the *Express* as 'the best Prime Minister we have got'! He was passed over for the unlikely aristocrat, Sir Alec Douglas Home, an egregious appointment which astounded everyone.

Years later when the bubble burst at Stormont I spoke to a top adviser of William Whitelaw at a reception and told him how the latter's task of trying to salvage something from the wreckage might have been averted if Butler had seized this great opportunity. He suggested that there might be another explanation rather than pure cynicism by 'Rab' Butler. 'Supposing', he said, 'Butler did raise this with the Prime Minister. It is quite on the cards that Macmillan gave him the brush-off reminding him that they had enough problems on their hands without opening the Pandora's Box of Northern Ireland.'

So at the end of the day nothing was done by these powerful politicians, whether Butler or Macmillan, to stave off the tragedy that was about to burst upon us in Northern Ireland. If conscience makes cowards of us all what of the consciences of politicians who contemplate the shambles and horrors of Northern Ireland in the years since 1969 and reflect on what they might have done when they had power in their hands? It was not an Irish problem, even the Orangemen were only the creatures of events set in train long ago by British politicians. It was a British problem and is still a British problem.

If Macmillan and Butler reacted in this fashion we could not expect much from Sir Alec Douglas Home. He too came to Belfast for the compulsory look at this curious appendage of the United Kingdom, the 'Province' that was not a province. When I met him face to face at a news conference his perky, grinning, skull-like countenance reminded me of one of Wodehouse's vague aristocrats whose hobby might be collecting butterflies.

Fate in the shape of the rival claims of Butler and the over-confident Hailsham had once again lumbered Britain with a compromise 'man-in-the-middle' who amiably confessed he used matchsticks to solve problems of high finance. His hobby was cricket or so it sounded. It soon became evident in reply to my questions about the scandals of religious discrimination in this outpost of the Not-So-United Kingdom that Sir Alec was a 'stone-waller'. He scored no runs but fobbed off all fast balls with a straight bat. He spoke with the arrogance of a belted earl, accustomed to talking even nonsense with a confident chin-up manner. He said all this talk of discrimination could be dealt with, hey presto, by recourse to the 'courts'. This had been proved demonstrably untrue by that excellent body, the Campaign for Social Justice in Northern Ireland, when test cases were thrown out by the local judges – but Sir Alec rabbited on as if he had found the simple answer to a problem which had defeated lesser minds.

When he went back to 10 Downing Street, the Campaign challenged him to prove his off-the-cuff assertion and a considerable correspondence ensued which ended in smoke when it emerged that the British Prime Minister had been talking through his hat.

A COLUMN TAKES OFF

AFTER MORE THAN than twenty years of anonymous journalism as a reporter I suddenly emerged sometime around 1950 as a Columnist writing under my own name. I have to thank Hector Legge, then Editor of the *Sunday Independent* who became my friend and mentor in what proved to be the most enjoyable phase of my career as a newspaperman. It's a phase which lasted 33 years. During all that time I was given complete freedom to write what I liked, a freedom which most newspapermen dream about. The column was first entitled 'Meet The People' but as my name became better known it was eventually featured as 'James Kelly's Diary'. In a way it was a pioneer effort, blazing a trail which others followed. It took a strong political line. Up until then the attitude to all politicians had been too deferential. The ruling establishment in the North had been treated with kid gloves by the Northern Ireland Press. I decided it was time to redress the balance. Sales of the *Sunday Independent* shot upwards. The column had taken off. I had always seen the humour of the pretensions of the local big-wigs and gave them hell every Sunday under splash headlines. I was amazed at the reaction and obviously Hector Legge was also, judging from the many letters he received, both praiseworthy and abusive. I was pleased by the response even from some of the establishment politicians themselves after I had lampooned them unmercifully. Some of them were not averse to tipping me off to the faults and foibles of their colleagues.

There are no real friends in politics. Most of them are individuals and out on their own and the devil take the hindmost. Inside the ruling government Establishment I was astonished at the rivalries and the way some of the leading personalities were stabbing each other in the back. Turning the spotlight on these intrigues made for absorbing reading and I laughed when a government minister complained that I was 'out-doing Madame Tabouis', the French international diplomatic journalist whose syndicated column was reputed to be written under Hitler's table!

I had some fun with my inside information on what was going on at Brookeborough's weekly Cabinet meetings. Letters started pouring in from all sides and all conditions of persons, high and low. I was flattered by the epithets 'pungent', 'hard-hitting', 'vigorous' and 'witty'. From the Royal Ulster Rifles in Cyprus came an expensive air-mail letter which I added to the pile of 'fan mail'. The writer said he had picked up my column in the lavatory and had 'never read such a lot of effing Fenian propaganda in his life.' To spend all that money to let me know that he had become one of my far-flung readers was stimulating. It reminded me of the Editor of the paper in Alabama, a cigar-chewing colonel, who when a volley of shots came through the window remarked, 'That editorial went down well!'

Many times subjects taken up for ventilation in the column were raised by MPs subsequently at Stormont but this led to a curious complaint from the then leader of the Nationalist Party, James McSparran, QC. The prior publicity in the *Sunday Independent* he claimed, was in effect 'marking the Unionists' card' in advance enabling their private secretaries to cobble up excuses!

Billy Douglas, the party boss, in a Telefis Eireann encounter in which the *Irish Times* described me as his 'most dangerous opponent' gave the column an unexpected boost when he confessed, 'I read you every Sunday'. He had to for he and his cohorts figured in it frequently as, for example, when I described the aftermath to his appearance at a seminar in Kilkenny. He was accompanied by Mr Ken Topping, QC, then government Chief Whip. Returning northwards at night they lost their way. Eventually these two defenders of Northern Protestantism found a signpost. It read 'Maynooth, six miles'. Needless to say they flashed past Ireland's celebrated Catholic clerical University.

Billy was troubled when I described him as chief Unionist 'trouble-shooter'. I also reported that when tickets for the All-Ireland Hurling Final in Croke Park, Dublin could not be got for love or money, wonder of wonders, the Bossman in Glengall Street was able to produce them! He went to the length of issuing a public denial.

The late Morris May, Minister of Education and the decentest man in the Brookeborough Cabinet before his untimely death from lung cancer, told me that the first thing he did every Sunday after attending the local Holywood Presbyterian Church was to rush round to buy the *Sunday Independent* to find out what I was 'up to'. Morris, an accountant by profession and a chain-smoker, was, I think, tickled by my 'revelation' that he was in fact the only man in the Cabinet who knew the difference between a decimal point and a full stop! When I told him that Machiavelli's *The Prince* was now prescribed reading for the men in the corridors of power in the Dail he confessed that he had never heard of the book. I was impressed by the quiet way he defused the Orange objections to the 65% grants to the Catholic voluntary schools and he once told me how profoundly affected he was when his son upbraided him over a speech he made at an Orange gathering in Scotland. Reading a report of the speech his son asked, 'How do you expect me to face my friends at Queen's University this morning if they read that stuff?'

My wife met him at a journalists' function in Belfast and in a heart-to-heart talk in my absence told him what she thought was wrong with the government. He listened quietly and joked, 'You are as bad as your husband' but then admitted that it was his ambition to beome Prime Minister. 'Things will be very different then I can assure you', he said. I believed him but fate intervened. His death which came with astonishing rapidity in the prime of life shocked everyone.

One of the last conversations I recall with him was after I had dreamed up an imaginary meeting of the Northern Cabinet in dialogue. It was at a time of internal crisis and intrigue when Brookeborough was becoming fed up with the job and longing to get out of Belfast, which he hated, for his beloved Colebrooke and his favourite hobbies, fishing and shooting rabbits. Morris May followed me out of Stormont to my car to tell me how he enjoyed this satirical spoof. 'I laughed', he said, 'you could have been under the Cabinet table'. Madame Tabouis again!

Catch-phrases which I invented were often quoted back to me by people in the street long after I had forgotten them. Government policy at that time seemed to be to cram all incoming new industry into the Protestant heartland within a thirty miles radius of Belfast and to neglect the majority Nationalist areas on the far side of the River Bann and Lough Neagh. For convenience I lumped the neglected industrial desert of Derry, Tyrone and Fermanagh together as the forgotten region 'West of the Bann'. The description caught the imagination and thereafter Brookeborough heard plenty about his policy of allowing 'West of the Bann' to languish in the western mists.

Eoin O'Mahony, better known as 'Pope O'Mahony', that remarkable lawyer turned journalist, told me that Sean MacBride was credited with the gloomy reflection that the problem of the North might eventually be resolved by a 'Gibraltar solution' with a Unionist government left to hold the enclave of Antrim and Down and Greater Belfast. When I protested and asked where that plan would leave the huge Catholic population of West Belfast, Eoin replied, 'I am afraid James you would have to be sacrified for the greater good of the greater number!' I said, 'Bully for MacBride. He would not have to live under such a regime.' At the same time I could not help thinking that in the South of Ireland such an idea might have its attractions. In West Belfast there has always been an under-current of suspicion that in the end they could be the sacrificial lambs in some so-called 'settlement'.

Many times I wrote scathingly about the situation in Derry where the ancient walls were retained along with the curfew bell to remind the majority Nationalists that they were the underdogs. The fantastic gerrymandered political boundaries to maintain the local Orange chiefs in power in the Guildhall I re-named 'Derry-manders' and this term stuck. Derry was the Achilles Heel of Unionism. The local Bossmen, Major This and Major That, (the Unionists loved to hold on to these military titles in peace-time) were almost unbelievable. To them the siege by the troops of James II was just yesterday and they looked down on the despised Nationalists of the Bogside from the old walls in much the same manner as the US cavalry looked over the palisades at the besieging Red Indians. Even in the later years of Stormont ministers confessed that they could do nothing to curb the bigotry and political chicanery of their supporters in places like Derry and Dungannon.

One thing I was proud of, and that was the spotlight which I turned on the notorious Springtown Camp where Catholics denied homes by the ruling clique in the Guildhall were housed in conditions not unlike the camps provided for the displaced Palestinians. The pictures we ran of this hell-hole finally forced the authorities to take action at last. I was aided very much in this and other investigations in Derry by Eddie McAteer, MP, the leader of the Nationalist Pary and I felt it was a matter of great regret that the rift between him and that other outstanding Derryman, John Hume, MEP, led to McAteer's departure from the political scene in the North. In the years that he led his party at Stormont Eddie McAteer tried every peaceful plan and strategem that was humanly possible to rouse the guilty men at Westminster to exercise their responsibilities in the Six Counties but was thwarted at every turn. The voices they listened to were the wrong voices. In sheer desperation he appealed to the Privy Council but this august body of prominent men proved to be a powerless pantomime show masking the fact that the 'active Privy Council' was in fact the same 'do-nothing Cabinet' which had already turned the deaf ear to all the warnings that resentment was gathering like a flood-tide in the hapless last Colony across the Irish Sea.

Hector Legge came to Derry to 'see for himself'. I suspect that he wondered if we were being too tough with the powers-that-be there. In the event he found that if anything we were not tough enough and he wrote a scorcher of an article describing the attitude of the party bosses he met.

Some hilarity was introduced into the political scene around this time by the sudden appearance, like a shooting star, of a young law lecturer, Tommy Teevan from Limavady, County Derry. The Unionists had won back West Belfast and the seat had then been declared vacant because of the ineligibility of Rev. Godfrey Macmanaway, MP. His departure from Westminster had been hastened by the brilliant legal arguments of Mr Geoffrey Bing, MP, one of the Friends of Ireland group who had begun to focus embarrassing attention on the activities of Stormont. Bing had completely out-classed the Attorney General, Maxwell-Fyfe of the War Crimes Tribunal fame, in the legal battle over Macmanaway. Glengall Street was in a quandray when Teevan dropped out of the heavens, as it were. They did not know it but Teevan who was a drinking man had entered into the fun of the thing when a group of conspiratorial Queen's University graduates, including a clever Catholic lawyer and lecturer, suggested that he should go forward as a Unionist candidate. They calculated that Teevan would prove a kind of time-bomb under the table of the sedate and strait-laced Ulster Unionist Party at Westminster and would pull the rug out from under this group of largely silent party hacks. They prepared a powerful address and Teevan was duly selected and elected. His rambunctious speeches and behaviour disconcerted his colleagues. He was the original bull-in-the-china-shop of the ever-so-cautious Unionists anxious to escape attention at Westminster.

A special meeting of the Party was called in a House of Commons Committee Room to censure Teevan after some misdemeanour but he was not the type of man to sit silent and accept criticism from these old fuddy-duddies. The meeting broke up in confusion when he sailed into the Chairman, Professor Savory. 'You old goat', he roared. 'How dare you attack me. You're not even an Ulsterman.' Professory Savory, although a long-time Unionist from Queen's University Belfast, was in fact born in the Channel Islands.

Teevan hated pomposity and after a celebration with his friends landed in trouble with the ultra-dignified Glasgow-born Vice Chancellor of Queen's University, Sir David Lindsay Keir, by driving over the flower beds on the university lawn. Summoned to the great man's presence, Teevan dressed himself in farmer's garb and hobnail boots and stomped noisily into the Vice Chancellor's office determined not to take any nonsense from this 'non-Ulsterman'. The upshot of this stormy interview was that he was suspended from his law lectureship. The conspirators retaliated with an anonymous newspaper correspondence for and against the Vice Chancellor who was not universally loved by his staff. Copies of the local Derry paper containing the letters were pushed under the doors of the senior staff to provide many a private guffaw. Phone calls and lurid postcards also arrived and at one time Teevan was visited by the police Special Branch.

When Lindsay Keir soon afterwards wiped the dust of Belfast from his feet to take up the post of Master of Balliol it is said that postcards kept coming allegedly from racing tipsters advising him to back this and that certainty in the 2.30 at Newmarket! Teevan's career as a politician came to a sudden end within a year when he was beaten in an election by Jack Beattie by a bare 25 votes. He was then just a young man of 24. Not long after his friends were shocked when he contracted a grave illness and died. Teevan, with his wild speeches and stout and unpredictable figure like the fat boy of Charles Dickens, made the respectable Unionists' flesh creep. His meteoric rise was startling and his end equally so.

A SEA TRAGEDY

AN OLD-TIME journalist, Alec McDonald, a former *Irish News* Chief Reporter, advised me years ago never to forget that newspapers are always on the look-out for 'a good sea story'. One of the most tragic I ever reported was the sinking of the Larne ferry, the *Princess Victoria* in the narrow seas between Scotland and the Antrim coast with the loss of 130 lives.

On the morning of 31 January, a Saturday, I was told that the Larne ferry was in trouble. Tommy McMullen, assistant editor of the *Belfast Telegraph* who covered routine stories for the Dublin *Evening Herald* was reassuring when I checked with him. 'It's all out on the P A', he said. 'It's a Scottish story so we can leave it to them.' The ship had lost its rudder in a gale off Corsewall Point and no doubt rescue ships were on the way. As an afterthought he mentioned that a Stormont Minister, Major J Maynard Sinclair, Minister of Finance was aboard as also was Sir Samuel Smiles M.P. for North Down at Westminster.

About an hour later before driving home for lunch, as a double check I phoned the Donaghadee (County Down) lifeboat and was surprised when someone there said my inquiry was the first they had heard about the incident. I took it from this that matters must be under control at the other side of the channel and went home.

There was a full gale blowing by this time. My lunch was interrupted by a phone call from the United Press of America in London. I could not believe it when the news desk said they had monitored an SOS call from the Larne ferry, *Princess Victoria* , stating that she was sinking fifteen miles off the Copeland Islands.

I drove immediately to Donaghadee where the gale was blowing hard from the sea. All the metal signs were swinging on their hinges over shops and as I braked near the massive pier sheltering the little enclosed harbour I felt my new car lifting from under me. I joined a *Telegraph* reporter, Jimmy Harrison, who was running along the seafront to the home of Mr McKibbin, the secretary of the local lifeboat which had gone to sea shortly after my phone call. The secretary came to the door smoking his pipe and said, 'Come in. It's all on the radio upstairs.' We followed upstairs to a front sitting room, puzzled by his mention of the radio. From the staccato messages coming from an ordinary radio on a table it suddenly dawned on us that we were actually listening to what amounted to a running commentary on a tragedy which even now seems unthinkable, the sinking with heavy loss of life of a big passenger ferry almost within sight of land, a ship that had for hours been within reach of ships and aircraft but through a chapter of errors and Saturday off-duty lassitude ashore, had listed and listed until she eventually toppled over upside down.

The radio was picking up loud and clear the radio telephone exchanges between a tanker, the *Pass of Dromochter* and a Belfast-Glasgow cargo boat the *Lairdsbank* . The skippers who had arrived on the scene just as the ferry turned turtle were giving a graphic description of the tragic scenes as the Donaghadee lifeboat picked up survivors in the raging seas. I recall one of the captains saying that he had spotted a life-raft with two girls, both WRENS in naval uniform, clinging on for dear life. Then he exclaimed, 'Oh my God. They have been swept into the sea.' Both were puzzled by the fact that they could see no women and children on the ships' life-boats and kept asking each other if they could see any sign of such survivors in the heavy seas. They did not know then but apparently one of the first of the lifeboats hit the side of the ferry as it was being lowered, throwing women and children into the water to their deaths.

Our shorthand was tested as we took rapid notes of these dramatic exchanges and kept rushing to the phone to relay them to our respective papers. At the Independent Belfast office my colleague, Denis McGrath, an old Irish News man, a great man in a crisis with vast experience in Reuters and Fleet Street behind him, was as excited as I was at this unexpected scoop with first-hand descriptions of a major sea disaster. He kept phoning my messages, minute by minute, to the Evening Herald in Dublin. We both pictured the big headlines the story would demand at the other end. The last message that came across was from the tanker's bridge suggesting that both ships should provide shelter for the lifeboat back to Donaghadee harbour. Dusk was coming on as we hurried over to the harbour where a small knot of people was gathered near the steps of the pier. There was a fierce gale blowing, harder than ever, and I recall a policeman's cap blowing into the harbour despite the fact that he had it strapped under his chin. I shifted my car as it was lifting and swaying too close to the pier for safety.

Meantime in the failing light the lifeboat pulled alongside and up the steps came the folk who had been rescued, led by an elderly grey-haired man in his bare feet, wearing only a shirt and trousers with a blanket thrown over his shoulders. They were all in various states of distress and were rushed in a van to the nearby Imperial Hotel. Here hot drinks and basins of warm water for frozen legs were provided in the lounge while crowds of agitated relatives who had arrived from Belfast sobbed loudly as they scrutinised the rescued people and found that their loved ones were not among them. It was a heart-breaking spectacle. Moving in the background I spotted Sir Richard Pim, Inspector General of the RUC and former Naval Commander in Churchill's famous war-time Map Room. He was inquiring quietly if anyone had seen Major Maynard Sinclair. But nobody had seen the minister. Later it was said that someone had observed him on the swaying deck before the ship plunged down to the depths.

Sir Samuel Smiles MP, descendant of the famous author of 'Self Help', had apparently not come on deck. His body was never found. His picturesque home was situated on the water's edge of the County Down coast a few miles from the Copeland Islands. The windows looked out on the seas where he and the other victims lie entombed in the sunken ferry. Captain Ferguson and the wireless operator, who kept sending distress messages all the time, remained at their posts to the last and went down with the ship. She was so far off course that it was surmised Captain Ferguson had been trying to bring the listing ferry, almost completely out of control, to the North Down coast to beach her at Ballyholme sands.

It must have been near midnight when we learned that a British naval destroyer had picked up some more survivors and bodies near where the ship had sunk. There was a mad rush by the press to Belfast docks to which the destroyer was heading at top speed. Relatives of workmen from the Belfast aircraft factory who had been returning on the ferry from a job in England were already waiting anxiously at the dockside as the destroyer pulled alongside. There was confused shouting of names and nicknames between them and a small group sheltering from the wind and rain on the deck. Everyone wanted to know who had been picked up and who had been lost. A few bodies lay on the deck under tarpaulins. From under one of the tarpaulins a pair of highly-polished shoes stuck out. Unmistakably this was the body of Major Sinclair, the Minister of Finance. Perhaps it was a habit cultivated during his army career but we always observed that his shoes were brilliantly polished. Normally, I was told, Major Sinclair travelled back from government business in London by air but because of an air crash at Belfast Airport, then at Nutts Corner, in which a number of people were killed, he had been asked by his wife to travel the 'safer way' by train and ferry.

Through the fickle hand of fate that was the day on which the unthinkable would happen. Who would have imagined that the big ferry which ploughed back and forth over the 18 miles' short passage between Larne and Stranraer several times a day, almost like a bus-run, would not alone get lost in a storm, out of reach of rescuers, but would eventually plunge to the bottom miles off course with heavy loss of life?

HANDS ACROSS THE BORDER

BEFORE MR DE VALERA 'went to the Park' as President of Ireland in 1959 he was invited to Queen's University in Belfast, an unusual and hopeful event in view of his recent history as a man who had been banned from the North for many years, and regarded by Northern loyalists as the devil incarnate. There was a tremendous turn-out at the spacious Whitla Hall for the occasion and Dev had every reason to be pleased with the reception he received. He was accompanied, as always, by his faithful lieutenant and 'minder', Mr Frank Aiken.

I was curious to meet Aiken, one-time leader of the Northern Division of the old IRA and native of South Armagh, but when I was introduced I found him dry and taciturn, with little to say beyond an occasional 'Yes, yes, yes', one of the most ill-at-ease politicians I have ever met. This was in complete contrast to Dev himself who met us in an ante-room and was quite chatty, charming the Belfast newspapermen with his warmth and friendliness.

It was an historic occasion and the packed audience was agog to hear what Dev, survivor of the 1916 Rising, would say to a Belfast gathering, and a mixed one at that. 'It is', he said, 'not the first time I have come to Belfast'. He paused and we wondered if he was going to tell about his experiences in Belfast Gaol. 'I came here as a young student. It was on the Twelfth of July', he continued, and the crowd laughed. So he was going to tell us about his reaction to the great march of the Orangemen on that day of days in Belfast when everything stops for the besashed brethren parading behind massed bands and the big drums. But no, Dev was keeping us in suspense. He had not seen or heard the Orangemen and their music, 'The Sash', the 'Lily-O', 'Derry's Walls' and 'No Surrender' or even 'Kick the Pope'.

He confessed that he had spent the day at McArt's Fort on Cavehill, communing with the spirits of the 1798 Presbyterian United Irishmen, Wolfe Tone, Henry Joy McCracken and the rest. The crowd gasped and broke into chattering reaction and no wonder. Here was one of the mistakes of history. No Southern Ireland politician facing the realities of a dissident Protestant population inmmersed in different folk-ways and traditions can afford to ignore this manifestation of the tribalism which gave the colour of orange to the Irish Tricolour. The symbolism of the flag is white for peace between the Orange and the Green. Was that not a mistake anyhow, a recognition of the division? Was the old Hibernian flag of green surmounted by the golden harp not a more inspiring national emblem? The symbolism of the Tricolour was lost on the Northern Protestants anyhow. They insisted on calling it a flag of 'green, white and yellow' and when it was banned by Sir Dawson Bates he made the mistake of so designating it. This enabled James McSparran, QC to drive a coach-and-horses through a prosecution in an Armagh court where a defendant was charged with the illegal display of the Tricolour. Thereafter cowardly sounding 'Yellow' was altered in the Special Powers Act to loyal 'Orange'.

Republican dreamers in Dublin who talk nostalgically about the Presbyterians of the North one day awakening to their great Republican heritage should come North on 12 July but go straight to Royal Avenue and forget about Cavehill. Better to face the truth and take it from there. In other words, don't make the mistake Dev did.

When Prime Minister Terence O'Neill set about organising Ulster societies in the United States from the descendants of Washington's 'Scotch-Irish' from Ulster, he had his critics at home. The late James Faulkner, the affable linen shirt manufacturer, father of Brian Faulkner, and whom I knew very well, met me one morning in a Fountain Street coffee house and made me laugh at his reaction to the Premier's 'Scotch-Irish' plans. 'What's he talking about?' he snorted. 'Sure his bloody ancestors drove them out of Ulster.'

Another time when Dev was due to travel North for the unveiling of a memorial to Roger Casement at Murlough Bay near Ballycastle we were tipped off that Northern Republicans were preparing a hot reception for him. Republicans like Jimmy Steele and his friends decided that it was time to confront the 'Chief'' over his tough treatment of the IRA during the war years when there had been executions, internments and deaths on hunger strike. The death of Belfastman Sean McCaughey after 23 days without food or water at Portlaoise Prison particularly rankled and the plan was to shout Dev down when he rose to speak. Dev and the organisers were blissfully unaware of the plot to cause sufficient disruption so that he would ''never dare to show his face in the North again'. We were told the night before that this would be the end of the 'big fellow'.

Needless to say we were close up to the platform with our pens poised, but whether it was cold feet, the enthusiastic reception of the crowd or the semi-religious background to the memorial unveiling, the expected rumpus never materialised. We could see some of the Republican demonstrators moving among the spectators but when we caught their eyes they shook their heads and later confessed that they had come to the conclusion on the spot that the uproar they had planned would not have been appropriate in the circumstances!

The occasion passed off quietly, Mr de Valera making his usual impassioned appeal on behalf of the Irish language which hard-line

Republicans dared not disrupt. Dev never knew how close he came to one of the most embarrassing moments in his long life.

After denying rumours that he intended to resign on health grounds Lord Brookeborough suddenly decided to give up the Premiership in March 1963. Late at night on 25 March the Unionist Party woke up to find that the Governor, Lord Wakehurst, had appointed Captain Terence O'Neill. Although Brookeborough had promised Morris May that his successor would be decided by a full meeting of the Unionist Parliamentary Party no meeting was called and the *fait accompli* began the Faulkner-O'Neill antipathy which was to have far-reaching consequences in the years ahead.

Morris May told me about the Brookeborough assurance before he died twelve months before. As contender for the Premiership he was confident that he would obtain majority backing in the Party including that of Faulkner who recognised his outstanding ability. Captain O'Neill was virtually smuggled into power overnight by means of a questionable straw-poll conducted by his supporter, Chief Whip William Craig, subsequently rewarded for his efforts by promotion to Cabinet rank. It was claimed that Craig rang round Party members assuring wavering M.P.s and 'Don't Knows' that all the rest were voting for O'Neill. In this way he was able to claim that O'Neill had majority backing in a three-way contest between O'Neill, Faulkner and rank outsider John Andrews, whom nobody considered a serious contender. Some members of the Party were livid and blamed Brookeborough for the apparent refusal to permit political power to get out of the grip of the County families.

It was generally conceded that by collusion at the top Brian Faulkner had been 'ditched' and it became more and more glaringly evident that he bitterly resented O'Neill's fast foot-work, as did his admirers inside and outside the Cabinet. Thus it could be said that the power battle between two ambitious men led up to the vicious blood-letting inside the Unionist Party with the eventual break-up of the old monopoly establishment into warring factions.

The tragedy was the timing of the split. Brookeborough had held on too long. He had held out against reforms of any kind, a stubborn and stupid politician with a mind set in the mould of the Thirties. Twenty years was too long for any politician to hold power. With Brookeborough, Grand Master of the Orange backwoodsmen of Fermanagh, it was a disaster. The legacy he left behind was a government of part-time politicians, responding not to the rising tide of liberal opinion and the demand for a wind of change, but to the whiplash of the antediluvian drum-beaters of the Orange Order, the Black Preceptory and the Apprentice Boys of Derry.

The O'Neill sprint to the corridors of power was so precipitate that he hurriedly gulped down the whiskey and soda offered by the Governor, Lord Wakehurst at Government House, Hillsborough and rushed back to Belfast to phone his fellow Cabinet Ministers to ask if they wished to stay in the new Government. What the shocked Mr Faulkner said has not been recorded. Lord Glentoran, the Leader of the Senate, could not be told. His butler told Jim Malley, O'Neill's secretary, that his Lordshsip could not be disturbed as he was in his bath! When he asked to speak to Lady Glentoran he was told, 'Her Ladyship is also in her bath'! There were two men named Morgan in the Parliamentary Party at that time, one William Morgan, a member of the Cabinet and the other a back-bencher. Through a mix-up in phone numbers the back-bencher was nearly offered a place in the government, such was the haste to re-construct a Government in time for an announcement in the morning papers.

The sudden resignation of Billy Douglas as boss of the party Offices in Glengall Street was taken by the Press to mean a complete change of style from the old regime but there was a puzzling hiatus and one minister who ran a shop on the Antrim Road, Belfast, on the side, told me that he and the others expected big things from the new Prime Minister but that nothing was happening. They were all bewildered, he said.

Eventually the new Prime Minister started visiting Catholic

schools and shaking hands with nuns. In his mind this was a major breakthrough. Paisley was suitably outraged at this flirtation with Papists. Catholics, however, wanted something more tangible than public relations exercises and were disgusted to find O'Neill doing a balancing act by joining the arch-bigots of the Apprentice Boys of Derry and posturing in an Orange collarette and bowler hat with his local lodge. They had expected something better than this apparent apeing of the Brooke tactics. In some ways he seemed to mean well and talked about the stupidity of the old type Unionists in their failure to recognise that the operation of the Butler Education Act was producing a new *intelligentsia* among Catholics in Queen's University and elsewhere who would not tolerate being treated as second-class citizens.

But the rising expectations of the minority were hardly satisfied with empty gestures and the apparent belief among his advisers that obvious reforms, particularly in the Augean stable of local government, must come, if at all, at a snail's pace so as not to disturb the local Orange factions who were not enamoured of this English-born old Etonian anyhow. Where bold decisive measures might have succeeded teetering caution failed. The anti-O'Neill lobby which could have been dispersed by resolute action gathered strength from the waffling and soon the back-stabbing began.

Some of O'Neill's ideas were off-beat. He tried to scoop the Irish government by persuading President Kennedy to fly to the North first to 'open the Giant's Causeway'. But the President, who later confessed that his Irish visit was 'the most moving experience of my life' was not to be nobbled in this way. He sent a polite refusal. Another daft notion was to revive the idea of an 'Irish Balmoral', a Royal residence where the Prince of Wales might reside for part of the year. Queen Victoria rejected a proposed residence 'half-way between Belfast and Dublin', which would have placed it somewhere near Dundalk, because she hated things Irish. O'Neill had started the ball rolling for an 'Ulster Royal residence' when the roof fell in on Stormont. Buck House, like Victoria, was probably 'not amused'. The idea that the 'peasantry' of Crossmaglen, South Armagh, might be wooed away from Republicanism by the wave of a gloved hand from an Irish castle could only be conjured up by someone far removed from reality in this day and age.

With a Catholic President in the White House and Pope John's death bringing about the miracle of the flag at half-mast over Belfast City Hall, so great was his esteem even on the Shankill Road, it seemed to us observers that a wind of change was blowing over the land, even over the 'Ulster' outpost. There was also the exciting prospect of the entry of both parts of Ireland into the European Community and the suggestion that the Irish Border would simply 'wither away'. When de Gaulle earlier said 'No' to Britain's entry, a numbskull MP had proposed that a statue to the General should be erected in the Stormont grounds. But Europe was now beckoning to the off-shore Islands to join Western Europe in a great crusade for peace and prosperity. If the French and Germans could bury the hatchet after centuries of warfare, had not the time come for Irishmen to do likewise. I thought it appropriate at this time to voice such thoughts in my Sunday column. As they say, 'Ideas have legs' and I found more and more people coming round to this perception of events. At Stormont, however, to a Cabinet hag-ridden by its past, 1690 was a greater reality than 1960. O'Neill was still depending heavily on gimmickry, shaking hands with celebrities at home and abroad.

In the dining room at Stormont one evening an M.P. in the course of some gossip told me that Edmund Warnock, QC, an admirer of Faulkner and a thorn in the side of both O'Neill and Brookeborough, confessed that while he was Attorney General he always thought it ludicrous that he had never at any time met his opposite number in Dublin. 'Summits' were very much in vogue at this time and Kruschev had just made his famous visit to London.

I thought it was time there was an 'Irish Summit' between

Brookeborough who was in the last days of his Premiership and Sean Lemass, the Taoiseach in Dublin. I wrote this in the *Sunday Independent* Diary and consulted with Brendan McCann, our intrepid and prize-winning cameraman. Brendan produced a photograph of Lemass and Brookeborough shaking hands to illustrate the piece. To do this he had to resort to a clever bit of montage. The hand which Brookeborough was apparently stretching out for the handshake was taken from another picture.

In fact it belonged to Mr Sam Clarke, Secretary of the Royal Ulster Agricultural Society, who never realised the part he had played in this first 'Hands-Across-The-Border'. The story and picture caused quite a stir and obviously set some minds alight on both sides of the Border. In fact it turned out in the end to be O'Neill's best gimmick of all and one with far-reaching consequences.

Elaborate arrangements had been made by O'Neill to keep his invitation to Sean Lemass to lunch at Stormont a close secret. Even his Cabinet colleagues were kept in the dark. The news broke at 1.00 pm on 14 January, 1965 and I recall that when Denis McGrath phoned me from the office to my home where I had just typed the last page of my Sunday Diary, I exclaimed, 'Oh hell, I'll have to do a new diary!' This remark reached Stormont Castle by bush-telegraph and I was afterwards twitted by O'Neill who enjoyed the report that I had been 'scooped'. But what he did not know was that the night before Lemass's dramatic drive North to Belfast, my cousin, Michael McGarry, a member of the Special Branch at Dublin Castle, had tried to contact me to tip me off. Michael had been detailed to travel with Lemass as his special bodyguard. He had mislaid my phone number and told me that he telephoned the *Independent* office in Dublin but someone there told him that, for security reasons possibly, they did not give callers the private phone numbers of staff! From Lemass I received a cryptic message through a priest – 'Congratulations'.

Two years later when Jack Lynch came to Stormont there was

less secrecy and someone tipped off Paisley. We were all on the spot for the arrival this time and witnessed the ludicrous spectacle of Paisley and his fellow political parsons throwing snowballs at Lynch's limousine as it rounded the Carson statue.

Nudged by Lemass, Eddie McAteer, the Nationalist leader, had agreed to become the Official Leader of the Opposition for which a salary was paid. Eddie played the part, even to the extent of smoking a big cigar, and I remember calling to interview him in the impressive office which had been put at his disposal on the ground floor around the corner from the entrance to the Senate.

It was a honeymoon period in which we expected big things. But malign influences on all sides were at work. In Dublin there was the daft period of the 1916 celebrations playing neatly into the hands of Mr Paisley. The IRA, almost moribund, was given an unexpected boost by the Press glorifying the old days of the derring-do ambushes, raids on police barracks and so forth while boozy ballads brought patriotic passions to the boil with pop stars encouraging a new generation to emulate Tom Barry and the heroes of old. I often wondered how many of those 'turned on' by this madness in their youth became victims of the turmoil that was to come? How many young men of twenty ended in early graves or in the 'human zoos' called prisons, all for what?

Paisley, also looking backward, wanted to ride the headlines with a raging tearing campaign to commemorate Carson by naming the new bridge across the Lagan in Belfast after the old rebel. He failed but he was more successful in pre-empting serious riots in Divis Street by forcing the weak-kneed RUC chiefs to order the police to smash down a shop-window and seize an election flag, the Irish Tricolour. In this case I heard that Paisley had been led into the situation. A Unionist newspaper Editor, Cowan Watson, told a reporter to ring Paisley and tell him that a Tricolour was being displayed openly in Divis Street. Paisley in a quote for the paper then threatened to march through Divis Street to seize the offending flag if the police did not act. They did, as they so often did, in response to his threats. That was the first night we saw petrol bombs used as weapons of attack in one of the fiercest riots I have ever seen. It was to be the beginning of many other violent confrontations in which the imported weapon, the Molotoff cocktail, was to be used.

After that Paisley, hungry for headlines whatever the cost, became the mob leader crying 'O'Neill must go' or the Governor, 'Lord Erskine must go'. His tactic was to go for the jugulars of the top men so that the unthinking mob would have a simple war-cry. After his resignation O'Neill in his autobiography confessed 'If Ulster does not survive, then historians may well show that it was the Protestant extremists yearning for the days of the Protestant Ascendancy who lit the flames which blew us up. This, of course, was coupled with the fact that for far too long no effort had been made to make the minority feel that they were wanted or even appreciated.'

During the 1916 march in Belfast we noted that Padraic Pearse had been demoted and his place had been usurped by James Connolly and that the Communist spokeswoman in Belfast, the late Betty Sinclair, was given pride of place at the head of the procession along the Falls Road. Some keen observers wondered were the 'Reds' taking over. Others wondered if the Church leaders had left a vacuum after the Vatican Council. Liturgical changes had been made but the 'people of God', the laity, who were supposed to come to the fore, had virtually been pushed aside. In West Belfast, once the great Citadel of Catholicity, the 'Coms' and their fellow-travellers were infiltrating everywhere and appearing in many guises as 'patriots'. Bishop Philbin, translated from a rural diocese in the West of Ireland, a strange and unexplained appointment at a crucial time, appeared overwhelmed by the enormity of the situation.

On the Protestant side the clergy of the principal denominations appeared equally inept and incapable of standing up to Paisley. In fact they acted as if they were frightened to death by a monster. There were a few honourable exceptions who had the courage to speak out but the abuse they received publicly and the intimidation by phone calls only served to warn the rest to keep their heads buried in the sands. The few voices of reason were drowned on all sides by the howls of the extremists.

Newspapermen have the reputation of cynicism but most of them are romantics at heart presenting the outward shell of toughness. It is hard not to show this cynical side, however, in a job where too often one sees the feet of clay of our so-called leaders. The 1916 leaders have almost been deified in the South but I wondered about them when in the midst of our rattling of the bones of the dead no less a person than the late Ernest Blythe revealed that at one stage the 1916 leaders had seriously considered the establishment not of a Republic but of a monarchy in Ireland!

Blythe, himself an Irish language enthusiast and former organiser of the Gaelic League, had a strange tale to tell. His experiences travelling around Ireland for the Gaelic League had convinced him apparently that there was something in this monarchist idea because he felt the apathy about the language would turn to enthusiasm if the aristocrats and the people in the 'big houses' could be interested in the Gaelic revival. The revelation that the 1916 men had seriously considered the possibility of a Gaelic-speaking monarch was said to have been confirmed from another authoritative source.

The further suggestion that a German princeling by the name of Joachim was seriously advanced as a candidate for King seemed preposterous. 'King Jo The First' would have been tutored in the Irish language in time for his coronation! That an International Socialist like James Connolly should condone such a hare-brained idea was breathtaking. One awaited indignant denials but none ever came. No-one wanted to probe this bizarre episode any further.

THINGS FALL APART

THE FAT WAS in the fire with a vengeance when O'Neill, tired of the back-stabbing and conspiracies in the Party and the Cabinet, resigned on 1 May, 1969. The last two years of his six years in the Premiership had been hectic. The whole sad saga has been chronicled over and over again. The Civil Rights marches, the Burntollett ambush by 'loyalists', the end of the bigoted Derry Corporation, the rise of the unknown Bernadette Devlin, the sackings of Harry West and Bill Craig, the resignations of Faulkner, Morgan and Chichester Clark and the various summonses to 10 Downing Street to be told what to do by Harold Wilson. Finally O'Neill claimed that the end came when the UVF decided to 'blow him out of office' with a series of explosions damaging electricity and water supplies.

It did not help O'Neill when he was voted Ireland's 'Man Of The Year' in a *Sunday Independent poll* – at least not with the extremists in the North. To them that was proof positive that he was a 'traitor'. His successor was Major James Chichester Clark, another County family squire. Once again Faulkner was 'dished' in the contest by one vote – O'Neill's vote. A South Derry farmer, Chichester Clark left home that morning for Stormont but first decided to clean out the byre, a Freudian note to his day of destiny. Chichester Clark's appointment was an absurd one. It made no sense except to the county folk who still believed that they had a prescriptive right to run the country and that the 'lower classes', including the jumped-up nouveau-riche, must be kept in their place. Forced by Downing Street to make the changes which had come too late, including the dismantling of the notorious 'B' Specials, 'Chi-Chi', as he was nicknamed, literally sweated blood. He was caught between the devil in Downing Street and the deep blue sea of Paisleyism and dissident Unionism.

The story going the rounds of the news-rooms in Belfast was that the unfortunate Prime Minister was continually ringing Home Secretary Reginald Maudling at night and telling him that he wanted to resign. Maudling, it was alleged, would try to soothe him, saying, 'Now James, go to bed and get a good night's sleep and things will look different in the morning.' But things did not look better in the morning. They got worse and worse and Maudling, during one of his quick visits to Northern Ireland, was widely quoted as groaning on the aircraft returning to London, 'What a bloody awful country. Quick get me a double whiskey.'

It was said that when Chichester Clark finally gave up the ghost and resigned in March 1971, Downing Street heaved a sigh of relief and hoped that his successor, the more experienced Brian Faulkner, would have a steadying influence. His package of reforms would have been impressive if they had been produced four years before but already they were too late. Pandora's box had burst open and all hell had been let loose, with bombings and killings, a nightmare of violence. Ignoring his Cabinet, Faulkner turned to the awful British Army GOC, General Tuzo, and his police chiefs, and the supreme blunder of one-sided internment was decided. This was Faulkner's 'Doomsday' and the beginning of the end of the sectarian-dominated RUC. The UVF bombers and killers were not included in the long lists of people to be interned. It was a disaster in every way, in its execution and its intention of hoodwinking the world that the violence was traceable to the one side only. Old-time Republicans were scooped up while the more active IRA men escaped. Horror stories abounded of brutality by the army, men blindfolded and taken in helicopters where they were told they would be thrown out in mid-air, others forced to run at the double in their bare feet over glass and cinders, and torture and beatings in the barracks before they were lodged in a prison ship in Belfast harbour or in Crumlin Road Prison. At Stormont the Unionist pressure for strong measures by the British Army resulted in January 1972 in the infamy of Bloody Sunday in Derry. This was the end. Shortly afterwards came the suspension of the Stormont Parliament.

I was present at Stormont when huge crowds gathered to hear Faulkner's impassioned address from the balcony, flanked by his rival, Bill Craig and others. It was the end of an era. The crowds could not believe that Heath had already decided that enough was enough and that it must now be Direct Rule from Westminster. Faulkner could not believe it either and accused the British Premier of establishing an 'Ulster Coconut Colony'. For me history had come full circle. I had been there at the opening of Stormont and here I was forty years later witnessing its dissolution.

From that day on 'Ulster' became in truth a Colony. The agreeable former Tory Chief Whip, William Whitelaw was installed at Stormont Castle and for want of a more appropriate title, we dubbed him 'Supremo'. This, in fact, was what he was becoming, with his high-powered staff, some borrowed from the Foreign Office. Now we had a one-man Government, or Colonial Governor. Willie Whitelaw had a style of his own. A man of obvious good intentions with a friendly, big-hearted manner, he typified the best type of Englishman, 'a decent chap who wanted to treat everybody decently'. At a press luncheon at Stormont when I was Chairman of the Stormont Lobby, he seemed pleased when I likened him to the 'white man in the jungle trying to bring peace to the warring tribes.' Consensus was his objective and his experienced Foreign Office men, in best cloak and dagger style, saw everyone concerned – politicians, IRA guerrillas and Paisleyites, in all kinds of secret hide-outs. In Britain's colonial history they had plenty of precedents for such secret negotiations. They had only to look up the files back in Whitehall for guidance. Rumours abounded and Paisley began his familiar line about a 'sell-out'. At the Darlington Conference, Faulkner came round to the idea of a Partnership Government and later at Sunningdale broad agreement was found for a new beginning in the North.

During all this time interest in the North in newspapers, television and radio had built up to a crescendo and Belfast became a Mecca for journalists. One American hot-foot from the horrors of the Vietnam War, arriving in the middle of the bombing and violence on the streets of Belfast, said he felt more afraid for his personal safety here than in Saigon. They came from the BBC, ITN, Radio Telefis Eireann, the US and Canadian networks, New York Times, Time Magazine, Newsweek, Le Monde, Paris Match and scores of Continental news organisations.

I had already made a number of appearances on UTV's 'Behind The Headlines' and the BBC's 'Political Panels' and began to enjoy a modest popularity as a hard-hitting broadcaster with a long experience of the local political scene. Once or twice I smiled grimly when I heard that certain local public figures had backed out when they were told that I would be among the journalistic inquisitors on a few of the panels. I took this as a back-handed compliment. It was less enjoyable to be jeered at outside the City Hall after an election count by some of those who did not appreciate my efforts on the box.

At one crisis press interview at Stormont after hundreds of Catholics had been burned out of their homes, I interrupted a Government Minister to ask why no provision whatever had been made at that time to find accommodation for these unfortunate people. There was an awkward pause and clearly the Ministers were taken aback by this sudden thrust. The spokesman, I think it was Brian Faulkner, stumbled and finally promised that something would be done but claimed that the question was 'unfair'. I did not realise that this interview had been televised live that morning until I arrived back at my office. On the way there from the car-park, I was amazed and not a little pleased, when all sorts of men and women stopped me in my tracks to thank me for my action! I was moved too when I got home at lunch-time to find a telegram there from a homeless family congratulating me for my humble efforts 'on behalf of us and the rest of the homeless people'. Later, after a similar news conference, Prime Minister Chichester Clark told me that he had 'expected a block-buster' from me but it never came. I must have been in a lenient mood!

Perhaps the most satisfying encounter I ever experienced was on a UTV Journalists Panel to question Enoch Powell about his quest for a Northern Ireland seat in the British Commons. This was the time when Enoch was known as the 'Wolverhampton Wanderer' after his row with the Tory Party over his racist speeches. Enoch had the reputation of eating interviewers alive so I did some homework and found that in all his previous years as a Minister and MP at Westminster he had not uttered a word about Northern Ireland. I threw this at him and accused him of touting for a Unionist seat and asked by what right he had come over to intervene in Northern Ireland affairs. Clearly this touched Enoch on the raw and he became quite heated and made the mistake of retorting what right I had 'coming up from Dublin' or words to that effect! As a native of the North, this struck me, and many other people, as rich.

Returning home that night I received a quick reaction. Several TV viewers rang to say how much they enjoyed my joust with the prickly Mr Powell and one lady said she had watched him closely during the encounter and to her mind he had aged by a couple of years before it was over! However, it clearly did him no harm for his search for a seat was successful. The maverick M.P. became the unlikely representative of the South Down constituency, turning up at intervals to lecture the local Unionists in their Orange Halls on the latest Foreign Office 'plot' to wrest Ulster and the Mountains of Mourne from the cherished 'Union'.

Another face-to-face encounter which sticks out in my memory was with Bill Craig when he was taking the salute, Fascist-style, at weekly parades of marching Vanguard followers. Craig had perpetrated a foolish speech to the Right-wing Tory Monday Club in London and I likened his 'shoot to kill' remarks with 'Sharpeville' which prompted him to accuse me of using 'picturesque language'. This was hardly an answer. The trouble with Craig was that he was so soft-spoken that it was difficult to believe that in the presence of a crowd he could use such chilling words of incitement. Afterwards he could be so pleasant over a drink in the television station's Reception Room that you wondered whether he and others of that ilk had a problem of dual personality, the Jekyll and Hyde syndrome.

Ian Paisley was the same. His technique was to try and shout you down and he was well equipped with a guldering voice to do it. It was hopeless trying to get in a supplementary question. You were drowned out in long rambling answers until the red light showed that the time was up. The most I could get out of him after one such interview was, 'Jimmy, you and I will never agree'. Afterwards the mask of the tough politician would drop and he would become the genial Minister in the dog-collar as he consumed UTV's offering of a large plate of ham sandwiches, specially prepared for his benefit.

Of the many alarming experiences I encountered back in Belfast, perhaps the most testing was the afternoon when Paisley's forces armed with sticks, cudgels and other weapons took over in the narrow streets of Armagh to prevent a legal Civil Rights march. The press and television men were in bad odour with the Paisleyites at the time because of the show-up they were getting so when a group of media men came to close quarters with them there were hostile shouts. A particularly villainous-looking aide of Mr Paisley called

John McKeague came forward with a deadly-looking cudgel and warned us that he could not be responsible for what might happen if we did not clear off.

The police had meantime hemmed us in with the demonstrators by placing barricades across our only line of retreat at the end of the street. A Dublin Herald man was told by a stony-faced RUC man that if he attempted to mount the barrier in the event of the mob attacking the press, he would be 'emptied back on his effing head'. The Charlemont Arms Hotel mid-way down the street seemed the only place of refuge for the press as the men with the cudgels jostled us and looked itching to use their weapons as we crowded inside. The proprietors looked worried at this invasion and promptly bolted and barred the front door. We were told there could be no bolt-hole through the back so we remained under siege for a couple of hours until darkness fell. Meantime on the Armagh Mall a visiting television cameraman who had become isolated from the rest was badly beaten up and had his camera and equipment smashed.

How Paisley was able to checkmate the police plans to 'protect' the Civil Rights march on that day was never explained. But through time it became apparent that there was a 'mole' in police headquarters who kept him apprised of confidential police arrangements.

The Stormont grounds which through the years had become sacrosanct against the intrusion of unruly elements were no longer safe when the loyalist dissidents took to the streets. The gates which used to be locked and guarded against protesting unemployed marchers were thrown open to the mobs of protesting Loyalists although the word 'loyalist' had meantime lost all sense of meaning as the Union Jack was jettisoned for the Ulster flag, the emblem some felt would eventually become the flag of UDI, for an Independent Ulster, cocking a snoot at Westminster. They surged through and into the holy-of-holies, the main hall and lobbies of the Parliament itself. From the Press Gallery you could glimpse the ring-leaders of the mobsters outside the hallowed precincts at the entrance to the Commons Chamber itself. Anarchy seemed just around the corner.

Newspapermen moving around in the grounds covering these crowd scenes did so at their own peril. A respected reporter from the Observer was attacked one afternoon near the Stormont steps as he moved through an excitable crowd shouting slogans and waving Union flags. Why was he singled out? Some of the demonstrators thought this Englishman had 'insulted the flag' as he passed. His explanation afterwards was that he had been chewing a chocolate bar and spat out a nut!

If the crowds who besieged Stormont were unruly they could hardly be blamed considering the example they were given by so-called political leaders inside the Parliament itself. An eccentric professor wearing an African shawl presented to him in Ghana, dancing on the table of the House and actually spitting in the face of Brian Faulkner shouting 'Lundy', and Paisley and his fellow-members being ejected bodily, roaring and bawling, stands out in my mind as one of the rowdiest scenes I have ever witnessed in any parliament. As burly policemen lifted Paisley from his seat one of his henchmen, spotting the rest of us leaning over the Press Gallery in amazement, pointed in my direction and to my embarrassment roared, 'Throw rebel Kelly out too!' When he himself was being bundled out, Paisley shouted at the police, 'Leave that man alone. He has a heart condition'!

The Irish Times which at that time prided itself as a 'paper of record' reported the whole rumpus ad lib including the 'rebel' jibe which I had used my discretion to exclude from my report. So I was not denied my small mention in what could be a footnote to history!

There were times during the turmoil of the '70s in Belfast against the background of riots, bloodshed and terror when you felt that what civilisation we had left was collapsing around our ears and that all moderate opinion and decency was being swept aside by evil forces of death, destruction and horror. A friend of ours, a gentle lady, a widow who lived with her two spinster sisters in North Belfast, ordered out of their home by a howling Orange mob during one night of terror in the district, told me about her feelings as they fled without even a change of clothes to shelter in a welfare home with other homeless refugees. This innocent victim, whose husband, an Irish war-time pilot officer, lost his life in the suicide mission of the frail Swordfish aircarft sent out from the North of Scotland against the German battleshslps heading for Norway, was left with a young son and returned to the family home in Belfast. She wrote to me telling me that all through that night of fear she could not get out of her mind WB Yeats's poem 'The Second Coming'. The words seemed uncannily appropriate to the inferno of Belfast at that moment.

> 'Things fall apart; the centre cannot hold.
> Mere anarchy is loosed upon the world,
> The blood-dimmed tide is loosed and everywhere
> The ceremony of innocence is drowned;
> The best lack all conviction, while the worst,
> Are full of passionate intensity.'

The poem which ended with the doom-laden words: 'And what rough beast, its hour come round at last, Slouches towards Bethlehem to be born' was written fifty years before but for our friends, like many others who have quoted it since, it could have been written when the dogs of war were unleashed in Belfast.

HOPE DEFERRED

SICKENED BY THE the violence and hate-mongering of years without hope the public in Northern Ireland were at first astonished and then delighted when William Whitelaw, that political wizard, announced on 21 November, 1973 after weeks of intense negotiations with the political parties that agreement had been reached on a power sharing 'Community Government' for the North. A few weeks later the British Government, led by Ted Heath, convened the Sunningdale Conference to be attended by the government of the Republic and elected representatives of Northern Ireland at which it was hoped to hammer out a settlement. Hopes were high as those two opposites, Faulkner, the young hard-line Unionist, and Gerry Fitt, SDLP leader, prepared to bury the hatchet in an amazing turn-around.

I realised that this could possibly be one of the most historic confrontations since the days of the Irish Treaty and when invited by my editor, Aidan Pender, to go to Sunningdale with our Dublin political correspondent, Chris Glennon, I accepted this as a major challenge. I knew that the negotiations would be top-secret and that it would be difficult to probe what was happening until the agreed communique, if any, was issued. I had made no secret of my admiration for the leaders of the SDLP, men of outstanding ability, many of whom had sacrificed lucrative posts in other fields to devote their time, and even risk their lives, in the service of the Northern minority and this was to stand me in good stead. Before flying to London a good friend in the delegation showed me, in the utmost secrecy, the draft documentation for the negotiations. The meeting was a hurried one and I had just time to take a quick shorthand note of the salient points. The result was that I went to Sunningdale probably better informed than most in the small army of media men detailed to cover this major attempt to bring down the curtain on the Northern conflict.

The politicians at the Berkshire location were separated from the press who were accommodated in a compound cut off from contact by barbed wire and police with guard-dogs from the Thames Valley constabulary. My hidden 'confidante' told me to telephone him close to the end of the conference but, on no account, to use my own name. 'Just tell them you are a friend of mine', he said. 'What name will I use?' I asked. He thought for a moment and then suggested the name 'McGrory', adding 'My father was a great admirer of Glasgow Celtic and they had a great star called McGrory. They even wrote songs about Paddy McGrory, renowned in song and story. If you use that name then I will contact you.' At the press compound the hours of waiting for releases were put in either playing poker or snooker in a relaxed club-like atmosphere. We knew that something big was on the way when we heard the unmistakeable sound of a helicopter over the roof-top and learned that it was Ted Heath, the British Prime Minister, in person, coming in, as it was reported, to give the conference a 'gee-up'. On the Saturday afternoon I was engaged in a heavy poker school when Michael McGarry appeared to tell me that I was wanted on the telephone. Earlier I had phoned my man at the negotiations. A civil servant with a clipped accent had answered, 'Yes Mr McGrory, I will get him to contact you later. He is very busy at the moment.'

The message I received was an exciting one. All the points detailed in the document I had copied had been agreed and just one remained to be hammered out but it was expected that this too would be agreed inside 24 hours. I phoned the Sunday Independent immediately with what I felt would make front-page news but alas, Hector Legge was no longer there, having retired, and this major break-through in Anglo-Irish relations was amazingly consigned to an inside page! However someone in External Affairs in Dublin spotted the story in an early edition and telexed back to the Irish delgation. There was some fuss about a 'leakage' and poor Michael McGarry laughed when someone told him that he was suspected! The previous night there had been a hilarious session at 10 Downing Street, at the invitation of Ted Heath, with the delegations participating in a night of Irish songs and entertainment. This had leaked out and apparently Brian Faulkner was just a little perturbed about the reaction among sober-sided Unionists in Belfast. He had blamed the Dublin secretariat and hence the dismay at this even more serious 'leakage'.

However what really amused me when I put down the phone was the sight of a number of my unfortunate colleagues standing before a television set taking down what must have been a personal 'think-piece' by Martin Bell in the BBC Six O'Clock News, suggesting a possible break-down or snag in the negotiations. When I returned to the poker table the man who had taken my seat was glad to allow me to take over again, confessing that since I had gone he had lost a packet. 'The cards were terrible', he groaned. The luck changed. I won £35 by dinner-time. That was clearly my lucky day.

It was late on Sunday evening when the conference terminated with a long agreed communique giving the exciting news of an Anglo-Irish Agreement for a future power-sharing administration in the North, with a two-tier Council of Ireland legitimising the Northern minority's aspirations for a United Ireland. All the leading figures, Fitt, Hume, Currie, Faulkner, Heath and Cosgrave smiled under the blazing white lights of the television cameras and we felt a great turning point in history had been reached. I recall Cosgrave's words,

'There are no winners and no losers'. He said, 'All of us who live today on the island of Ireland have inherited an immensely difficult and complex problem which has brought suffering and death to innocent men and women in each generation. It is a problem which no previous generation in our history – whatever else may have been achieved – was able to resolve. The way is open to us who live in Ireland at this particular time to resolve it.'

These were brave words and we all felt Heath had scored a major triumph by utilising the skill which had been brought to bear on so many difficult colonial problems around the world to bring a ray of sunshine into the darkening scene in Northern Ireland. The Sunningdale Agreement was a brilliant attempt to solve the seemingly insoluble. We all realized that but later we wondered if perhaps it was too soon. All the lessons had not been learned by December 1973.

Back in Belfast to a new uproar at Stormont so bad that the Speaker adjourned the Assembly inside two minutes. It soon became evident that the Sunningdale Agreement was in for a rough passage with the extremists on all sides united once again like baying wolves to tear the hopes of peace at last to ribbons. The new Executive of six Protestants and five Catholics took office on 1 January, 1974 amidst a chorus of goodwill and offers of help from Europe and America and for a time the new Ministers impressed everyone, except the begrudgers and malcontents, with their fresh approach to the problems facing them. Higher civil servants confessed privately that they were impressed with the new intake from the Opposition benches and it seemed that a wind of change was blowing through the fusty atmosphere of the 'Protestant Parliament for a Protestant people' at long last. Some said the SDLP men in the power-sharing Cabinet were, if anything, 'too good', arousing jealousy and envy with their enthusiastic reception in the press at home and abroad. Fitt, Hume and Currie seemed to be monopolising the headlines and one could hear murmurs that they were 'running the show'. Paisley and the rump of the old Unionist Party, the splintered forces of bigotry and stupidity, joined forces in a coalition which had only one thing in common – a blind and insensate hatred of Catholics attaining positions of influence in their own ommunity.

The shadowy Council of Ireland was seized on to stir up the mobs. All the old war-cries of 'Sell-Out', 'Betrayal' and 'Lundies' were revived by this cabal of disgruntled and bitter 'left-overs' from the old regime, West and Craig, and their new-found mouthpiece, Ian Paisley. They were less concerned with the Council of Ireland than the deep down primitive old instinct, born and bred and fostered in their Orange lodges to 'Keep the Mickies out'. They saw the Mickies not only 'in' but making a good job of it.

Meantime Harold Wilson was back at 10 Downing Street and had appointed Welsh miner's son, Merlyn Rees, a school-master, as Secretary of State for the North. He came in with the right credentials, having been active for a considerable time on the fringe of the situation in Belfast and Dublin as an interested MP. I interviewed him in his office in London and was impressed by his claim to have studied the whole history of the Irish problem. But first impressions are misleading. In office he lacked resolution and seemed at times overwhelmed with the complexity of the job. He presented the appearance of a weak man, a bumbler under the thumb of a cynical bland Prime Minister at Number 10.

When the loyalist conspiracy to subvert the will of Westminster reached a climax, Edward Heath was interviewed as he left for a trip to China and was asked what he would do in such circumstances. He replied curtly that Labour was now in power. 'They are the government. It is up to them to rule.'

But back in Belfast while the Executive waited for action to back them, all they got were ineffectual gestures. Anarchy had been let loose and the British Army seemed too paralysed to stop the blatant mass intimidation. Their ineffective role has never been explained. Were the military chiefs re-enacting the posture of the Curragh

Mutiny all over again or were they 'standing-to' on orders from London? A veil has been drawn over that quesion.

Once again it was 'Cry Havoc' as the dogs of war were let slip. Ignoring Secretary of State Merlyn Rees, wringing his hands and shaking his head in despair, Faulkner, Fitt and Napier of the Alliance Party flew to meet Wilson who was resting on the Scilly Isles. He had already decided he was not going to risk his neck in a confrontation with the Army bosses over the Stormont Executive, and in any case he, who had boasted that he could settle the Irish problem, looked with lack lustre eyes on Ted Heath's Sunningdale creation. Faulkner and the Unionists in the Executive could get no support, not even from the panicking Protestant middle-class business interests or Churchmen, so they resigned. That brought about its collapse.

The loyalist politicians who had remained cautiously in the wings fearing that the entire Ulster Workers' Council would be arrested suddenly appeared on the 'Strike' platforms to join in the rejoicing at this pyrrhic victory and claim part of the credit for bringing about another tragic political vacuum. The loyalist workers and farmers, who stood to gain more than the politicians from the new era of stability which had just appeared on the horizon, cheered with the rest. It seemed to me a classic case of cutting your own throat.

Direct Rule was re-imposed. The 'Coconut Colony' was presented with a new 'Supremo' after Merlyn Rees was kicked upstairs to become Home Secretary. The new incumbent, a bumptious little man named Roy Mason, from the mining town of Barnsley, arrived at the steps of Stormont Castle where the snarling animals in stone accord a typical 'Ulster' welcome to strangers. The solemn farce of the Constitutional Convention and its 'No Surrender' Majority Report had ended up in the Westminster waste-basket. Its sole purpose clearly was to give Wilson a breather. The classic Westminster ploy for doing nothing was always to set up a Royal Commission or a Constitutional Convention or some such time-consuming body. An 'Ulster UDI' was floated again and one of Paisley's collaborators dared to hint at Soviet assistance for a six-county Cuba. Hare-brained ideas were never lacking among the new brand of politicians who rose and sank into the ground like mushrooms.

Mason scored his one success. Paisley's attempt to stage another rebellion, this time against 'the Mother of Parliament's, on foot of his demand for a return to 'majority rule' was crushed with the aid of the police and the army, not to mention the reluctance of the power workers to be used again as dupes for political purposes. The 'Putsch' was an inglorious flop. One wondered if the same resolution had been shown at the top in defence of the Sunningdale Agreement would history not have taken a more hopeful turn.

When Wilson decided to slip out and hand over the burden of governing with only a tiny majority to Jim Callaghan, he forgot about his ambition to clear up the mess in Anglo-Irish relations. I recalled my brief meeting with him during a National Union of Journalists Dinner in Manchester some years before. As he turned to go after a few pleasantries he nudged me and remarked with a wink, 'Don't forget Roger Casement'. Evidently his decision to return the bones of Roger Casement from his prison grave to Dublin had loomed large in his mind as a big break-through in Anglo-Irish relations! Against the horrors of what was to follow it was in retrospect a pitifully inadequate gesture.

The misplaced faith in a Labour government bestirring itself to tackle the problem, not the 'Irish' problem but the 'British' problem of the ramshackle statelet Lloyd George had carved out of an ancient province across the Irish Sea, finally died in the hearts of even the most dedicated Irish socialists. The bizarre back-stairs intrigues which Michael Foot conducted with Enoch Powell and the Ulster Unionists to secure their votes in a Parliamentary show-down was the last straw. The 'deal' to increase the 12 'Ulster' seats to 17 seemed, back in Belfast, to be the limit in treachery and many people recalled the words of Foot's hero, Nye Bevan, when he described the 'Ulster' anti-Labour group of Unionists as a 'dagger' in the back of British Labour. That was in the context of another razor's edge Labour majority. Bevan's view was that sooner or later this threat would have to be 'liquidated'. He must have turned in his grave when the threat was intensified.

I remember visiting the House of Commons about this time and being greeted in the Press Gallery by a Guardian man who did his stint in Belfast during the worst days of the violence. 'Here comes Jimmy Kelly', he remarked loudly, 'a man from a far-off country, of which we know nothing!' His quotation of the words of Runciman during Hitler's rape of Czecho – Slovakia I felt was very apt.

OXFORD, BRUSSELS AND STRASBOURG

O N A HOT July day in 1976 I found myself walking up the High in Oxford with John Hume and Ruari Brugha, Fianna Fail spokesman on Northern Ireland to attend a discussion on the seemingly hopeless situation in the North. Invitations had come from Lord Longford's British-Irish Association to attend a weekend at Oxford at which all sorts of personalities from Britain and Ireland could let their hair down on the Irish situation without fear of being reported.

It was my first visit to the city of the 'dreaming spires' on the banks of the Isis and the Cherwell. The famous 'Union', scene of many famous debates and nursery of political leaders of all parties, looked disappointingly small and unpretentious. When I reached the entrance lounge I met Tom Driberg, one of the few working journalists to be elected to the Lords. He was brewing coffee and I joined him in a cup. Driberg, a 'big-wheel' in the Labour Party, laughed when I recalled his visit to Belfast away back in the Thirties as the original William Hickey columnist for the Daily Express and quoted his actual words describing his walk up the Falls Road past Frank O'Neill's Rock Bar. He remarked in the column that all the men in the Falls Road walked with their hands in their pockets 'as if fingering their gats'! He had forgotten that and was clearly pleased that I had remembered.

Inside the debating chamber under the stern gaze of a statue of Gladstone was an extraordinary gathering of politicians, historians and members of the House of Lords, drawn from all shades of opinion on both sides of the Irish Sea. Lord Longford was presiding and Merlyn Rees, within a few months of the end of his inglorious sojourn as Secretary of State for Northern Ireland, was to deliver a key-note speech. Garret Fitzgerald was sitting with his wife in the front row. It was a hot day and I noticed that he had taken his shoes off and lolled back comfortably in his stocking-soles.

Merlyn's speech was a typical muddle-headed one in which he skated over the thin ice of the failure of Wilson and himself to deal effectively with the loyalist uprising against Sunningdale and the power-sharing Executive, the best chance for a peaceful break-through in a decade. The more I listened to his evasions the more annoyed I became, especially when subsequent speakers, including Dublin TDs, seemed prepared to let him away with it. I tried to intervene but Lord Longford kept calling more politicians, none of whom appeared to know much about the situation in the North. Eventually, on a point of order, I asked the chairman if he was going to confine the discussion to politicians only as up to that point it seemed that the Oxford Union was being turned into an ante-room to Leinster House and the House of Commons. Longford took my point gracefully and ignoring the small group of economists and others who had queued up to speak, said 'As this gentleman seems to have something to say I propose to call him next.'

I don't know whether it was the inspiration or atmosphere of the celebrated Union or my abiding memory of Labour's betrayal of the Sunningdale Agreement but I had plenty to say. In fact I surprised myself for I sailed into Rees and his boss, Harold Wilson, to such effect that Rees, red-faced and angry, demanded and got permission to answer my charges of dereliction of duty. While the rest of the audience, including SDLP members, were amused, Rees kept on loudly quoting me, 'Jimmy says this' and 'Jimmy says that'. I cannot remember the gist of his heated reply except one telling phrase where he asked if I expected him 'a Welsh miner's son' to order the troops in to stop a 'workers' strike'. This was where most people would part company with Rees. This was no 'strike'. This was a deliberate conspiracy to smash the first community government in Northern Ireland's history. To call it a 'workers' strike' was a misuse of words.

I received several pats on the back for this unplanned intervention from, among others, Donal Barrington, SC, and Garret Fitzgerald who reminded me, 'He (Rees) did not answer any of your questions.' A few of the English invitees were kind enough to say that my contribution had brought the debate alive. So ended my first and, no doubt, last speech in the Oxford Union.

Out again into the hot sunshine and with Ruari Brugha we sought out a quiet pub in the High Street to cool off with a couple of glasses of iced lager. We had been accommodated in St Edmund's Hall and that night dinner was laid on in the historic dining hall with the wine running freely. One of the speakers at the dinner was monocled Christopher Ewart-Biggs who had just been named as the new British Ambassador to Dublin. He seemed an extremely odd figure and he made a rather peculiar rambling speech. To me he appeared like a Wodehouse character and I voiced this opinion. I recall Liam Hourican of Radio Telefis Eireann who sat opposite correcting me and hinting that the new man for Dublin was no fool but a very important man in the British Diplomatic Service. Looking up his record later after the poor man was killed in that appalling land mine explosion as he drove into Dublin, I could not but agree.

Sometimes when I reflected on the violent clashes that go on in Ireland over the Irish and British 'Dimensions' and the so-called 'Sovereignty' issue, I felt that we were losing sight of the over-riding importance of the 'European Dimension' and the evolving pattern of a European Community containing Britain and the two parts of Ireland.

At the height of the nightmare on the bitter streets of Belfast I joined a party of journalists who were invited to Brussels to see for ourselves the modern vibrant headquarters of the European Community – home of the much-abused bureaucrats. This temporary escape from a political mad-house was like opening a window on another world, a world in which the total irrelevance of the conflict in the North stood out like a patch of unsightly weeds in a well-kept garden.

All the people we met in Brussels wondered how we had been able to stick the horrors of the years of urban guerrilla warfare. They wondered that Ireland had not learned the lesson of the Europe of Belsen and the millions who died in Hitler's war. At the same time there was a genuine desire to help in a positive way and they saw economic development and re-construction as the key to the door of reconciliation. We flew back to Belfast but after our escape for a few days into another world it was a case of coming down to earth with a bump. Nobody wanted to talk about Brussels or Europe. While we were absent the UVF miscreants had made their murderous journey over the border to wreak vengeance on innnocent people for the crimes of the IRA The horror bombings in Dublin and Monaghan were all over the front pages.

From London Michael Lake, thanking me for my Independent special article, 'How Brussels Views The Violent North', wrote: 'I felt so sorry for you all returning from such a happy trip to what you call this "nightmare city". The Dublin bombings and the subsequent events in Belfast have gripped us all here with the deepest depression. On the other hand the spirit you all showed in Brussels is a reminder that most people in Northern Ireland clearly deplore the situation and I was myself full of admiration for the group's attitude.'

At the end of June 1976 a large group of European journalists came over to Northern Ireland to study the political and social aspects of the seven years' nightmare of terror which political intransigence had unleashed. The consensus was that the most depressing aspect of their itinerary was the meeting with some of the politicians of the North. The majority did not appear to belong to this century and yet these were the people who were throwing up road-blocks to every attempt to escape from the morass of their own creation.

At the invitation of Rev Bill Arlow of the Irish Council of Churches, I appeared on a panel of Belfast journalists to answer questions from the European journalists on the role of the media in the situation in the North. Bill Arlow was a man for whom I had a great deal of respect as a peace-maker. He had played a noble part in bringing about a short-lived truce in the North following a three-day secret meeting between leading Protestant clergymen and the Provisional IRA in Smyth's Village Hotel in Feakle, County Clare. High hopes arose at the time that something tangible would come of what amounted to indirect contacts between the British Government and the IRA but by Easter 1975 the Provos believed that no progress was being made and the violence increased steadily. The Unionists as usual were up in arms at such contacts and did their best to torpedo them.

I arrived at the Queen's University building where the seminar was held about half an hour too early. As it happened I was just in time to hear the noted Belfast hospital surgeon, Dr Bill Rutherford, one of the heroic figures behind the scenes in both the Royal Victoria and the Mater Hospitals during the conflict, giving a lecture on the price of terror on human life. It was illustrated by coloured lantern slides, so horrific that at times one had to avert one's gaze.

Dr Rutherford, a kindly avuncular figure who had spent years as a missionary in India, made a deep impression on the journalists from Europe and on me. For years I had been reporting on the bombings and other acts of violence but this quiet and unemotional lecture brought home the full shocking and sickening results of the so-called 'war'. Never in my many long years have I seen anything so horrible and so shameful. Yet this was the daily round in our

211

hospitals dealing with the obscene slaughterhouse scenes, the end result of the explosives tossed into crowded pubs or secreted in cars owned by the 'targets'.

There were gasps of horror from the journalists at the pictures of bloody stumps which had once been limbs, the torn bodies, the ripped-open chests and abdomens, the skulls split open. We found the whole thing most affecting and once the surgeon confessed that he became personally emotionally involved as one terrible picture of a mutilated young girl recalled his awful experience of having to bring her father into a mortuary for identification. In a choked voice he excused himself and said that for a terrible moment he saw the face of his own young daughter in the poor tortured face of another innocent victim, one of hundreds.

Describing this experience afterwards in my Sunday Diary I wrote: 'If there was one wish we could all have been granted at the end of a brief glimpse of violence it was that the faceless men on all sides who are ordering the dupes to go out and commit these atrocities should be shown these pictures, morning, noon and night until they finally conceded that no cause in the wide world could justify such unmitigated tragedy and misery. It was a truly revolting and shaming experience to be forced to sit there among fellow Europeans and admit that this was happening in so-called Christian Ireland AD 1976.'

In the intervening years I have had no reason to alter this conviction or this feeling of shame.

In the panel discussion afterwards it soon emerged that nearly everyone was agreed that Britain appeared to have virtually washed its hands of its responsibility for what was happening. There was that awful cynical Ministerial talk of an 'acceptable level of violence', a holding operation while waiting like Mr Micawber for something to turn up while London proceeded with its own pressing problems.

In those circumstances I resolved to throw the ball back into the

European journalists' court. I asked them collectively if now that both parts of Ireland were in the European Community, and with London in despair, did the European Community not feel some sense of responsibiity or feel the need to exercise its influence or goodwill for an attempt to end the horror and slaughter by a peaceful solution.

I reminded them that the bleached bones of thousands of Irishmen lay buried in Flanders, the Somme and elsewhere, men who had died in Europe's many wars and that therefore Europe owed Ireland something in return.

There was a long and thoughtful silence. Clearly I had made a point which I hoped would be remembered. Then two journalists answered. One suggested that when the elections for the European Parliament took place then there could well be something done about the residual 'war' in Northern Ireland. The other journalist said he came from a part of Belgium which felt it owed a lot to Ireland for it was missionaries from Ireland who had brought Christianity to that part of Europe.

Some months later I was a member of a small party of Belfast journalists invited to Strasbourg to see the European Parliament in action. This was before the election of John Hume, MEP and the appearance there of the reluctant Loyalist MEPs, John Taylor and Ian Paisley to introduce their own export version of the 'Ulster' attitude to the 'Treaty of Rome'.

Although the Assembly was that afternoon discussing some of the trouble spots of Europe I noticed that not one Irish or British voice was raised about the appalling loss of life in the unresolved situation back in Northern Ireland. It was as if the most tragic situation in Europe since the end of World War II was not happening. They sang dumb.

Later I met a few of the Southern Ireland TDs flying home from Strasbourg. I was not impressed. One of them, a real culchie, smelt strongly of whiskey and regaled me with his boasts that the expenses he was paid paid his drinking bills! I made a mental note that direct elections could not come quickly enough. Surely the electors in Ireland would eliminate such political passengers?

On the other side of the coin Ireland was well represented by its Commissioner, Dick Burke and his staff which at the time included John Hume. It was obvious that Hume was already well known and respected and I noticed that when he appeared in the Parliamentary main hall he was button-holed by Foreign Ministers and other notabilities who recognised him instantly. No doubt this could be attributed to world-wide television coverage of the many events in which Hume and the other SDLP leaders figured over the years.

DELAYING THE INEVITABLE

LOOKING BACK AFTER I had finally said 'Goodbye' to my friends in Independent Newspapers, after nearly 50 years – some kind of a record – I felt no regrets. In spite of the ups and downs it has been a great life, full of excitement and interest. Money could not buy the rich experiences you gained over an active life in journalism, the people you met, the saints and the sinners, the great and the lowly, the proud and the humble, the doors that were opened to you, the confidences gained and the friendships made. I worked with no fewer than ten editors, six on the daily paper and four on the Sunday so I know something about editors. I say 'with' and not 'under' for in the Belfast Office there was a kind of 'UDI' situation with the Northern editor given wide authority to act on his own initiative. Covering events for a national daily printed in Dublin with personal links to British and American newspapers and radio and television broadened one's outlook and scope. 'Bordermania' might be rampant in the North within the confines of the Six Counties but I never allowed the division of the country by the imaginary line drawn crazily through the green fields, rivers, lakes and villages from Carlingford Lough to Lough Foyle to shrink my all-Ireland outlook down to the miserable semi-provincialism of that British invention 'political Ulster'. I was born and spent ten years of my boyhood in an Ireland undivided and deep down, always resented the attempts to set up a false 'regional culture'. Belfast to me was an Irish city, with evidence all around of its Irishness, in the very names of the Shankill, Falls, Ormeau and Ballymacarrett in contrast with Dublin's Anglicised place names.

It amazed me that after nearly four centuries there were people who claimed in the presence of foreigners that they were not really Irish but some kind of hybrid 'Scotch-Irish'. It riled me that the awful inferiority complex of Unionism, their knuckling down to often arrogant, and frequently ignorant, English politicians rather than taking their places with heads high in an all-Ireland state, respected among the nations, should have prevented my generation and others from rising to their full stature as citizens not of an inferior, subsidised and mendicant state, but of an Ireland of which both Protestants and Catholics could be proud.

In my time I had seen at close quarters the six Prime Ministers who had presided over the counterfeit parliament at Stormont, depending for its existence on the most ignoble sentiments of religious bigotry and mean discrimination that had become a by-word throughout the world. Craigavon, Andrews, Brooke, O'Neill, Chichester-Clark and Faulkner had come and gone and left nothing behind but a sundered community of ghettoes, tribal hatreds, barbed-wire 'peace-lines' and a feeling of hopelessness, worse than any I remembered down the years. With the British troops sent over with guns, plastic bullets and helicopters to 'keep order' among the warring tribes as they used to do on the North-West Frontier, came the relays of 'Supremos' or colonial 'Pro-Consuls' and their attendant ministers to restore a semblance of order. Faulkner had likened the new regime in Stormont Castle to a 'Banana Republic' – the only difference was the colour of our skins. After Whitelaw and Heath had failed came the long procession of new boys – Pym, Rees, Mason, Atkins, Prior, Hurd, Brooke and Mayhew – bright-eyed at first and confident that with the good old spirit of British 'compromise' the local politicians would toe the line and 'share power', or what little of it remained, only to face the brick-wall of 'Not-An-Inch' and 'No Surrender', the dismal catch-cries of a dismal past.

It used to amuse me to attend the weekly lobby correspondents interview with Prior in the Conference Room at Stormont Castle and listen to the Fleet Street men parrying polite questions with the Secretary of State about a possible 'new initiative' and the intricate chess-game of his negotiations with Paisley and Molyneaux and the rest. It was all much ado about nothing and soon faded into mere snap interviews off-the-cuff on TV and radio over his shoulder at social engagements. Then came the colossal blunder of the Hunger Strike, Margaret Thatcher's unexpected fillip for the IRA, ignoring advice from Dublin, Catholic Bishops, the SDLP and all the people who knew what would result from the death-bed scenes in the Maze Prison. It was an age-old story and the new Bourbons had learned nothing from the past. As usual they listened to the wrong people.

Eventually James Prior's 'Plan' was unveiled and an Assembly was elected to Stormont. The naive idea was to get all the warring politicians together in a 'talking shop' without powers. Through time they would get to know and appreciate each other. Gradually they would be given back certain prescribed and limited powers if only they would agree. It was like feeding sugar lumps to performing bears. The trouble was that the type of people returned to the Assembly representing the Protestant majority were, if anything, more extreme and more dyed-in-the-wool than any of their predecessors. They wanted the old Stormont Parliament restored. Their simple answer was 'Majority Rule' or nothing. Wisely the SDLP decided that to appear in this Assembly was to give credence to a Mark II version of the parliament which had collapsed in disgrace.

I attended the new Assembly at Stormont occasionally and found it a depressing institution. The Assemblymen were mostly third-rate politicians about the political level of rural councillors. It was dominated by Ian Paisley and his lieutenants masquerading as an Opposition to a deflated collection of 'official' Unionists including a handful of Westminster MPs who seemed doubtful about the continued existence of this powerless Assembly. Some of these like their leader, James Molyneaux MP, the tight-lipped Chief of the Black Preceptory, put in token appearances before frequently rushing off to the London-bound afternoon plane. I felt sorry for the discomfited members of the Alliance Party who sat at the end of the semi-circular seating looking, as I wrote at the time, like visitors who had wandered accidentally into an Orange Hall.

The question in everyone's mind was where do we go from here? For years Orange politicians have been twisting the dial of the old time-machine, turning from the mundane affairs of the present and the future back across the centuries to 1690. Each Twelfth of July the Orangemen will be out marching along Royal Avenue, Belfast but as each year follows another we continue to wonder why they are marching.

Britain, meantime, was marking time in Northern Ireland, contenting itself with 'crisis management' while the situation worsened. SDLP leader, John Hume, MEP, spoke of a 'psychological withdrawal' by Britain from Northern Ireland.

Britain had other things on its mind such as the recapture of the barren Falkland Islands in the South Atlantic from Argentina, a Jingoistic prelude to a successful Thatcher election victory. Then came the disaster of the miners' strike and the spectacle of mounted police charging the miners' pickets like Peterloo all over again.

Against this background of British inertia the New Ireland Forum was born. It was the first time since 1920 that all the Irish political parties had the opportunity of coming together to spell out their views on how lasting peace and stability could be achieved in a New Ireland through the democratic process and report on possible new structures and processes through which this objective might be achieved. It was open to all parties who rejected violence but only the SDLP in the North agreed to take part, the rest of the parties there with astonishing stupidity sulked in their tents, leaving it to private individuals to put their case to the Forum. The Forum's deliberations lasted nearly twelve months.

Holidaying in Malahide, County Dublin the night before the Forum's Report was due to be launched, I called at Jury's Intercontinental Hotel in Dublin with Chris Glennon, political correspondent of the Irish Independent and there met John Hume who was generally believed to have master-minded the whole idea of the Forum, having often complained of the absence of any consensus by the Irish democratic parties on the problem of the North. When I congratulated him on his remarkable achievement of having for the first time in more than sixty years inspired this attempt to formulate a constructive approach to the New Ireland we all dreamed about, John suggested that this was an opportunity I should not miss as a journalist. Brushing aside my objections that I was now retired and therefore out of the swim, he said: You were present at the opening of the Stormont Parliament. You were also there at the closing of that Parliament. So it's only right that you should be present at the Forum tomorrow.'

So it was that the following afternoon I presented myself at Dublin Castle and met another old friend, Ted Smyth, promoted to the Foreign Affairs headquarters in Dublin after his successful sojourn at the Irish Consulate office in New York. Ted, who had been seconded to take charge of the media arrangements for this historic Forum, was surrounded by international press, television and radio men all clamouring for tickets. He had already arranged a front row seat for me in the gilded St Patrick Hall facing the party leaders. It was my first visit to this palatial hall with its wall of huge mirrors and hanging banners of the Knights of the Most Illustrious Order of St Patrick. The place was packed with a distinguished company of diplomats, ministers, TDs, Senators and a galaxy of 300 newsmen, television and radio representatives from all over the world.

Five-minute speeches were allowed by the leaders as the television cameras whirred under the arc lights. The Taoiseach, Dr Garrett Fitzgerald, said the report was an 'agenda for possible action'. Mr Charles Haughey, Opposition Leader, said it was an 'agreed basis on which peace and stability can be built'. Mr Dick Spring, Labour Leader, said the Report provided 'an element of hope'. John Hume, who had so often looked out on the agony of the North from Derry's embattled Bogside, said, 'This is an extraordinary day in the history of our island. It marks the culmination of an unique enterprise ... Things cannot be the same again.'

Just before the party leaders spoke a Radio Telefis Eireann producer took me by surprise by asking if I would hurry down afterwards to another room where John Bowman would like to interview me on my impressions of the Forum. I agreed and later found myself under the glare of the television lights in front of a huge assembly of press and media men waiting to grill the leaders in turn about their views. I recognised several of my colleagues who must have wondered what I was doing there. But there was no time for explanations for here was John Bowman introducing me to the viewers all over Ireland as the 'distinguished' ex-Political Editor of Independent Newspapers. They say 'distinguished' when your hair turns to silver. I have forgotten what I said about my impressions of this historic occasion but recall that I ended by telling Britain that it was now up to them to give a positive response to such an important document. The *Indo* headline next day was 'Up to you Maggie'. Meantime back at our holiday flat in Malahide my wife, just back from a hair appointment, switched on the television to see me giving forth, 'filling the screen', as she unkindly put it, with my burly six foot two figure. The world is full of surprises.

Unfortunately the rest of the press conference did not go so smoothly. Desmond Rushe in his descriptive piece in the Independent the next day described the press conference as a 'tactical blunder of considerable dimensions'. The tone of some of the questions became quite nasty as each of the leaders was questioned in turn without knowing what the others had said. I agreed with Desmond that they should have left the Report to stand on its own feet and speak for itself.

It was a blunder that was repeated in the Fitzgerald-Thatcher Summit at Chequers the following November when Mrs Thatcher's 'Out, out, out' to the Unity, Federation and Confederation, and Joint Authority suggestions for a New Ireland appeared to pour ice-cold water on the Summit's Agreed Communique, leaving Dr Fitzgerald's separate press conference under a cloud of ambiguity.

In recent years it has always seemed odd to me that politicians should go to such great lengths to hold their private meetings and 'Summits' in such secrecy and then blow it all under skilled cross-examination at the press conferences afterwards. The higher civil servants who spend so much time producing the bland communiques or official statements after such gatherings must squirm and sweat as they listen to their masters afterwards undoing all the months of diplomacy and negotiation in their desperate efforts to justify themselves – often along party lines – with off-the-cuff replies in necessarily brief television interviews. For every one politician who can handle a television interview and impress, there are five who emerge as shifty-eyed, bumbling or ill-at-ease. They should exercise self-restraint and keep clear of the x-ray eyes of TV but such is the fascination of the 'Box' that they keep coming back for more.

Before the Chequers meeting I was asked by Jim Fitzpatrick, managing editor of the Irish News to write a special article on the prospects for yet another exercise in Summitry. I wrote that each time a new Anglo-Irish meeting was announced I experienced a strange feeling of deja vu. The Summit had been delayed till November which Addison once described as 'the gloomy month when the people of England hang and drown themselves'. There were optimists like Tony Benn who prophesied that Northern Ireland might be ripe for the fade-out round about the time that those other outposts, relics of an Imperial past, Hong Kong, Singapore and Gibraltar gave up the ghost. But I struck a note of caution. What about the kelpers and sheep farmers of the barren Falklands where Lord Carrington's plans for a diplomatic retreat had been spoiled by the precipitate action of an Argentine military dictator?

The Unionists had extracted great comfort from the fact that monetarist and all as she was, Mrs Thatcher was now prepared to pour millions down the drain in the Falklands and that Carrington, whom they suspected of being fed-up with the dreary steeples of 'Ulster', had been allowed to go from the Foreign Office. For the moment 'Ulster' and the millions spent on its upkeep was safe. The fears that the Tories might be tempted to go along with the Forum Report were lifted and there was a new note of confidence from the Unionist leadership. At the back of my mind was the question which I often pondered over the years from the days of Churchill's war-time blandishments to Dev – in the last analysis do the politicians alone really decide such grave matters as the future of the island of Ireland? Where does the real power lie in such vital issues? Knowing what I did about the back-door hints, winks and nudges at Westminster, I wondered whether the Unionists had got the message via the corridors of power, NATO and the Pentagon, or perhaps from Enoch Powell, that 'Ulster' will be OK so long as the military chiefs advert to what they call the 'Iceland Gap' in the Atlantic Defences and the Republic asserts its ill-defined neutrality. Defence was not even mentioned in the Forum deliberations for a New Ireland – 'too sensitive an issue' I was told. But with the Irish Sea rumoured to be patrolled by unidentified nuclear submarines, regularly tearing fishermen's nets to ribbons, one wondered what is really happening and when the implications of Ireland's role in global strategy, discussed in secret, unfolds in the open. The Unionists wonder too, as the Cold War ends and the Iron Curtain in Europe collapses, they see their trump card disappearing at last.

Craigavon, gazing out of the window of Stormont Castle away back in 1937, confided his innermost belief that a United Ireland was bound to come eventually. The remark came out of the blue to G C Duggan, CB, OBE, LLD, former Principal Assistant Secretary in the Stormont Ministry of Finance. Duggan, who had come North from the old Dublin Castle regime and took a sardonic view of his new masters, must have been amused at the furore which his quotation of Craigavon's private opinion created when he reported it in a series of articles entitled 'Northern Ireland – Success or Failure?' published by the Irish Times in 1950. Duggan had retired by that time and was living in the South. Inevitably he was accused of 'biting the hand that fed him' and a later senior Stormont civil servant, Dr John Oliver, CB, in his book *Working At Stormont* claimed that Duggan had committed an 'egregious error' for revealing what was said in a 'totally privileged and confidential setting'. He added in a rather hoity-toity tone: 'As the subject was the extremely sensitive one of the border and the Prime Minister's views on its permanence or otherwise, few officials or ministers anywhere in the British parliamentary system would agree, even in the much more permissive climate of today, that Duggan was right to record it.' Fortunately Duggan disregarded the sensitivities of the Unionist mentality in his decision to uncover this interesting foot-note to history.

Bob Fisk who has done a remarkably able job of penetrating the fog of propaganda surrounding Anglo-Irish relations in his book *In Time Of War*, quotes an earlier view of Craigavon as given to Michael Collins in 1922. He told him that 'for the present an all-Ireland Parliament was out of the question, possibly in the years to come – 10, 20, or 50 years – Ulster might be tempted to join with the South.' In the context of Churchill's war-time offers to Mr de Valera, Fisk quotes Lord Brookeborough as saying, 'In one deal, at a moment of crisis in the death struggle, Northern Ireland could have been sacrificed. I had the awful feeling that had we refused, we would have been blamed for whatever disasters ensued – thank goodness it did not arise.'

Oddly enough my experience has been, in talking to Unionists off the record over the years, that most of them agree that, sooner or later, a United Ireland must become a reality. Their aim has been to put off that day as long as possible and hence what is known as the siege mentality. Mrs Thatcher's conversion from 'Out, out, out' to the Anglo-Irish Agreement signed at Hillsborough, was a shock. They are deeply suspicious of the British Foreign Office's hidden agenda to tidy up Britain's expensive involvement in the Six Counties, now that the barriers are coming down in Europe. The tragedy is that few, if any, Unionist politicians are prepared to take the risk of following the advice of a leading Protestant churchman who argued, quite reasonably, that as a United Ireland was inevitable in the long run, the Protestant population should be bending their energies to obtaining the best possible deal against the day when they would become a declining minority in an All-Ireland state.

Years ago, Sean Lemass prophesied that the Irish border would 'wither away'. That was when Britain and the Republic entered the European Community and wider horizons opened before us. Taking the long view, the upsurge of violence which followed the resistance to the Civil Rights movement in the North, if anything, merely delayed the inevitable.

If violence is the result of the failure of politics, where did they go wrong? Will a younger and newer generation, sick of the image 'To hell with the future and live in the past', sweep aside the turmoil of these years and demand a better life in a new Ireland, an Ireland in which the abilities and genius of the two communities is harnessed to produce a golden age of peace and prosperity such as we have never known?

A young man's vision or an old man's dream?

EPILOGUE

I T IS DARKEST before the dawn. Certainly that was a dark period when things looked hopeless. There had been the futility of the talks about talks and the meetings at Stormont between the political parties eventually ending in mutual recriminations, leaving the way open for the violent men on both sides to go on with the killing, tit-for-tat, the bombs on the 'mainland', and the wanton destruction of our own small towns and villages. Soon the loyalists of the UVF/UFF were killing more innocent people than the IRA. It was a stalemate. Violence had proved futile. If anything, the situation had worsened.

How to bring the insanity to an end? That was the great question. In the surrounding gloom there were suddenly gleams of light from afar off. Pope John Paul II had dared to return to his native Poland where the Communist regime was tottering.

Gorbachev, the man from nowhere, had appeared as a beacon light of an amazing change in Soviet Russia. The Berlin Wall was torn down and the Iron Curtain disappeared as the Communist bloc collapsed. The strategy of the Atlantic defences and NATO's secret documentation about the 'Icelandic Gap' was torn up overnight. Soon British Secretaries of State, Brooke and Mayhew, were pointing the lesson to the politicians of Northern Ireland. The IRA's 'Brits

Out' campaign was answered in an unexpected declaration that the British government had no longer any political, strategic or economic interest in remaining in the Six Counties if a majority of the population were to indicate that it was time to go by a democratic vote. The Irish border, the political bone of contention for 50 years, started to wither away as Sean Lemass had forecast. On 1 January 1993 the Customs border disappeared overnight. The change came unheralded and unsung as the European Community's Single Market came into effect throughout Europe. 'Anything to declare?' was a thing of the past and only the ramshackle British Army checkpoints remained along the invisible line as a temporary irritant until they too would go. Faltering British politicians and despairing commentators took refuge in the stupid comment 'The Irish problem is insoluble' but other insoluble problems were being solved elsewhere in the world, in the Middle East and South Africa. The input more often than not was coming from the US rather than Great Britain. In London they held up their hands in horror at the suggestion by the Clinton administration that an American 'Peace Envoy' such as ex-President Jimmy Carter might help to break the log-jam. But behind the scenes things were beginning to happen. The SDLP leader, John Hume, in private conversation with Sinn Fein President, Gerry Adams, brought his formidable knowledge of the shape of things to come in Europe to bear in the debate with the burgeoning political awakening in the Republican movement. Secret talks had also taken place between British civil servants and Republican spokesmen but they ended suddenly. When the Hume-Adams Accord, pointing the way to peace, was presented to the Irish and British governments there was a confused reaction at first by some of the politicians. The Unionists as usual were hostile and sniffed a conspiracy by what they labelled the 'Pan-Nationalist Front'. But the public reaction was more far-seeing. After 25 years there was war-weariness on all sides. By Christmas 1993 the two governments went public with the Downing Street Declaration which the SDLP

Deputy Leader, Seamus Mallon, said contained not a whisker of difference from the Hume-Adams Accord. John Hume's comment was that the Declaration removed any possibility of justification for the continuance of violence. We thought the end was in sight very quickly. But a frustrating eight months elapsed before the reply we hoped and prayed for came from the IRA, with the killing and outrages continuing on both sides, an obscenity against which we gritted our teeth. On Wednesday 31 August 1994 the IRA announced an unconditional ceasefire beginning at midnight. After 3,168 deaths and 25 years of terror the nightmare was over, or so it seemed until the loyalist killers announced that their copy-cat campaign would go on irrespective. The IRA statement said:

> Recognising the potential of the current situation and in order to enhance the democratic peace process the IRA will call a ceasefire from midnight, Wednesday, August 31. It will be a complete cessation of military operations and all units have been instructed accordingly. Our struggle has seen many gains and advances made by Nationalists for the democratic position. We believe we are entering a new situation, a new opportunity and we note that the Downing Street Declaration is not a solution nor was it presented as such by its authors. Solution will only be found as a result of inclusive negotiations. Others, not least the British government, have a duty to face up to their responsibilities. In our desire to significantly contribute to the creation of a climate which will encourage this we urge everybody to approach this new situation with energy, determination and patience.

The announcement made worldwide headlines and brought representatives of the media from as far apart as Japan and Finland to Belfast and Dublin. On the stroke of midnight my phone rang. It was my married daughter, Mrs Eileen McCrory, a teacher in Perth, Western Australia, preparing for the morning drive to her class in a local grammar school. 'Is it really true?' she asked. I assured her that it was but told her to keep her fingers crossed for it soon became clear that there were suspicious elements prepared to pour cold water on the prospects for peace. John Major at 10 Downing Street was

227

at first ready to join Taoiseach Albert Reynolds in welcoming the 'best news for years' but back in Belfast the Unionist and Paisleyite 'No men' had started to quibble. Did 'complete' mean 'permanent'? It was a good question from their point of view. There was no answer. Who could answer for future generations and say forever and forever. But it was good tactics for delaying the changes which everyone knew had to come, changes which those used to top-dog domination for more than half a century did not relish. The Tory party, beset by its internal squabbling over its role in the new Europe, took up the cry and the silly game of semantics and dilly-dally proceeded, postponing the inevitable recognition of Sinn Fein for the long delayed round table negotations between all the parties involved seeking the way forward in an agreed Ireland in Europe from which the spectre of the gun and the bomb had been banished at last. Nearly nine years had elapsed since the loyalists had erupted violently against the signing of the Anglo-Irish Agreement by Mrs Thatcher, the British Prime Minister, and the Irish Taoiseach, Garrett Fitzgerald, at Hillsborough on 15 November 1985. The explosion of resentment against what was an echo of the Sunningdale Agreement of 1973, giving the Republic an input into the affairs of the North through an integrated conference which was really nothing more than a foot-in-the-door for the 40% Nationalist minority, had blown up into a vociferous 'No' campaign. It came perilously near to civil disobedience. Paisley was in his element once more as a mob leader. British ministers at Stormont were publicly insulted and Unionist mayors and local office-bearers laid siege to Stormont hanging their chains of office on the barbed wire entanglements put up to keep them at bay. Even the RUC, caught in the middle, did not escape the abuse. Banners proclaiming that 'Ulster' and Belfast says 'No' hung over the Belfast City Hall and provincial buildings. Amid tumultous scenes in Donegall Place, Belfast the effigy of Mrs Thatcher was burned to loud cheers. For once Westminster refused to back down. The loyalists had over-reached themselves. The British public were becoming fed up and wiser heads in the Unionist establishment realised that they had scored an own goal. Soon the tattered banners had succumbed to the wind and the rain. The Agreement remained firmly in place and evidence of its efficacious intervention in areas of dispute began to show up. The wind of change had begun to blow. By the summer of 1994 it was blowing strongly across the Atlantic. The Hume-Adams Accord followed at last by the Downing Street Declaration signed by John Major and Albert Reynolds received the powerful endorsement of President Clinton at the White House. Soon the swithering Provisional IRA leadership was receiving electrical impulses from the united Irish-American lobby to seize this historical opportunity to end its campaign of violence and enable the peace process to begin. The 'Ceasefire' came and people were out in the streets of our cities, towns and villages enjoying the freedom from fear that they had not known for 25 years. There was no going back and woe betide those who would bring back the nightmare of those worst days in our history.